THE INTRANET DATA WAREHOUSE

Tools and Techniques for Building an
Intranet-Enabled Data Warehouse

RICHARD TANLER

WILEY COMPUTER PUBLISHING

John Wiley & Sons, Inc.

New York • Chichester • Weinheim • Brisbane • Singapore • Toronto

Publisher: Robert Ipsen
Editor: Robert M. Elliott
Managing Editor: Erin Singletary
Text Design & Composition: Ampersand Graphics, Ltd.

Designations used by companies to distinguish their products are often claimed as trademarks. In all instances where John Wiley & Sons, Inc., is aware of a claim, the product names appear in initial capital or ALL CAPITAL LETTERS. Readers, however, should contact the appropriate companies for more complete information regarding trademarks and registration.

This text is printed on acid-free paper.

This publication is designed to provide accurate and authoritative information in regard to the subject matter covered. It is sold with the understanding that the publisher is not engaged in rendering legal, accounting, or other professional service. If legal advice or other expert assistance is required, the services of a competent professional person should be sought.

Library of Congress Cataloging-in-Publication Data:

Tanler, Richard, 1950–
    The Intranet data warehouse : tools and techniques for building an intranet-enabled data warehouse / Richard Tanler.
        p.   cm.
    Includes index.
    ISBN 0-471-18004-1 (alk. paper)
    1. Intranets (Computer networks)   2. Data warehousing.   I. Title.
TK5105.875.I6T36   1997
005.75'8—dc21   97-17968
                                                                            CIP

Printed in the United States of America
10 9 8 7 6 5 4 3 2 1

CONTENTS

PREFACE

Data, simple facts, and figures, describe an enterprise and its competitive environment. Data warehouses can help organizations to safeguard their data assets and make data more accessible to decision makers. Yet, the true value of data can only be realized through the communication and collaboration that occurs among individuals. In just a few years, the Internet has created the largest information repository on earth and, in doing so, has dramatically changed the way in which individuals communicate and share information on a global level.

How Did We Get Here?

To place what we have each experienced in the past few years in perspective, consider that our ancestors used the first primitive implements of information technology to record their experiences on the walls of their caves. It was thousands of years before the Egyptians gave us a formal means of written communication (3000 B.C.) and not until 105 A.D. that the Chinese invented paper in roughly the form that we know it today. Guttenberg invented the printing press 1,300 years later, and Edison invented the telephone four hundred and fifty years after that (in 1876). All remarkable contributions to communications technology, but perhaps none more remarkable than we have experienced in the past 50 years with the development of computer information technology.

The history of computer information technology can be loosely classified into three major phases, or eras:

- The Hardware Era, which began in 1945 with the development of the Electronic Numerical Integrator and Calculator (ENIAC), focused on producing ever faster and more powerful computers for commercial data processing.
- The Software Era, which began in 1975 with the introduction of the Altair 8800, the first "personal" computer for the general public, and

gained momentum in 1981 with IBM's introduction of the highly successful Personal Computer. The new generation of "personal" computers triggered a corresponding need for a new generation of software—software that was both useful and easy-to-use and distribute.

- The Content Era, which represents one of the most significant changes wrought by the Internet, emphasizing the creation and management of content rather than application software logic, and improving collaboration and information exchange among users. The Content Era is, however, still in its infancy, growing and changing to respond to the information needs of the global community.

In reality, of course, there are no clearly defined starting or stopping points for any of the eras. During the Hardware Era, information technology provided an efficient means of processing business transactions such as orders, invoices, and reservations. The Software Era began as a result of changes in hardware technology—changes that enabled hardware manufacturers to build and market relatively inexpensive "personal" computers to the general public. At this point, computers were no longer the exclusive province of programmers and data entry clerks. The software industry had "users," nontechnical information-starved business individuals that needed practical, easy-to-use applications with which to exploit their new computer capabilities.

Responding to users' demands, manufacturers provided users with "personal" information processing capabilities in the form of software applications, predominantly spreadsheet and word processor programs, and distributed these applications on magnetic storage diskettes. As the Software Era progressed and users continued to demand more and more applications for business use, the "personal" computers became bloated with applications and files. As corporations "downsized" their mainframe computer systems, they continually "upsized" their desktop computers and networks.

The magnetic storage diskettes that provided the software industry with an inexpensive media for distributing applications software also contributed to a significant problem in the Software Era—the rise of "bloatware." The "universal" diskette enabled software developers to adopt a "one size fits all" approach to distributing software, creating applications that could meet the needs of a wide range of users—from novices to those at the extreme end of the technical proficiency curve—and roll the complete package into a single product. In reality, most users actually use less than 10 percent of the features that are incorporated in most applications packages. Software vendors typically include every feature of the application program on the distribution diskette, even though the vast majority of users will never need—or use—most features.

Formal and informal studies indicate that "bloatware" confounds (and annoys) the average user. In fact, most users never spend the necessary time to become completely familiar with Windows, the "standard" for ease-of-use, let alone each feature-laden application. It is now becoming clear that the major impact of the Software Era was not merely the empowerment of a large class of primarily nontechnical users seeking information and demanding applications, but the rise of "bloatware" which led inevitably to the Content Era.

The transition into the Content Era began with the popularization of the Internet and World Wide Web. In the Content Era, the focus shifts to the content rather than the hardware and software technologies that are used to deliver it. Unlike the Software Era in which users were tasked with loading applications from diskette (or CD-ROM) and then using the application logic to access or create useful content, the Internet (and the World Wide Web) presents users with content first, hiding the application software from view. Users receive only the application logic that they need to support the content and retain only the content and application logic that they require at their local workstation (i.e., PC).

The Content Era emphasizes the creation and management of content (i.e., raw data that is optimized through communication and sharing) and on improving collaboration among users. Although electronic mail is proving to be the first "killer application" of the Content Era, the era is still in its infancy and we are only now beginning to understand the potential of this latest stage in the information technology evolution. In many respects, Internet technologies are not an extension of client/server computing; they represent a fundamental and comprehensive shift to the next era in information technology—distributed network computing on a truly massive scale.

Where Are We Now?

Two significant technology trends are occurring in the Content Era:

1. Emphasis has expanded from On-Line Transaction Processing (OLTP) applications to On-Line Analytic Processing (OLAP) and Data Warehousing.
2. Client/server system architectures are going through a metamorphosis, often emerging as Intranets.

These two technology trends are intertwined in that they deal with the related subjects of information management and information dissemination. Data warehousing recognizes that data is a valuable asset that must be structured for On-Line Analytic Processing. The Intranet is creating a new model for communications and collaboration within the enterprise. Together, they constitute a fundamentally different information infrastructure for organizations seeking to achieve optimal return on their intellectual capital investments.

We all know how to measure and report financial capital using balance sheets. Unfortunately there is no quantifiable measurement comparable to the corporate balance sheet with which to evaluate and report changes in intellectual capital. It is virtually impossible to estimate the return on a planned investment in intellectual capital. (How can an organization measure the impact of better information on a management decision to be made sometime in the future?) Despite the lack of measurement tools however, most companies now recognize that there is a competitive mandate to invest in building intellectual capital. Organizations that do not stay intellectually ahead of their competitors may pay the ultimate price—failure.

Why Read This Book?

This book is about building the intellectual capital of a corporation in the Content Era. It is about the challenges of managing the raw data assets of a corporation and translating those assets into an even more valuable form of information. The transformation of data into information extends to the need for enterprise-wide communication and collaboration among decision makers. Ultimately, this book is about providing decision makers with more timely, accurate, and complete information to enable those decision-makers to make informed decisions faster and with greater confidence.

This book is intended to be a call to action. It is not enough to archive data in a warehouse. Organizations must find new ways to apply this data to improve decision-making. The Internet and corporate intranets represent fundamental shifts in information technology. Within the enterprise, the Intranet is far more than an improved electronic mail system. The real challenge is to provide true decision support over the Intranet.

I had two objectives in writing this book. First, I wanted to introduce a strategy for building intellectual capital on a new technology foundation—the intranet data warehouse. The audience for this message is anyone that must present to management the benefits of investing large sums of money in developing a data warehouse and delivering decision support applications over the intranet. Corporations are investing millions in data warehousing. How can they guarantee maximum return on their investment?

My second objective was tactical, to outline current "best practices" for providing data warehouse access to users of the Intranet. There are many reasons that intranet delivery of decision support applications is compelling, including cost-effectiveness, ease-of-use, and the pervasive nature of Web browser technology. There are also significant challenges, including competing technology "standards," scalability of the architecture, security, and meeting user requirements for dynamic analysis of structured (i.e., alphanumeric) content. The audience for this message includes anyone involved in the implementation of a data warehousing project for intranet delivery of applications.

The book is presented in two informal sections:

Chapters 1–4 are introductory, explaining the interrelationships among data warehousing, on-line analytic processing (OLAP), and intranet technologies. Chapter 5 introduces issues that are emerging in planning and implementing an intranet data warehouse that spans numerous technologies and areas of responsibility.

The second section of the book (chapters 6–11) provides a more in-depth technical discussion of the key issues that developers must consider in deploying data warehouse applications over an intranet. In order to present the most accurate and current information available on each of the technical issues, I enlisted the aid of experts in their respective technical fields.

Chapters 6 and 7 describe the technologies that developers must embrace in establishing a distributed network-based applications architecture. In these chapters, we describe the emerging distributing computing standards and messaging protocols required to execute server-resident data analysis functions from downloaded browser applets. The data warehouse contains raw alphanumeric data that must be converted into meaningful reports and graphs (text and image documents) as a function of various analytic processes. This middle-tier processing of raw data into textual information is the key to intranet data warehousing applications.

Because the intranet data warehouse will be accessible to hundreds, possibly even thousands, of users, the issues of performance and system scalability are magnified far beyond those of traditionl client/server computing. Chapters 8 and 9 provide two approaches to improving data warehouse performance. In Chapter 8, we explore Red Brick Systems' software approach to optimizing the database management system for data warehousing applications. In Chapter 9, we describe NCR Corporation's hardware approach for addressing scalability and performance concerns through parallel processing.

Chapter 10 deals with security—a critically important issue because the information contained in the data warehouse is one of the corporation's most valuable assets.

Chapter 11 introduces the requirement for background processing performed on behalf of users, so-called agents. The chapter also discusses methods for integrating data warehouses and OLAP applications with intranet technologies such as search engines.

Finally, in Chapter 12 we summarize the steps involved in building an intranet data warehouse and integrating OLAP functions by describing the creation of a business application for a hypothetical company.

Building an effective intranet data warehouse is not, as you'll see in the upcoming chapters of this book, an easy task. But it is an important step in building the intellectual capital of the enterprise and staying abreast of changes in computer information technology. Organizations that fail to keep pace with technology and optimize their investments in their intellectual capital risk failure. Perhaps a question that Scott McNealy, CEO of Sun Microsystems, posed to an audience of executives sums it up best, "Would you rather be the windshield of a fast moving car or the bug?"

ACKNOWLEDGMENTS

To all of the many individuals who helped me to better understand the impact of the convergence of three technologies—data warehousing, OLAP, and the intranet—please accept my deepest appreciation.

Five company representatives contributed case studies that identified the value of an intranet data warehouse within the context of their business management challenges:

Adam Krauter, Manager—Land O'Lakes, Inc.

Tim Davis, Director, Data Warehousing—Fidelity Investments

Daniel Greenberg, Vice President Marketing—A. C. Nielsen

Maggi Keith, Director, Development Corporate Services—Dayton Hudson Corporation

Rick Brattin, Project Leader—Tyson Foods

One of my objectives in writing this book was to cover a broad range of technical issues that together form the basis for creating an intranet data warehouse. I could not have done this without help from many individuals far more knowledgeable than I. Those individuals and their particular area of specialty include:

Chapter Six: The Microsoft Intranet Data Warehouse: Architecture and Tools
Steve Harsbarger, Director—Micro Modeling Associates, Inc.

Chapter Seven: The Sun Intranet Data Warehouse: Architecture and Tools
Donna Rubin, Data Warehouse Technology Manager—Sun Microsystems Computer Company
Dan McCreary, President—Integrity Solutions

Chapter Eight: Optimizing the Performance of the Intranet Data Warehouse
Paul Rodwick, Director, Product Management—Red Brick Systems

Chapter Nine: Using Parallel Processing for Scalability
Alan Chow, Vice President Parallel Systems—NCR Corporation
Dan Harrington, Vice President Marketing—NCR Corporation

Chapter Ten: Securing the Intranet Data Warehouse
Mark Zucherman, Internet Program Manager—Hewlett-Packard Company
Eric Livingston, Principal—American Management Systems

I am grateful to each of these contributors who devoted a large portion of their valuable time to preparing content for this book.

At Information Advantage, my colleagues, including Dave Alampi, Jim Frome, Michael Martin, Mary Trick, and Skip Valusek, provided invaluable help in expanding concepts.

Finally, I want to thank several individuals without whom this book never would have reached publication:

To Jan Wright, an extraordinary technical writer and editor, who guided me through the entire writing process;

To Isaac Cheifetz who counseled me on the organization structure and themes;

To Karen Drost and Dara Moline who coordinated the entire project; and,

To everyone else who provided encouragement and support, without which I could have easily succumbed to the temptation to give up:

My deepest gratitude is offered.

When I started this project, I thought the journey would be easy. I was unprepared for just how difficult it is to research a topic that is broad in scope and rapidly changing. The many contributors and supporters have made a difficult task a reality. Thank you.

CHAPTER ONE

Introduction: Outsmarting the Competition

Increasing the intellectual capital of an enterprise is a competitive mandate. Organizations that effectively use information technologies gain both the knowledge and speed to achieve overwhelming superiority within their markets. They become capable of outsmarting their competitors. An intranet data warehouse is one of those technologies that can give organizations a "leg up" on the competition. But despite all of its inherent advantages, an intranet data warehouse involves significant technical and management challenges that can prevent organizations from fully realizing its potential benefit. Providing decision makers with timely, accurate, and complete information with which to make faster, better-informed decisions is not an easy task.

What Is an Intranet Data Warehouse?

Specifically, an intranet data warehouse is a combination of technologies that enable users to dynamically generate a database query, conduct data analysis (i.e., execute mathematical functions), and format the results as text or image files for display in any Web browser. This is key in the ultimate utility of an intranet data warehouse; it does not require any PC software other than a Web browser. The warehouse and the analysis software are both easily accessible

1

via a Universal Resource Locator (URL). Users' queries to the data warehouse dynamically create reports and graphics for display in the browser, providing access to accurate, targeted information when and where users need it.

In many ways, the disciplines involved in designing and managing an intranet data warehouse are the same as those required of traditional data warehousing. What distinguishes the intranet data warehouse is that it meets the needs of a very large number of nontechnical users. In this respect, it magnifies the issues surrounding ease of use, performance, scalability, and security. Data warehouses designed for intranet deployment are likely to be used by a broad range of users, each with different technical skills and their own definition of "ease of use." This is one of the reasons that, in practice, an intranet data warehouse is likely to evolve into a combination of distributed databases. Performance and security can be enhanced by creating separate, potentially smaller data marts. But managing a distributed data warehouse and meeting the needs of a large and diverse user community remain two key challenges of an intranet data warehouse.

The applications architecture of the intranet introduces an additional technical challenge. Along with providing a solution for distributing data management across the network, an Intranet data warehouse requires that online analytic processing (OLAP) functions be distributed as well.

Why Build an Intranet Data Warehouse?

Military strategists use the term *overwhelming superiority* to describe what every army hopes to have prior to engaging an enemy. Overwhelming superiority entails having numerically and technologically superior assets with which to wage a battle and knowing how to effectively use them. One benefit of achieving overwhelming superiority is that it can serve as a deterrent; most adversaries will choose not to enter a battle if they believe that success is impossible.

Today the term overwhelming superiority is applied to corporations that have achieved so dominant a position of market leadership that they seem to be nearly invincible. Microsoft, Disney, and Wal-Mart come immediately to mind. These companies, and many others that possess overwhelming superiority in their industry segments, are able to make strategic and tactical moves at an extremely rapid rate. The pace of change is not going to slow; thus, the competitive advantage shifts to companies that can accelerate their decision-making capabilities.

At one time, overwhelming superiority was tied to an abundance of financial capital. Market leaders defended their position primarily by outspending their competitors. This strategy is no longer sufficient. In the current business environment, information is one of the most valuable assets that an enterprise can use to effectively wage competitive battles and defend its market position. Intellectual capital has achieved an equal—if not superior—status to financial capital.

Today's successful business leaders try to outsmart their rivals rather than just outspend them. Increasingly, industry leaders overwhelm their rivals by being faster and more nimble at setting new competitive agendas; they continually "raise the bar" for competitors. Consequently, the objective is to identify opportunities faster, plan actions with greater insight, execute more rapidly, and make course corrections sooner than competitors.

Perhaps the best example of overwhelming superiority in the computer industry is Microsoft Corporation, a company founded with virtually no financial capital, in a highly competitive industry overshadowed by IBM. Yet it took Microsoft only a little more than 20 years to pass IBM in total market capitalization (the dollar value that the stock market places on companies). Microsoft understood better than any other company the significance of the emergence of the desktop single-user computer, responded to this knowledge, and so came to dominate what would rapidly become the largest market for software.

Using Information Technology to Gain Competitive Advantage

The process of making and implementing decisions is largely dependent on effective communications and collaboration. Data warehouses contain information such as the measures of operating performance and competitive intelligence that facilitate decision making. But a data warehouse merely stores raw data in the rows and columns of a database; before that data assumes any informational value, it has to be analyzed and formatted for presentation. Then, of course, it must be communicated.

When we apply Internet technology—which is most notable for its ability to facilitate worldwide communications and collaboration—to data warehousing, we vastly improve our ability to communicate and collaborate within the enterprise (and, with the appropriate Internet links, outside of the enterprise). To implement a decision to temporarily lower price in order to reduce excessive inventory levels in selected markets, for example, may require numerous approvals and cooperation from multiple departments within the enterprise. A properly designed intranet data warehouse can accelerate effective implementation of such decisions by improving the quality of the data, adding informational value with analytic tools and speeding information flow throughout the enterprise.

A data warehouse stores the "raw" data as individual "facts." Unlike a relational database management system, a data warehouse stores facts for each time period, creating a historical perspective on performance. A data query might, for example, return the fact that 240,000 units were sold during the month of December. Some simple analysis can increase the informational value of this fact. Knowing that sales declined by 10 percent from the previous month typically initiates the rapid-fire questioning process that lies at the core of data analysis. The standard what, when, where, how, why, and what-if questions represent a business analysis process that is repeated many times every day in virtually every enterprise.

The Key Components

Three key technologies are converging to form the basis of a new information infrastructure for accelerating effective decision making, and investing in these technologies helps to build the intellectual capital necessary to overwhelm business rivals:

- **Data warehousing** is the creation of a complete and accurate repository of data. In the lexicon of the intranet, data warehouses manage "content." They contain *structured content*; that is, primarily alphanumeric data stored in the rows and columns of a database. In contrast, most of the data types on the Internet represent *unstructured content*, including image and audio data, as well as text.

- **Online analytic processing (OLAP)** provides the tools needed to access and analyze data. OLAP functions include query and reporting (which simplifies SQL code generation), multidimensional analysis (sometimes referred to as a spreadsheet on steroids), statistical analysis (also known as data reduction), and data mining (a type of data exploration).

- **Internet technologies, specifically intranets,** improve enterprisewide communications and collaboration. Intranets are at the forefront of a distributed network computing paradigm shift, redefining client/ server application development and deployment strategies.

The information infrastructure that emerges from the convergence of these three information technologies emphasizes data management on one dimension, data analysis in a second dimension, and data communications on a third dimension (see Figure 1.1).

[handwritten note: data management. data Analysis. data communication.]

Data Warehouses

Data warehouses are designed to meet decision makers' need for more and better-timed information about business performance. This information is typically expressed in terms of financial gain (or loss), measured by sales of product or service or numbers of customers. Data warehousing has gained much of its impetus for growth from the success of relational database management

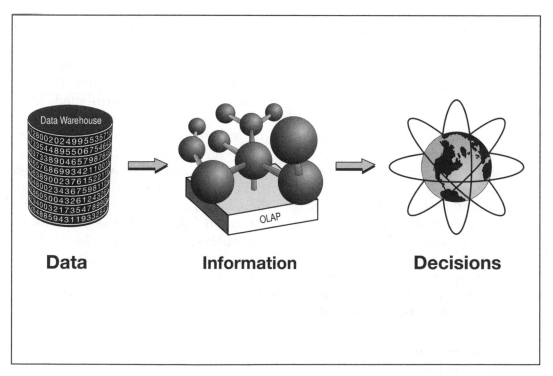

Figure 1.1   Three technologies converge to form a new information infrastructure.

system (RDBMS) software and the declining costs and higher performance associated with server hardware. Rather than redundantly storing data in multiple, single-application proprietary systems, a data warehouse is accessible by multiple applications that share an "open" central administration. In this context, open is derived from the fact that major RDBMS software vendors use SQL (Structured Query Language) as a common query language for their products.

A data warehouse enables users to access this central, multiapplication database with its vast stores of complete and validated data, and to apply a consistent set of raw facts to the standard business analysis questions that support decision making and decision implementation. Case in point: The CIO of a major manufacturer expressed the need for consistent data in his organization by observing that, "All of our reports differ by small annoying amounts. We spend the first part of every meeting arguing about who has the right information. The proliferation of spreadsheet applications contributes to the problem of data inconsistencies and accuracy. Users seldom submit their applications to rigorous testing before results are communicated. If data is to be useful in decision making, it must be trusted."

Bill Inmon, the author of several books on the topic, is widely recognized as the father of data warehousing. In *Building the Data Warehouse* (John Wiley & Sons 1992–1993), he defines a data warehouse as: "a subject-oriented, integrated, time-variant, nonvolatile collection of data in support of management's decision-making process." Expanding on Inmon's definition, a data warehouse should also contain complete and accurate data. It should be capable of supporting all of the users' analytical requirements to address subject-oriented business management issues that are critical to an organization's long-term success, rather than focusing on operational issues such as manufacturing scheduling or claims processing. A well-designed data warehouse contains all of the data needed to respond to business analysis questions (what? when? why? what if?), precluding the possibility of prematurely terminating the search for an answer because information is not available.

Three types of data warehouses result from users' decision support requirements and typical business issues:

- Financial
- Marketing
- Behavioral

Financial Data Warehouses

Financial data warehouses monitor business performance in financial terms; they contain "snapshots" of financial history, revenue, and expense data. Financial data is generally updated monthly or on another reporting period (such as every four weeks) that coincides with the enterprise's financial calendar.

A financial data warehouse contains a relatively small number of facts—the numeric performance measures. Often only a single fact such as dollars is used to describe revenue and expense measures. Facts are stored in the warehouse along with their descriptions, which are generally referred to as dimensions. Examples of dimensions describing the fact *dollars* include: account (e.g., travel expense), department (e.g., marketing), organization (e.g., business unit), and location (e.g., country). The analytic requirements of financial data warehouse users emphasize multilevel consolidation and comparisons of financial data over time. Rapid system response to questions is a prerequisite since users are accustomed to the nearly instantaneous response of spreadsheet applications. Financial data analysis also tends to be highly repetitive; thus, user requirements and associated database design aspects of planning the data warehouse project are generally less complex than those of other data warehousing projects.

Marketing Data Warehouses

Marketing data warehouses are designed to allow users to evaluate the business performance of a product or service from multiple perspectives. These data warehouses often contain rich *competitive intelligence*—the data needed to analyze the impact of each vendors' marketing activities on the sales of products or services. This type of information is updated frequently—often weekly, and in many cases, daily.

The marketing data warehouse allows users to analyze data at various hierarchical levels along each database dimension, typically geographic (e.g., store, service representative, territory, district, region, or country) and product (e.g., category, vendor, brand, or item). The analysis requirements are very complex and highly variable because the users' questions are almost impossible to predict. Many manufacturing companies, including Polaroid, and retail organizations, such as Target Stores, have very sophisticated product data warehouses that are designed specifically to support their marketing operations. Both organizations are attempting to improve total product sales by improving the quality of the information available for the thousands of decisions that are necessary to continuously improve the marketing of products in dynamic and highly competitive businesses.

Behavioral Data Warehouses

Behavioral data warehouses are used for applications categorized broadly as *database marketing* or *relationship marketing*, that focus on attracting new customers and maintaining loyalty among an existing customer base. The data warehouses associated with these applications contain information about individual customers and their behavior.

Behavioral data warehouses are commonly found in insurance companies, financial institutions, airlines, and health care providers, among others—all of which have an overriding need to understand their customers' behavior and to determine how best to provide product and services to meet individual customers' needs.

Data in a behavioral data warehouse is generally updated on a regular basis, but the frequency varies according to the specific application and environment. Because these systems contain detailed behavior data about many individuals, the data warehouses associated with this type of decision support system are generally much larger than the financial or product/services data warehouses. Tandy Corporation and MasterCard both have behavioral data warehouses that exceed one terabyte (1,000 gigabytes) of customer-specific data.

Because the database dimensions are different for each type of data warehouse (i.e., financial, marketing, or behavioral), the design considerations are also different. Most companies have a variety of tactical decision support requirements, which often lead to the creation of multiple data warehouses, each intended to support a particular decision support requirement.

Online Analytic Processing

Online Analytic Processing, or OLAP as it is more commonly known, provides the online data analysis capabilities required to answer decision makers' ongoing flood of questions. The initial questions are generally rather simple, but their complexity increases as the preceding questions are answered. The most difficult to answer are the open-ended why and what-if questions. Sophisticated data analysis functions are needed to answer these.

E.F. Codd introduced the concept of Online Analytic Processing in a white paper published in 1993. In that paper, Codd outlined 12 rules for OLAP that differentiated simple database query and reporting tools from more sophisticated analytic methods. The label OLAP was reserved for sophisticated *multidimensional* analysis. It was an attempt to segment (some would say fragment) an already confusing array of products designed to retrieve and add informational value to the raw data stored in the warehouse.

But because most vendors of data warehouse access and analysis tools have adopted the OLAP label and apply it to their technology with little regard to Codd's rules, throughout this book, we use the OLAP acronym to describe any software tool that facilitates the generation of a database query (simple OLAP) or supports more complex forms of data analysis. This broad definition allows a tight link to be established between the data warehouse (data storage) and OLAP (information processing for decision support) without limiting the use of the label OLAP to a small segment of analytic tools. In this way, OLAP becomes largely synonymous with tactical decision support analysis.

The broad OLAP market spans four separate capabilities (see Figure 1.2), even though specific vendor products often possess a combination of these analytic functions:

- Query and reporting
- Multidimensional analysis
- Statistical analysis
- Data mining

The query and reporting class of OLAP tools enable users to formulate database queries without having to interact with the SQL database programming language. These tools provide rich report formatting and graphical presentation capabilities, which are executed on the client workstation, and conform to the Microsoft Windows model for an easy-to-use interface. Most vendors of query and reporting tools are adding more computational flexibility to each new release of their software in order to move up the OLAP "food chain."

More complex OLAP functions involve multidimensional data analysis, which includes a robust set of data computational and data navigation capabilities. Multidimensional analysis enables users to enter a data warehouse from any single dimension to begin the analysis, then navigate to other dimensions to further analyze the information. For example, a user might initiate analysis from a product perspective, then repeat the analysis in each market segment. The ability to navigate within the report shell (i.e., to drill up, down, and across dimensions) is a key characteristic of multidimensional analysis, as

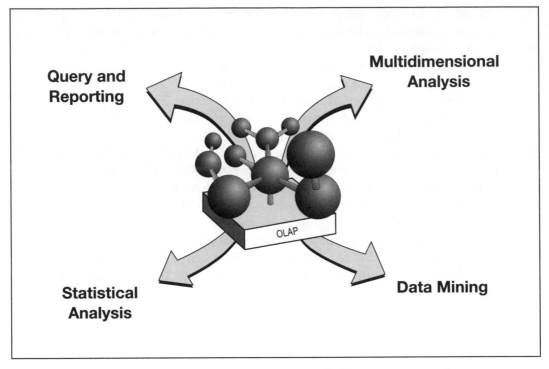

Figure 1.2 OLAP functions provide four capabilities to respond to user queries.

is the ability to modify report parameters to isolate the information that best responds to the query. In other words, the first report that a user produces may be merely the starting point in a multistep analysis process.

Multidimensional analysis provides the analytic flexibility to answer such questions as:

- How have advertising expenditures affected sales?
- Where are competitors making inroads?
- Which products are losing market share?
- Which customers are most loyal?

Answers to these types of questions require a computational layer of software to transform the data stored in the warehouse into information. The computational layer produces calculated measures and aggregations using the raw data facts stored in the warehouse. The computational layer can easily generate four to five times more computed measures and aggregations than the data facts stored in the warehouse.

Statistical analysis represents the next level of OLAP complexity. It attempts to reduce a large amount of data to a simple relationship, which is often stated as a mathematical formula. Calculating an average, for example, represents the most basic form of statistical analysis. More sophisticated statistical functions include regression, correlation, factor, and cluster analysis. Statistical analysis techniques are important for generating models that are used in projecting sales or customer behavior based on historical trends and relationships. Models are essential for answering the what-if? type of questions.

Data mining, the most complex type of OLAP analytical function uses sophisticated pattern recognition and learning algorithms to identify relationships among data elements. Data mining models nonlinear problems with large numbers of variables, automated multivariate analysis, using techniques such as decision tree algorithms, neural nets, fuzzy logic, and genetic algorithms. Statistical analysis is user-directed in the sense that the user specifies the dependent and independent variables included in the analysis, whereas data mining applications act in the role of an agent working on behalf of the user to discover hidden insights that may go unrecognized by the user. One of the best examples of a data-mining application is the determination of factors associated with credit card fraud and risk assessment.

com → OLAP functions reside between the data warehouse and the presentation/ user interface components of an application. Intranet and browser technologies provide the development shell for creating the user interface and presentation functions that must interact with OLAP functions. The OLAP functions themselves link to the data warehouse to retrieve the raw data required for analysis and perform the data analysis. The result is a three-tier partitioned application (see Figure 1.3). Although the data, analytic logic, and presentation/user interface tiers are separate, they must work together.

Intranet and Web Technologies

Most people are now at least somewhat familiar with the World Wide Web. Its underlying Internet technologies support a public network of interconnected servers that comprises the largest information warehouse on earth. The Web's infrastructure relies on a set of widely supported standards, including:

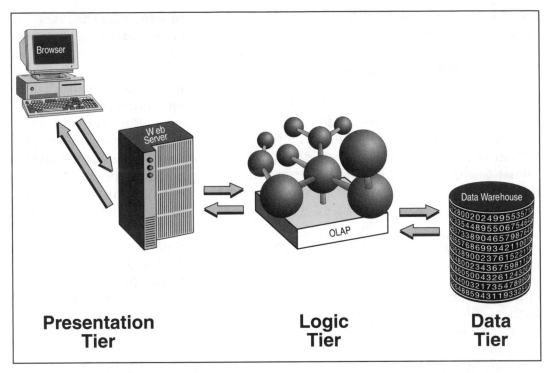

Figure 1.3 OLAP functions as part of a three-tier intranet architecture.

- **HyperText Markup Language (HTML)** is the language used to create information for display.
- **HyperText Transfer Protocol (HTTP)** is the method of transferring and linking information.
- **Universal Resource Locator (URL)** provides the means for locating information within the Web.

Intranets are an enterprise-secure variant of Internet technologies that operate over internal TCP/IP networks and are separated from the public networks by security firewalls. Although intranets may incorporate Internet access, intranets are private and secure. They offer companies the potential to achieve enormous gains in the speed with which information is disseminated throughout an enterprise. All of the advantages of the Internet technologies apply to intranets; furthermore, intranets benefit from the higher performance of private internal network architectures. Intranets offer compelling cost advantages and an applications software distribution model that can greatly simplify the challenge inherent in supporting large numbers of users.

Like the Internet and the Web, intranet applications provide users with access to unstructured content (text documents and images) that can be continuously updated to provide users with the most current information available about a given topic. Many companies publish product specifications, price information, marketing collateral, training material, operations manuals, and employee phone lists on their corporate intranets. Intranet content is following the same path as Internet content; that is, most information content is text and image data. Intranets provide business users with a simple means for sharing information, thereby simultaneously improving communications and collaboration.

Internet technologies offer many significant cost benefits, primarily a result of their "thin" client requirements that often eliminate (or at least delay) the need for expensive hardware upgrades. The simplicity of the Web browsers further promises to reduce the costs associated with user support, and the network-centric architecture reduces the complexity of managing software distribution and data synchronization.

In addition to the economic benefits, the intranet alters a basic tenet of computing. It is organized *for* all users, not *by* individual user. In other words, the intranet shifts the focus from "personal" computing and supporting the needs of individual users, one at a time, to network computing and supporting the needs of multiple users simultaneously. The intranet facilitates mass deployment of applications rapidly and cost-effectively.

Merging the Concepts

The intranet, or more precisely, the Web browser software, can provide a universal interface to all of the information resources of the enterprise. An intranet data warehouse exploits Internet technologies by providing a simple interface to OLAP functions, which perform database queries and analytic processing to convert the raw data contained in the warehouse into formatted reports and graphic images. If the information resource is a static document, users need only specify its location via a URL. If, however, the information resource is raw data that is stored in the warehouse, users must also send an SQL query or program call to the server-resident OLAP functions to translate the data into usable information for inclusion in a text or image file. While there are a number of ways that SQL queries can be embedded in browser interface components and/or program calls can be issued over the intranet, the technique is largely dependent on the intranet architecture and its use of components represented by either the Microsoft network computing model or the broadly supported CORBA (Common Object Request Broker Architecture) network computing model. A detailed description of these models is presented in Chapters 6 and 7, respectively, but what is important to understand at this point is that the user need not be concerned with the actual data analysis or retrieval methodology. These activities take place "under the covers," delivering reports or graphics for display on the Web browser.

Web browser software, acting as the universal client interface to both the structured and unstructured content available on the Intranet, changes the way OLAP functions are provided to users. In client/server data warehousing, vendors extend the functionality of the client, adding retrieval and analysis tools to the PC-based applications. An intranet data warehouse, on the other hand, shifts the emphasis to server-based computing, and encourages the development of interface and display components that are easily downloaded from the server to the Web browser on the client.

The primary advantages of an intranet data warehouse include accelerated information flow throughout the enterprise and decreased costs for application deployment, particularly when the costs involved in intranet deployment are contrasted with those of client/server computing. These advantages significantly increase the benefits of data warehousing, providing decision makers with timely, accurate information and access to the OLAP capabilities that add informational value through data analysis.

When thinking about the value of information, it's useful to remember that information is much more like cheese than wine: It *doesn't* improve with age. The value of information in a business environment is largely a function of *when* it is delivered to the appropriate decision maker. Information that is available to a decision maker before a competitor has the same or similar information is a significant competitive advantage, because decisions can be preemptive rather than reactive. Information acquired at roughly the same time as a competitor may be useful only for defensive purposes; and information that arrives late, after a competitor has already acted, is tantamount to a report card—typically one with unsatisfactory grades. So, the longer it takes to get critical information to decision makers, the less value that information is likely to have for the decision maker.

Combining intranet capabilities with the vast stores of a data warehouse accelerates information flow in several important ways. An intranet can greatly improve information flow throughout an enterprise, ensuring that decision makers have ready access to the information they need, regardless of its physical location in the enterprise; or, if the intranet is linked to the Internet, virtually anywhere on the World Wide Web. And, new information can be quickly and easily deployed throughout an organization. The collaborative nature of an intranet often encourages users to share their personal insights and experience. Together, these benefits help organizations to develop effective processes to integrate decision making with decision implementation. One common objective of an intranet data warehouse is to reduce the gap between decision making and decision implementation from days or weeks to hours.

Because intranet architecture uses network computing resources efficiently, it also offers the potential for reducing many of the costs associated with user support and application deployment. The costs associated with client/server computing have ballooned during the past 10 years, often as a result of the increasing demands of desktop software products. The "bloatware" requirements of popular desktop packages combined with the costs inherent in supporting nontechnical users on sophisticated, feature-rich applications are driving hardware and support costs through the roof in many organizations. Although an intranet can't provide a complete solution to rising support costs, it can greatly facilitate application deployment and encourage information exchange. Applications that previously required months for a complete rollout to users can be deployed almost instantaneously, with a full complement of user support information.

User support requirements are also minimized because Internet technologies, including intranets, encourage developers to create applications for mass deployment rather than creating feature-rich applications for technical users. While this is not a new concept, it is one that was lost as developers focused on "personal" computing rather than meeting the information needs of the enterprise.

Costs of an Intranet Data Warehouse

Although costs vary widely depending on scale of the initial effort, there is little doubt that the steps involved in building a data warehouse, acquiring OLAP tools, and deploying applications represent a significant investment. The budget, including hardware, software, and resources is frequently in the $3 to $5 million range for a complete enterprise system. Fortunately, there are many ways to limit the scope of the effort to significantly reduce the initial expenditure while still achieving substantial economic benefit. Once the commitment is made, the insatiable appetite of users for more and better information is likely to drive the need for an enterprisewide solution and a long-term commitment of resources.

Adding intranet access to a data warehouse typically reduces the per-user cost, because applications can be shared by a larger numbers of users. The costs associated with user support and application software development are also lower for an intranet data warehouse when they are measured on a per-user basis.

Of course, the costs associated with any major investment in technology must be weighed against the anticipated returns. Because intranet data warehouses do not *directly* translate into improvements in operational efficiencies costs, they are difficult to cost-justify. The value of the technology is derived from decisions that managers will make in the future, decisions that will demonstrate their economic value only after they are implemented. It is nearly impossible to predict what information will be derived from the analysis of warehoused data or how it will improve an organization's competitive effectiveness. Small gains in market share or customer loyalty, successful business expansion from new products or services, and minor operating cost reductions can all have enormous financial benefits that easily justify the investment in intellectual capital formation.

Although it is often difficult to cost-justify an Intranet data warehouse investment during the planning stages, dramatic returns on the investment are occasionally recounted after the effect of decisions can be quantified. One of the most remarkable stories I've heard was related by the CIO of a major retail company. The company's investment in its intranet data warehouse, which will ultimately serve the information needs of store managers in 6,000-plus retail outlets, exceeded several million dollars. But the CIO estimates that the entire investment was returned in just a few day of analysis that correctly guided the company's marketing decisions for an annual promotional program. The CIO notes that this type of promotional event happens only once a year; if the company had missed its opportunity, it would have lost valuable time as well as significant revenue gains.

An intranet data warehouse project must be directed at clearly defined business objectives that are based on a realistic assessment of the enterprise's critical success factors. By aligning the information needs of users with the business objectives, it often becomes clear that investing in the intellectual capital of the enterprise is nothing less than a competitive mandate. To remain viable, most business enterprises need to grow (in terms of revenues) while becoming more efficient (i.e., lowering costs).

Planning and Implementing an Intranet Data Warehouse

Planning a data warehouse project for the intranet involves three separate, but highly interrelated sets of strategic decisions. The starting point, as with any major information technology initiative, should be a clear outline of business objectives' criteria for success. The most important question to ask at the start of the project is, What are the critical success factors for the enterprise? This question should be answered by the organization's executive management group. Executive support is essential to the success of the project to ensure the commitment of all required resources. Even at the initial stage of project planning, the scope of the project may be limited due to resource or budget constraints.

Once the project scope and objectives are documented, it's time to begin determining user information requirements. To do this, organizations typically rely on a project team composed of managers from the departments that will be using the intranet data warehouse. The project team needs to understand the decisions that users are making and implementing. This, of course, requires an understanding of what information is available or is lacking for effective decision making, as well as how long it takes to identify a problem or opportunity, and to make or implement decisions. At this stage, it is often advisable to expand the project team to include representatives from the user community. Remember that users typically focus on solving current problems, rather than on technology infrastructures intended to support long-term business requirements. This is a major source of conflict within many project teams but much of the conflict can be overcome with guidance from an effective, understanding project coordinator who is knowledgeable about the needs of the various user departments and familiar with the long-range goals of the organization.

After the user requirements are documented, the project scope should be reviewed in the context of budget and timing considerations, then broken down into phases to ensure that users realize some benefits during the first several months of project initiation to motivate their continuing commitment. Typically, three strategic planning efforts proceed in parallel:

- **Applications Strategy:** The applications strategy flows directly from an analysis of the organization's critical success factors and user information requirements. The applications strategy is tightly coupled with the database strategy, in that the application strategy helps to clarify the information requirements to determine what data should be stored in the data warehouse. Priorities set during the applications strategy phase establish the parameters that influence database design. The applications strategy also defines the applications programs that are needed to meet user reporting and analysis requirements.

- **Database Strategy:** The database strategy addresses database design and quality assurance issues, as well as data warehouse creation and maintenance. Important purchase decisions include the selection of database management system software and hardware. Issues of scalability are also important as they relate to size of the database, number of users, and complexity of the analysis requirements.

- **Deployment Strategy:** A deployment strategy is crucial to the success of a data warehousing project. It should consider such questions as: How will users with a wide range of technical abilities receive information? How will mobile or remote users receive information? How will users collaborate, sharing their experiences and ideas with others, in cooperative problem resolution? How can routine analyses be automated and sent to users on a need-to-know basis (i.e., software agents working on behalf of users)? How will users be alerted to a serious business issue in a timely manner?

Certainly, ease of use is also a critical factor in the success of an intranet data warehouse project. To some extent, ease of use can be measured by the amount of training that is required for the average user, as well as the amount of documentation that is needed to support that user. By this measure, Web browser software achieves a near-perfect score for ease of use, especially when it is compared with the majority of Windows-based application programs.

The final budget and development time lines will grow out of the integrated strategic planning processes. The scope of the project may be redefined several times to remain within the budgetary constraints, but the planning process must not lose sight of the business objectives and user requirements.

Once the strategic plan, budget, and time line are approved, it's time to plan the implementation. Here, the lessons of the Internet and Web are important.

The largest information warehouse on Earth exists in its current state because hundreds of thousands of developers built it piece by piece, allowing it to continually evolve to respond to ever-changing user requirements. The intranet data warehouse must also be allowed to evolve to meet user information requirements. Referring to the work as a "project" is misleading in that the intranet data warehouse will never be truly finished; instead, it must be designed with change in mind. In this way, an intranet data warehouse is "organic"; that is, it is constantly growing and changing to meet the needs of users. The highly adaptable nature of the Web browser development environment provides developers with the means to rapidly add new applications. The implication is that the intranet data warehouse should be staffed as an ongoing effort, a new Information Services department.

In the next chapter, we discuss the architecture of the intranet in more detail, building the case for how an intranet can affect both data warehousing and OLAP applications deployment. As we begin to drill down into the technology layers, it is important to remember that the objective of combining data warehousing, OLAP, and intranet technologies is to create intellectual capital that results in overwhelming superiority.

CASE STUDY

Land O Lakes

Land O Lakes, with headquarters in Minneapolis, Minnesota, sells more than 400 dairy products through 30,000 retail grocery stores and wholesale club stores nationwide. Dairy foods account for half of Land O Lakes $3 billion annual revenues in the United States.

In an intensely competitive battle for retail shelf space, Land O Lakes identified three strategic growth opportunities. The first opportunity is to leverage its national brand strength, especially for butter. "Butter is making a strong comeback now that people are rethinking their health perceptions concerning margarine," observed Adam Krauter, marketing manager for information and technology in the Land O Lakes Consumer Division. "We want to capture as much of that growth opportunity as we can."

The second opportunity concerns cheese products. "In the northeastern United States, people ask for our deli cheeses by name," Krauter explains; "in the Midwest and western states, they don't. To us, this indicates a major opportunity to expand our cheese sales on a geographic basis."

The third strategic challenge flows directly from the first two: the need for rapid, economic expansion of its field sales effort. "We have a dedicated field salesforce, primarily in the regions where we have historically been strong," Krauter explains. "To expand in other geographic areas, we decided it was most economical to leverage existing broker organizations." Land O Lakes now works with more than 50 food brokers, whose sales representatives call on retail outlets.

The decision was made to use a solution that leveraged both Windows and Web interfaces to the data warehouse in an attempt to cost-effectively integrate the brokers into the company's overall sales effort while also providing all of the representatives with better tools for selling its products.

Land O Lakes now makes its case to retailers more rapidly and more persuasively. Previously Land O Lakes had established the data warehouse using IBM's Metaphor tools. "They were a great advance 10 years ago," Krauter says, "but we felt we had to leap ahead to the latest generation of data warehousing technology.

One of the key reasons Land O Lakes selected a solution that provided Web and Windows integration for data analysis was the ability it gave the company to rapidly and economically scale up the data analysis environment to include brokers located across the United States. "With the existing system, it was very complicated to get data out to the field," Krauter notes, "and we weren't comfortable with future prospects for doing that more easily. Also, our data environment is becoming increasingly complex, with a combination of proprietary data, syndicated data, existing Metaphor data, and new-customer shipment data.

Land O Lakes created a complete infrastructure for scalable, optimized multidimensional analysis enabling the data environment and user community to grow without affecting the data analysis architecture.

The data warehouse contains four databases: three categories of syndicated bar code data plus Land O Lakes' own proprietary customer shipment data. Syndicated scanner data is aggregated for the current week, 4 weeks, 12 weeks, and 52 weeks. "We use the scanner data to measure the success of our products against those of our competitors," Krauter explains, "or to project how a new product of ours might perform in an existing category. We do this by geographic market and by key account."

If a new product is introduced in Los Angeles, for example, sales representatives can immediately show grocery managers how the new product is selling at other stores in the same chain, at stores in competing grocery chains, and against comparable products from other dairy manufacturers.

Because users can customize reports and drill anywhere in the data hierarchy for specific data within aggregate categories, representatives can easily tailor their presentation before each sales call.

"The intranet data warehouse and OLAP capabilities help change our customers' buying decision from one based on instinct, personal experience, or incomplete information to one based on real and accurate data," Krauter observes. "That's why our brokers are so happy to have fast, flexible remote access to the data warehouse—they need it in order to do the job we're asking them to do. We are excited about the capabilities of integrating the data warehouse with the Web, which enables end users to access and analyze the data warehouse using standard Web browsers. Broker organizations have the ability to use either the Windows or Web interface into the data warehouse. The Web enables the brokers' sales representatives to analyze data without learning a new tool. They can access and analyze our data warehouse using browsers they already have and know how to use, which means the number of people working on our behalf can increase without requiring an equivalent investment in training and support."

Both the Windows and Web interfaces give users the ability to customize reports, request different categories of information, and drill anywhere to specific data. In addition, users can easily exchange reports without special translation software. "This flexibility ultimately makes for very impressive presentations to our customers," says Krauter, "and it can all be done through the Internet and our corporate intranet."

Land O Lakes also takes advantage of agent technology, which continuously monitors the data warehouse for out-of-range conditions and automatically delivers alerts or reports to those who need to know. For example, agents are set up to detect price and volume variances that indicate market opportunities, and to raise alarms concerning widening price spreads relative to competitors' products.

In a mature, competitive consumer marketplace, the ability to change product, pricing, and placement strategies—and execute those strategies successfully—is one of the only available avenues for growth. "It all boils down to reacting more quickly to the market, with more information about what is actually happening," Krauter explains. "Now our field salespeople no longer have to wait days for data analysis in response to a request, or go with a gut feeling and hope it's right. They can get the data and the answers they need, when the question arises.

"Some of the results we've experienced include: Field sales and brokers can perform immediate analysis of current competitive data by product, re-

gion, and key account; reports can be customized and detailed with drill-anywhere data to support specific selling situations and opportunities; and rapid, economic, deployment of high-function data analysis capabilities to a fast-growing number of remote users via the Web. Compared to the old way of operating based on outdated or unsupported information, immediate analysis of current data using Windows or the Web is a far more productive way of working." ∎

CHAPTER TWO

CREATING AN INTRANET DATA WAREHOUSE

An intranet is far more than the application of Internet and Web technologies on private TCP/IP "corporate" networks. Intranets can fundamentally change the way in which business applications are developed and deployed within a server-centric distributed computing architecture. An intranet data warehouse exploits this technology to allow information-rich communications and collaboration to occur throughout the enterprise. It relies on Internet technologies moved inside corporate firewalls to provide secure access to information that is essential to decision makers. Developing business applications for intranet deployment introduces new approaches to distributing computing tasks among the client and networked servers. The distributed computing architecture of the intranet is particularly relevant to intranet data warehouse applications. An intranet data warehouse requires sophisticated database query, analytic processing, and formatting logic in order to turn raw data into reports and images that can be displayed on a Web browser.

This chapter focuses on the technologies that permit the data warehouse to be integrated with intranet technologies. It provides some basic definitions of Web technology and reviews the technology components and software standards that support the intranet. The chapter emphasizes the need to balance client-side processing and what appears "on the glass" (application components executed on the client) with server-side processing or what is performed "over the wire" (application components that are executed on one or more servers on the network). Finally, the chapter offers a brief overview of the technologies that define a network operating system, which allows distributed components (i.e., components executed on various hardware platforms with different operating systems) to communicate with one another.

Before we explore Internet and intranet technologies and their impact on the data warehouse environment, it may be useful to review the evolution of the data warehouse itself. Early practitioners of data warehousing focused on database design, development, and management, communicating the message "Build it!" As the organizations that were building and using data warehouses began to realize the value of the vast information stores at their disposal, the challenge shifted from "Build it!" to "Analyze it!" The rapid growth of online analytic processing (OLAP) software applications reflect this need for more sophisticated data analysis.

Although there is still much to do in building more reliable and efficient data warehouses and developing applications that better support decision making, the focus is now shifting to deployment. Too often, decision support applications were the province of a relatively small number of technically competent "power" users, the business analysts assigned to the marketing, sales, and finance departments. But a key goal of data warehousing is to provide broad information access throughout the enterprise to support decision making at each management level. The intranet provides the technology to achieve this goal, providing enterprisewide information deployment to support effective decision making.

Client/Server versus Intranet Deployment of Data Warehouse Applications

If data warehouse access is limited to a relatively small number of power users residing at corporate headquarters, the basic technologies associated with a client/server deployment strategy and an intranet deployment strategy are virtually identical. The network architecture, database content and design, and OLAP functions required to support users' decision support information needs are essentially the same, because the simplicity of the Web browser interface is not a particular advantage for technically proficient power users.

Pursuing an intranet deployment strategy is a commitment to extending data warehouse access to users throughout the enterprise as well as to users that may be external to the enterprise, such as suppliers, wholesalers, retailers, affiliates, and so forth. The differences between client/server and intranet deployment begin to snowball as a result of the need to support a very large user community.

Both types of data warehouses—client/server and intranet—rely on relational database management systems to manage the database. In fact, the same data warehouse can be used to deploy traditional client/server applications or intranet applications. Both types of applications generally share TCP/IP networks for internal access to the data warehouse. And the OLAP functions issue SQL queries to the data warehouse in one way or another, regardless of the deployment strategy. So what's the difference between the two types?

In many respects, the differences between an intranet data warehouse and a client/server data warehouse are philosophical rather than technical. They relate to the information needs of the user community and to the method used to deploy that information to meet users' decision support requirements. One goal of an intranet data warehouse is to improve information-rich communications and collaboration in order to accelerate decision making and decision implementation throughout the enterprise and often beyond the bounds of the enterprise. Within this context, an intranet data warehouse places greater emphasis on operational and tactical decision support than does a client/server data warehouse.

In general, the following considerations distinguish an intranet data warehouse from a client/server data warehouse:

- User requirements
- Data warehouse content
- Application architecture
- Scalability
- Security

User Requirements

The economics and simplicity of intranet deployment of data warehouse applications eliminate many of the barriers to providing information access to relatively nontechnical users within and outside of the enterprise. The intranet data warehouse is also a catalyst for creating entirely new applications capable of accelerating decision making and decision implementation. Using a Web browser to provide data warehouse access to vendors and/or suppliers can, for example, significantly lower the cost and support barriers that exist with traditional deployment of PC applications to a large number of individual users working in a variety of computing environments. But providing such access to vendors and suppliers can offer a number of very real advantages in managing inventories and responding rapidly to market trends.

Client/server data warehouses often focus on the needs of power users, who possess both technical and analytic skills, but often lack access to the appropriate data sources. So-called power users tend to perform comprehensive data analysis to support *strategic* decision making. They may spend many days or even weeks analyzing trends and competitive data to prepare their findings for presentation to management. Thus, power users need and want a robust ad hoc *data analysis tool set.*

The intranet data warehouse user community, on the other hand, often consists of users who want *information* that is related to topical business issues rather than the *tools* for ad hoc analysis. Power users express their decision support requirements in terms of required analytic functions such as, "I need the ability to perform nonlinear regression analysis." The majority of business managers describe their needs in terms of required reports within the context of a business problem; as new business issues arise, they request additional reports.

While power users tend to emphasize requirements for *strategic* decision support, the larger business community requires *operational and tactical* decision support. Intranet data warehouse deployment serves the needs of users who need and want quick answers to business issues for immediate decisions. Consequently, to successfully deploy the data warehouse and OLAP functions over the intranet, we need to address the information needs of the nontechnical (i.e., casual and active) users as well as those of the power users.

Casual users are the executives and front-line managers who have specific information requirements; but because they tend to use the data warehouse rather infrequently, they have difficulty remembering how to efficiently retrieve the information they need. In this situation, "ease of use" translates into "difficult-to-forget." In other words, applications should be designed to be intuitive—easy for infrequent users to remember how to use. Active users are those who rely more heavily on the flow of information to make the daily decisions that affect operations. In the retail world, a store manager concerned with overall operations management is an example of a casual user. The merchandising manager tasked with making frequent decisions about product stocking, pricing, and promotion is an example of an active user.

An intranet data warehouse is ideally suited to respond to the needs of both active and casual users who make numerous tactical and operational decisions on a daily basis. It enables the interface and display components of the application to be adapted quickly to the unique requirements of users and the relevant business issues. The intranet focuses on providing users with content and the ability to quickly navigate among pages of content. Because most non-technical users are familiar with the Web browser, which is rapidly becoming the universal interface for online information access, they are able to efficiently retrieve the specific content they need.

Intranet data warehouse developers are less concerned with providing reams of raw data and a wide range of sophisticated analytical tools to power users than are the developers of traditional, client/server data warehouses. Instead, intranet data warehouse developers are more interested in the deploy ment issues associated with getting information to decision makers in a timely manner to influence tactical and operational decisions. This is not to imply that the analytic capabilities delivered to active and casual users are any less sophisticated than the applications used by power users, but they are generally less interested in flexible ad hoc analysis of raw data; tactical and operational decisions require information presented in a way that addresses the user's business issue, as opposed to "open" data warehouse access.

Ideally, all data warehouses should be designed to support strategic, tactical, and operational decision support. To do this, the data warehouse must be accessible by both traditional client/server applications and intranet applications; however, in practice, this may not always be feasible because the applications' focus, security, and performance issues may dictate a separate data warehouse or data mart for intranet users.

Data Warehouse Content

The content of an intranet data warehouse (i.e., the data sources, level of detail, and database design) reflects the needs of a diverse user community with a wide range of technical skills, and emphasizes operational and tactical decision support.

Performance and security issues also play major roles in determining the content of an intranet data warehouse. These issues influence content decisions (i.e., what information to actually retain in the underlying databases) and the level of detail to be maintained, as well as the design of the data warehouse. We'll address both of these issues in greater detail later in this chapter and in Chapters 8 and 10, but it is important at this stage to understand that because an intranet data warehouse is intended to serve a larger and more diverse user community than a client/server data warehouse, it involves more—and more complex—security concerns.

The size of the intranet data warehouse user community and the diversity of the applications deployed have a similar effect on the performance issues surrounding a data warehouse. Furthermore, performance concerns are magnified by a need to support high user concurrency at peak load times, which tend to correspond with each new update of the data warehouse. In many cases, organizations find that a decentralized data warehouse design (data marts) addresses both the security and performance concerns and provides efficient access to the information sources and applications that users need for their specific decision support requirements. Data marts can also be very effective for providing access to users who are external to the enterprise, enhancing the security of the underlying databases by allowing users access only to summary information rather than providing an entry into a central data warehouse.

Although a single, complete data warehouse is often an attractive solution for centralizing data administration, the need to maintain a reasonable level of performance and safeguard valuable data resources while responding efficiently to user information requirements makes data marts practical in many situations. But distributed data marts may introduce many of the managerial nightmares that centralized data warehouses are designed to remedy.

Applications Architecture

The most obvious difference between an intranet data warehouse and a client/server data warehouse from the users' perspective is what appears "on the glass." Again, code developed for client/server data warehouse applications *can be* duplicated within a Web browser. It is possible, for example, to take the code developed as a Windows application and execute it from a browser using plug-ins. However, the simplicity of the browser interface affords developers the opportunity to focus on the most appropriate user applications interface for an intranet data warehouse, discarding design concepts that were implemented merely to conform to the Windows application development model.

In addition to changing the way applications are developed, Internet and intranet technology changes the way applications are distributed. Traditional client/server applications are designed as mass-market products and distributed via diskette or CD-ROM. They incorporate a single, generalized set of features that over time and multiple upgrade cycles are often poorly focused for user needs. Studies indicate that most users of PC applications use less than 20 percent of an application's functions.

But when applications are deployed over an intranet, users can select the level of functionality they want, retrieving only the features they need, when they need them, to perform a single task. As a result, the information that appears "on the glass" in an intranet data warehouse application differs greatly from that of most client/server applications. The evidence is compelling. Contrast the challenges that most nontechnical users face each time they install a new application on their PCs with the continuous downloading of applications from the Internet. Of course, applications deployed over the Internet or an intranet are smaller and less functionally rich than most traditional client/server applications, but that's the point! Simplicity is an advantage rather than a disadvantage, when users have ready access to additional functionality.

Two-Tier Application Partitioning

Most first-generation client/server OLAP data warehousing applications conform to the Windows client/server model. They perform all of their OLAP functions (i.e., interface, query generation, data formatting and display) on the user's PC—the client side. When the user requests information or analysis, an SQL query is transmitted from the PC to a network server that manages the data warehouse. In this case, the data warehouse is truly just a data server that transmits the query result set back to the user PC for formatting and display.

The result is a very client-centric application architecture that is based on a two-tier application partitioning scheme. In this arrangement, both the presentation (interface and display) and logic processing (query and formatting) are performed on the client. The presentation and logic processing are in fact a single tier, with the client-side computer code functioning as a single program. The data warehouse comprises the second tier in this two-tier architecture, which still forms the basis for most client/server data warehouse applications. Figure 2.1 illustrates a typical two-tier architecture.

Three-Tier Application Partitioning

The distributed computing model of the intranet encourages the transfer of some or all of the analytic processing from the PC onto the application servers. To accomplish this, the application logic components are partitioned from the presentation tier, resulting in a three-tier architecture. The intranet also allows interface and display software components (i.e., the presentation tier) to be electronically delivered to the user's desktop on demand. When users request information from a server by issuing a URL, they typically retrieve a page of HTML text. The HTML page may, however, contain application components that allow users to establish communications with an external program to, for example, invoke an OLAP function. With this arrangement (i.e., downloading

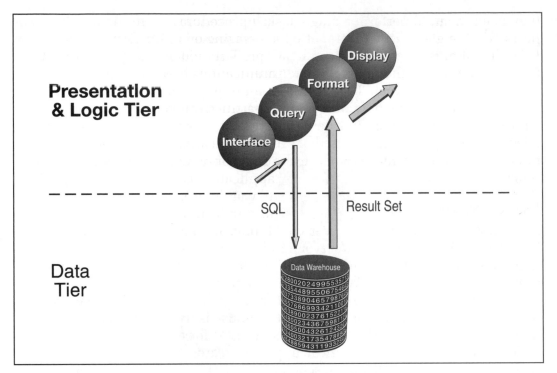

Presentation & Logic Tier

Interface Query Format Display

SQL   Result Set

Data Tier

Data Warehouse

Figure 2.1 Two-tier application partitioning of data warehouse applications.

application components to the Web browser), there is no need to permanently install any of the OLAP application code on the client.

Application developers favor a three-tier application model because, by separating the logic components from the presentation tier, they can modify the presentation tier (the interface and the display components) without impacting the underlying logic tier. Much like the data warehouse represents a shareable data tier, the logic tier also becomes shareable by multiple applications. The key benefit of a three-tier partitioning scheme is that the presentation tier can be tailored to needs of users while sharing both consistent data (data tier) and OLAP functions (logic tier).

One characteristic of a true three-tier application is that developers of the application computer code often use different programming languages for each application tier. In a three-tier model, applications developers create the database using SQL. Programming tools such as Microsoft's Visual Basic or Sun's Java are well suited for creating the code for the presentation tier; and developing the logic tier generally requires a robust procedural language like C or C++. An API—typically one based on object messaging or remote procedure calls—manages communications between the presentation tier and the logic tier, while SQL continues to handle the communications between the logic tier and the data tier. Figure 2.2 illustrates the three-tier partitioning model.

The value of the three-tier application partitioning model becomes particularly apparent when considering the architecture of the intranet. The Web browser becomes an important part of the application presentation tier, serving as the shell within which application components are presented. The browser is the only piece of client-side application code that is necessary and common to every user of the intranet data warehouse. Additional components that represent the presentation tier of an application are downloaded to the browser. It was noted earlier that none of the component pieces of the application need to be permanently installed on the client-side; however, browsers

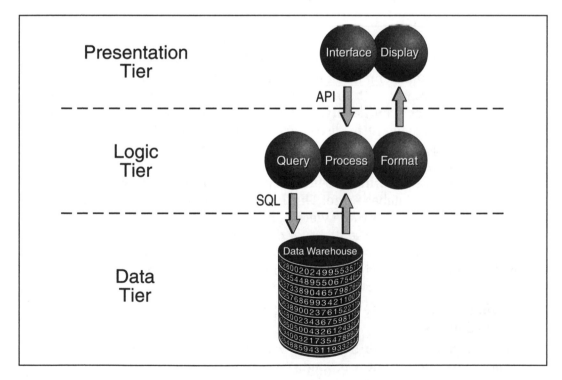

Figure 2.2   Three-tier application partitioning for data warehouse application development.

support the caching of downloaded components to the PC. The term *plug-in* describes this capability. Using plug-ins improves the performance of an application that requires downloading a substantial amount of code to the PC. Once downloaded, the code can be reused without having to repeat the download process each time.

By providing the ability to download interface and display components on demand, the presentation tier becomes highly adaptable to meet the needs of users, a critical requirement for meeting the more specific information needs of active and casual users. The three-tier application partitioning model also allows the logic components to be executed on a server, which is essential for supporting the thin-client requirements of the intranet. The three-tier model does, however, raise many new issues with respect to managing the communications among components of an application that are distributed between the client and one or more servers. These issues are discussed in some detail later in this chapter; specific vendor solutions are given in Chapters 6 and 7.

Scalability

Despite all of its inherent advantages, an intranet data warehouse involves some very real management challenges, many of which result directly from the dramatic increase in the number of users accessing the system and performing data retrieval and analysis. The additional processing load magnifies the need for management to devote careful attention to the scalability of the database management platform—the hardware and software, as well as the network and OLAP tools.

Discussions of scalability, particularly with regard to data warehousing, often focus only on database size. Until recently, this was the only dimension that was of concern since there were relatively few power users in any organization actually using the client/server data warehouses on a regular basis. Certainly, database size is an important factor in scalability, but we need to consider three other issues with respect to intranet data warehouse scalability:

- **Capacity:** The ability of the warehouse to effectively manage very large databases.
- **Concurrency:** The ability of the warehouse to effectively support a very large concurrent user load.
- **Complexity:** The ability of the warehouse to facilitate comprehensive OLAP functions.

Providing access to the data warehouse and OLAP functions via the intranet presents a range of scalability challenges, but the intranet's distributed applications architecture provides a very workable solution. Consider the Internet, essentially a huge worldwide information warehouse that supports the largest user community on Earth. By adopting Internet technologies, intranets meet many of the challenges of large-scale deployment. Successful intranet deployment does, however, require discarding the client-centric application development approaches defined by Windows in favor of the server-centric architecture of intranet technology. The various issues related to scalability are explained in more detail in Chapters 8 and 9, focusing on the selection of appropriate database software and server architecture.

Security

As mentioned earlier, widescale Internet or intranet deployment of data warehouse access raises important issues regarding security. The intranet data warehouse architecture must enforce database security through multiple layers of network security. Without question, the liberal sharing of information among intranet users causes some very real concerns about data security. In one sense, these issues are not unique to the intranet data warehouse since client/server data warehouses must also enforce database security. In both cases, users are generally granted read-only privileges and are authorized to access only a portion of the contents of the data warehouse.

But the issues associated with security are amplified by the exposure of the data warehouse to a larger user community and are further compounded when users can enter the intranet from the Internet. Network security is a serious issue, not only to protect the intranet data warehouse from incursions from the "outside" but also to safeguard all other valuable information assets of the enterprise. We'll deal with the security issues in more detail in Chapter 10, but for now, it's important to recognize that while the data in a warehouse must be secured, if it is too tightly controlled, the true value of the warehouse cannot be realized.

Database security issues are particularly complex with respect to the intranet data warehouse goals of sharing information and improving collaboration among users. If, for example, a vice president of sales has authorization to view all financial data at the national, regional, and territory levels, he or she can create reports for distribution to the regional sales managers. But, if the regional sales managers are authorized to view detail information only for the territories within their respective regions, the vice president may inadvertently share sensitive information (such as salary data) that the regional sales managers are not authorized to view or access. At some level, management must determine the value of sharing information among users; if the links to the data warehouse are maintained to support true collaboration, it is necessary to establish specific authorization and access privileges for each user. Database security should not be compromised at the OLAP application logic tier.

Structure of the Intranet Data Warehouse

The basic structure of an intranet is a private TCP/IP network connecting servers and clients using the same standards and protocols as the Internet. The intranet is often connected to the Internet through a firewall that limits external access to the secure intranet, while still permitting access to the public Internet. Users already familiar with the basics of Web technology may want to skim this next section and the accompanying sidebars to review the major concepts and/or to familiarize themselves with the terminology as it relates to the data warehouse and OLAP applications.

Initially, intranets were primarily intended to store static text pages such as price lists, training manuals, and information bulletins for retrieval from a browser. The ability to easily update and deploy these pages throughout the enterprise using the basic Internet technology components (see the Sidebar "Key Components of Internet and Intranet Technology") made the early intranets extremely popular with large organizations. Figure 2.3 illustrates the basic architecture of the intranet for retrieving unstructured content.

Organizations are evolving intranets to serve a wide range of business applications, including Intranet data warehouses to provide users with access to structured content. Intranets are superseding client/server applications development, which placed the computing burden on the client, in favor of server-centric applications development that distributes computing across the network. In this way, the Web browser is becoming the universal interface to a wide range of business applications and information resources.

This is an important distinction between the intranet and the Internet: Internet technologies are moving to support electronic commerce, while intranet technologies are moving to support a new distributed, network computing applications development model that is capable of addressing a wide range of business needs. Although intranets and the Internet are based on the same technology and adhere to the same protocols and standards, they are on two distinctly different evolutionary courses.

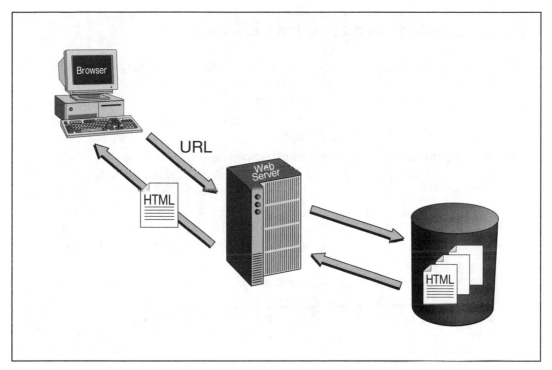

Figure 2.3   Intranet architecture.

Applying Intranet Technology to the Data Warehouse

Creating the underlying database for an intranet data warehouse involves essentially the same steps as for creating a client/server data warehouse database. Issues associated with source data extraction, validation, data cleansing, and maintenance are identical. Generally, a data warehouse developed for client/server access can also support intranet access. However, the user information requirements (i.e., tactical and operational decision support versus strategic decision making), coupled with greater performance, scalability, and security concerns, may result in the need to create a separate data warehouse or data marts for intranet deployment.

The OLAP functions that reside between the browser and the database in an intranet data warehouse system represent a unique aspect of an intranet data warehouse. The acronym itself well defines the technological requirements: the data warehouse needs to be *online* to the Web browser, and an *analytic*

Key Components of Internet and Intranet Technology

- **Cookies:** A mechanism developed by Netscape to accommodate the "stateless" nature of the Web. Cookies, which are now widely supported by other Web browser software, allow server-side connections to store and retrieve information at the client, thereby creating a persistent client-side state.

- **DNS (Domain Name System software):** A system of hierarchical names and name servers that translates host names into Internet addresses.

- **CGI (Common Gateway Interface):** The first widely supported standard for linking external programs to HTTP; it provides the link between HTTP and HTML to external programs that dynamically generate documents

- **HTTP (HyperText Transfer Protocol):** One of the most common methods of transferring documents across the Internet. The syntax of a typical HTTP URL is http://host/path. For example, the URL http://www.microsoft.com defines the browser protocol as HTTP; the host hierarchy is a named server "microsoft" within the World Wide Web domain. Because HTTP uses a standard port number (80), no port number is specified.

- **HTML (HyperText Markup Language):** The language commonly used to create text pages for Web display. HTML incorporates codes that define fonts, page layout, embedded graphics, and hypertext links. These codes, which are generally called *tags,* instruct the browser on how to display content.

- **Hypertext links:** The pointers that link HTML pages for display on Web browsers. Hypertext links include the destination URLs. The

process must be executed to create information for display in the Web browser.

OLAP applications must execute computer code for both the presentation and logic tiers. From a user perspective, the most obvious difference between client/server and intranet data warehouse deployment strategies is what appears "on the glass" with respect to the presentation tier. On the intranet, the

Web browser highlights text that has a hypertext pointer and interprets a click on the text as a request to access the referenced document.

- **IP (Internet Protocol):** A low-level communications protocol that creates the basic links between nodes. Most Web servers rely on IP.

- **Search engines:** Web tools that enable URLs associated with content stored on an Internet or intranet server to be registered for efficient retrieval. The registration process involves storing descriptive information about the content in an indexed database of URLs. The search engine examines the database to locate all URLs containing information associated with a user-specified search topic. Search engines are important because they provide an extremely useful form of metadata, that is, the data about the information resources available to users.

- **TCP (Transmission Control Protocol):** A higher-level communications protocol that operates in conjunction with IP to provide a reliable virtual connection between two applications situated anywhere on the network. Together, the IP and TCP protocols are commonly referred to as TCP/IP.

- **URL (Universal Resource Locator):** Essentially, the address of an Internet resource, along with information about how it can be accessed. The URL uses a *schemepath* syntax in which *scheme* identifies the protocol that the browser uses to access the resource (e.g., HTTP), and *path* is a hierarchical name that includes the host name and an optional port number.

- **Web browser:** A program that issues requests for resources across networks and displays the resources when they are returned.

presentation tier is—at least initially—simply the browser that retrieves the enterprise's home page (in HTML), which provides a high-level overview of the information resources available to the user. Many organizations include a search engine to assist users in locating specific information resources by topic. The Sidebar "Retrieving Information from an Intranet Data Warehouse" describes what happens when an intranet data warehouse user issues a request for information.

Retrieving Information from an Intranet Data Warehouse

The following is an example of how a user's request for data contained in the intranet data warehouse is processed "over the wire." From the enterprise's home page, which is coded as an HTML document and presented "on the glass," the user enters "Phoenix Sales Report" in a box labeled "Search for available reports." The browser then sends the topic "Phoenix Sales Report" to the search engine program that resides on a server, which in turn issues a query or a directory listing to the search engine's database. The search engine query identifies all matching report entries in the database and sends a list (in HTML format) back to the browser, indicating a URL for each report on the list.

Once again "on the glass," the user selects a report from the list by clicking on its description. Clicking on the item issues the URL to the appropriate Web server. In this example, the Web server sends a component of an application interface that looks like any other document that may be displayed in the Web browser. This is one of the unique aspects of developing applications for the intranet: The application logic is often disguised, appearing to the user as just another page of text. At one level, this is not all that different from presenting a user with a "menu" of choices common in mainframe applications development.

In this example, the Web server is an applications server that returns an HTML page containing a list of available markets (a menu of selections) for which the sales report can be generated, along with the URL associated with each market listed on the menu. When the user clicks on Phoenix in the list, the browser issues the selected URL to the applications server containing

In a traditional client/server data warehousing system, users begin the information retrieval process by booting client-side application code. The user then interacts with the application code to produce content. The reverse is true of the intranet, where the application code disappears behind the content. In the client/server environment, the user is often provided with an array of standalone applications. In the intranet world, the user has an enormous amount of content that is organized behind a single universal entry point—the browser. The challenge for intranet developers is to maintain the simplicity of the browser interface while delivering the comprehensive analytic processing the OLAP logic. In this case, the URL contains a CGI script that provides a reference to a UNIX or NT file that contains a program (i.e., the logic components) that generates an SQL query based on the user's selection. An example of the URL issued from the browser, based on the user's selection of Phoenix from the list of available markets, is as follows:

www.server_name.com/cgi_ibin/report_market.cgi "market=phoenix"

When the Web server receives this request, it locates and starts the executable report_market and substitutes the parameter Phoenix. The executable generates an SQL query, once again substituting Phoenix in the SQL code. (e.g., select date, product, units, from fact_table where market like phoenix). The database then returns the query results to the executable on the server. The executable performs any processing that is required to construct a report. The report, which is now simply formatted data in the application server memory, is next converted into an HTML document by another server-based program—the format component of the application.

The process of transforming the report file into an HTML document that can be read by the browser requires adding HTML tags to the row and column headings and the data itself. The formatting component of the application applies HTML tags based on the requirements of the application. For example, a column heading in the report "Phoenix" would become <td>Phoenix</td> when placed in an HTML stream. The executable returns the HTML stream to the Web server, which sends it back for display in the browser as a columnar report.

Of course, this example has been simplified to illustrate the key processing layers and one method (CGI scripts) of establishing communications between the Web browser, a server resident program, and the data warehouse.

needed to extract data from a relational database (i.e., formulate an SQL query) and process the raw data for display in the browser.

A less obvious difference between client/server and intranet data warehouse systems is the role of the server in processing users' requests for information "over the wire"; in other words, processing requests on a server somewhere on the network. We use the term "on the wire" to emphasize that the user need not be concerned with where on the network the process is actually performed.

Most client/server applications rely on communicating SQL queries generated from client-side OLAP functions directly to the data warehouse via Microsoft's open database connectivity (ODBC) protocol for managing communications with a server-resident database. A client/server application is designed to help the user construct a query to produce a report online (to author new content), while most intranet applications are designed to retrieve static content.

The value of the intranet data warehouse is in providing users with dynamic content creation by inserting OLAP functions between the browser and the data warehouse. OLAP application vendors use either of two approaches to accomplish this. One approach is to download the logic components of an OLAP application and cache the components on the client-side (i.e., plug-ins). The approach offers an efficient means of delivering software to users, invoking electronic transmission rather than requiring users to install software distributed via diskette or CD-ROM. The client then issues SQL calls in much the same manner as any client/server tool.

The second approach is to process the logic components on an application server. This reduces the network traffic and provides a more scalable three-tier distributed application solution than does the first approach. This approach provides an efficient method of distributing processing "on the wire" (executing OLAP logic functions on network-resident servers). Distributed processing reduces network traffic by minimizing the amount of code and data (query results) that are transported between the client and server. The server itself can be scaled more effectively to meet the processing load than can individual PCs throughout the enterprise. In addition to reducing network traffic and increasing server scalability, this approach partitions the application interface from the logic, allowing developers to adapt the interface to the needs of a diverse user community. Figure 2.4 illustrates how the presentation tier can be tailored to suit specific user requirements while sharing logic components on the server.

Figure 2.4 also illustrates that, rather than issuing SQL code from the client-side, messages or remote procedure calls are being issued to server from the client-side browser-resident interface. The server-resident OLAP functions send a query to the data warehouse, process and format the results, then send the output back to the browser, generally as an HTML document. This arrangement permits the presentation tier to be changed or customized without rewriting the underlying application logic.

Integrating Search Engines into the Interface Component

The search engine is an essential part of the interface component of an intranet data warehouse. In fact, it is the combination of the browser and a search engine that represents the universal client interface to the full range of

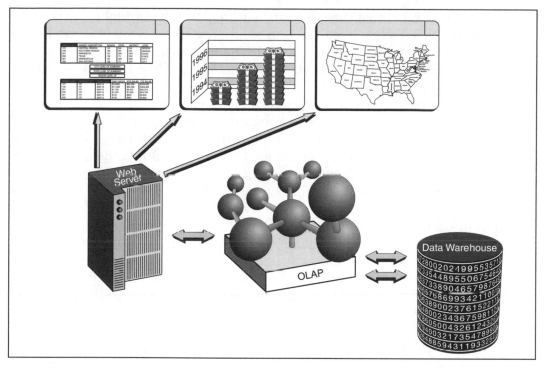

Figure 2.4 Intranet data warehouse applications feature an adaptable presentation tier.

information resources. A number of companies including Fulcrum Technologies, Excalibur Technologies, Verity, and Excite offer industrial-strength search engines for intranets (Fulcrum Surfboard, RetrievalWare, SEARCH97, and Excite, respectively). Search engines provide metadata about the information resources available to users, typically about the unstructured (static) content available on Web servers.

To effectively integrate the data warehouse with Internet and intranet technologies, search engines must be capable of navigating information that is dynamically extracted from the data warehouse (i.e., structured content), enabling a user to enter a search phrase like "Sales and Phoenix" to discover that a sales report can be produced from the intranet data warehouse. It is possible to perform this type of retrieval today from an intranet data warehouse, but the process is not a particularly simple one. Users must create "virtual reports" (report templates) that can be dynamically generated on demand by the OLAP functions. The users must then describe and register the virtual reports to the search engine, just as they would describe and register a static information resource. When the virtual reports are subsequently requested, the search engine downloads components of the user interface to allow the user to further refine the information request.

The information request ultimately results in the dynamic creation of the report as an HTML document. The user can then drill up or down within any dimension that is marked up in the report, thereby reinitiating the dynamic generation of yet another report at the next level up or down the dimensional hierarchy. For example, after reviewing sales data for Phoenix, a user may want to retrieve more detailed information about the sales region, in this case drilling up to the western region sales report, and then, if necessary, back down to the details concerning the Albuquerque market. In this way, users can navigate the structured content contained in the data warehouse in much the same way as they navigate the unstructured content on the Internet. A Web browser allows the user to return to the search engine at any time to shift the analysis or information search to a new topic or to retrieve text or image information.

Using Agent Technology

Search engines make it easier to "pull" information from a large information store by serving as a guide. Agents, on the other hand, work on behalf of users to "push" information based on a user's need to know. Because they provide a means to automate routine analytical processes, agents are a valuable means of alerting users of critical situations—once again accelerating the decision-making process.

While agent technology is certainly applicable to client/server data warehousing systems, the need to support operational and tactical decision making of intranet users makes it essential for intranet data warehouse systems. In particular, casual users need to be alerted to changes in business conditions that demand immediate attention.

As discussed in more detail in Chapter 11, an agent process is triggered by some predefined event or at a specified time interval. The agent then sends an alert to notify users on a need-to-know basis. Triggers, agents, and alerts must be able to run continually as background processes somewhere on the intranet.

A sales forecasting application being developed by a major manufacturer of consumer products provides a good example of the use of triggers, agents, and alerts. When each week's actual sales are updated to the data warehouse (trigger), the system automatically calculates the mean absolute percent error between statistically forecasted sales and actual results for the latest six-week period for every product (an agent process). The mean absolute percent error is a simple way of representing forecast error over time. The system sends an alert to each marketing manager responsible for the product forecast whenever a threshold for the mean absolute percent error calculation is exceeded. The marketing manager can then take appropriate actions to avoid out-of-stock situations or excessive inventory buildup.

Longer-term, agent technologies are likely to support closed-loop decision support and electronic authorization. Closed-loop decision support is a process by which agents trigger other agents to actually formulate a recommended action for user authorization. In the sales forecasting example, the system might trigger a second agent to recompute a statistical forecast based on inclusion of most recent data or to increase the safety stock level provided to manufacturing.

Developing Intranet OLAP Applications

Although developers often use tools such as HTML and Java (see the Sidebar "Component API Standards") to build the presentation tier of the OLAP application for intranet deployment, technology alone does not represent the major difference between developing applications for intranet deployment and those for client/server deployment. Remember that the design goal of most client/server applications, including OLAP applications, is to make a complex computing process easy to use, which generally means conforming to the Windows model of file structure and icons. The application developer adds numerous features that may (or may not) be required by users and distributes the shrink-wrapped product to the mass market.

In contrast, providing OLAP functions for the intranet data warehouse requires the developer to hide the application code behind the content. In many cases, the content is the only aspect of the application visible to the user. A report displayed as a page of HTML text often acts as the interface for executing calls to an external program to perform the next step in the computing process. At one level, the application interface becomes irrelevant because it is both highly adaptive to an individual user's needs and, if the developer is successful, it is nearly invisible to the user. For example, many Internet users cannot distinguish between the role of the browser and that of the search engine in retrieving text documents. If the browser issues a URL that contains a CGI script, then an external process is executed to fulfill the user's request.

But, for the most part, users remain blissfully unaware of (and unconcerned by) the underlying processes.

The components of the application logic tier should be developed in a high-level programming language such as C, C++, or Java. SQL, which was developed primarily to retrieve data organized in tables, columns, and rows, is poorly suited for coding complex multstep analytic logic. Although the application logic components can be downloaded to the browser, this tends to result in the type of application design that is reminiscent of Windows applications. Therefore, the recommended approach is to employ a distributed application model where the logic components are executed on a server. Distributed processing "over the wire" is key to achieving scalability of the intranet data warehouse.

One important aspect of a distributed applications environment is that it allows users to implement multiple vendors' tools at various tiers; for example, OLAP tools developed by one vendor communicate with the databases provided by another. As applications are partitioned further, the (server-resident) logic components are integrated with client-side applications that provide a wide range of client-side services, including more robust display options. For this reason, standards play a major role in the success of Internet and intranet technologies; they ensure that code developed by one vendor (e.g., a three-dimensional data visualization capability) can access server-resident databases and analytic functions developed by another vendor. The result is an "object-ware" software market that supports applications assembly from component parts.

Building a distributed intranet data warehouse application (one that allows components to be processed on servers "over the wire" as opposed to centralizing processing on the PC) requires three key technologies: a cross-platform development language, a component API, and a distributed component architecture.

Cross-Platform Development Language

In order to develop programs capable of running on multiple operating systems and hardware platforms, programmers need a standard development language that can run on every platform without modification of their code. Sun Microsystems' Java promises to be such a language. Java is an object-oriented programming language that supports platform-independent application development of code as applets. The advantage of coding a Java applet is that HTML documents can be dynamically enriched with sophisticated user interface, information display, or application logic components. Most current operating systems and hardware platforms are designed to provide high-performance execution environments for Java bytecodes.

There is no doubt that Java will be a major factor in intranet application development, especially in cases where cross-platform independence is required. However, Java is a relatively new language and still has a way to go to equal the power and capabilities of more mature development languages like C++. Also, true cross-platform compatibility comes at a price. Java itself, and programs written in Java, must always take into consideration the "least common denominator" platform intended for its deployment. In many cases, developers will not trade off rich functionality to support multiple platforms. Where functionality is more important than support for multiple platforms, development languages like C++ and Visual Basic will continue to have their proponents.

Component API

Programmers also need a specification for encapsulating their program's functions and making them available for use by other software programs. In particular, OLAP logic components should be shared by components used at the presentation tier. By changing the interface or display components, an application takes on an entirely new look and feel, even though the query and processing logic remains the same. This type of relationship between the presentation tier and the logic tier permits software vendors to develop products that adhere to a common standard, thereby shortening the development time for applications that address the needs of different users and business problems. In other words, a wide range of business applications can be assembled from existing components rather than being hand-crafted from scratch. With an effective component standard for application development, the Web can realize its potential for rapid development as well as rapid deployment of intranet applications. Once again, it is important to note that a component model is not a unique requirement of intranet applications development; the distributed applications architecture of the intranet simply emphasizes its importance. Similarly, OLAP applications place greater emphasis on a component model because data analysis requires developing a substantial amount of code.

Two component API standards are currently emerging: Microsoft's ActiveX and Sun's JavaBeans. Both have particular relevance for the Web and specific relevance to how OLAP functions are coded, although they tackle the problem from very different perspectives (see the Sidebar "Component API Standards").

Component API Standards

- **Microsoft ActiveX:** Microsoft's ActiveX API assumes that leveraging the investment in existing PC and OLE technologies is more important than cross-platform support and calls for components that can be combined with other ActiveX components. The advantage of ActiveX is that it extends Microsoft's popular OLE component model to the Web. Thus, existing Microsoft desktop applications will be able to move to ActiveX with limited effort. Furthermore, Microsoft's dominant share of the desktop market and existing client/server applications give ActiveX instant credibility. The major disadvantage of ActiveX is that it is supported only on Microsoft platforms, although this factor is mitigated somewhat by the fact that ActiveX supports Java, enabling ActiveX desktops to request services of powerful server-based JavaBean components. Microsoft also claims to also be building its own version of Java runtime for UNIX. This version will probably run Java code built into the ActiveX model on any operating system and hardware platform. (Refer to Chapter 6 for additional information.)

- **Microsystems' Sun JavaBeans:** Sun's JavaBeans API assumes that cross-platform portability is more important than extreme functionality and calls for components that can be combined with other applications in other component architectures, even ActiveX. The beauty of JavaBeans is that it is written in Java; consequently, an application studded with JavaBeans can run anywhere, and because of its compact nature, will work even on hardware with minimal resources. The major disadvantage of JavaBeans is that it is lagging behind ActiveX in market acceptance and momentum. JavaBeans became available in late 1996 and has no legacy applications to leverage. (Refer to Chapter 7 for additional information.)

Distributing Presentation Components

Although applications developed for an intranet data warehouse can take advantage of distributed computing by moving major portions of the application processing to servers, there is still a need to electronically transfer application components from the server to the client. At a minimum, portions of the presentation tier (the interface and display components of the OLAP application) must be downloaded to the browser. The presentation tier provides the link to a browser-resident interface that controls server-based OLAP components that reside "on the wire" (i.e., processes executed on the server). The downloaded presentation tier components (computer code) may be cached on the PC for future use, but more often the code is discarded when the application is completed. The result is that applications become "objectware"—the user interface and display components are downloaded to the browser to instruct application logic components that remain on the server. Users adapt the interface to the application logic by selecting and downloading only the user interface components that are relevant. Sun Microsystems created its Java development language specifically to facilitate the development of objectware. Figure 2.5 illustrates a typical objectware model for distributed computing.

The developers of OLAP software are tasked with determining *if* components will be distributed to a server, *which* components will be distributed

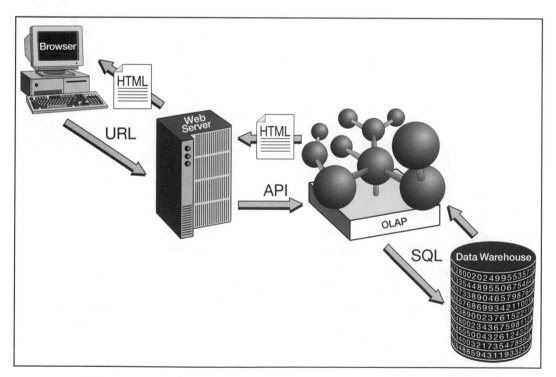

Figure 2.5   Objectware model for distributed computing.

Distributed Component Architectures

- **CORBA (Common Object Request Broker Architecture):** At a high level, CORBA, developed by the Object Management Group (OMG), is very similar to DCE (see next entry) in that it is intended to support the construction and integration of client/server applications in heterogeneous distributed environments. At a lower level, however, CORBA is specifically designed to support distributed object programming. The benefit of CORBA is its technology; on paper it calls for a pure, distributed, object-oriented approach that is truly platform independent. Its main drawback is the absence of available components to run atop the platform and a lack of momentum in attracting development atop its platform.

- **DCE (Distributed Computing Environment):** Like CORBA, DCE, developed by the Open Software Foundation (OSF), aims at making the network computer look like one ubiquitous server so that applications need not concern themselves with where the clients and servers are located on the network, or with differences in operating systems, hardware platforms, languages, or network protocols. Unlike CORBA, DCE is designed to support distributed object programming.

- **DCOM (Distributed Component Object Model):** DCOM is a Microsoft technology loosely based on DCE's RPC (Distributed Computing Environment/Remote Procedure Call) technology. DCOM is specifically designed to support distributed processing of OLE/ActiveX components. A major disadvantage of DCOM is that it is currently supported only on Microsoft platforms, although Microsoft is discussing the possibility of releasing the DCOM specification to a standards body. (Microsoft uses ActiveX to link Java to DCOM in order to support distributed object communications.)

- **IIOP (Internet Inter-ORB Protocol):** IIOP allows ORBs from different vendors to communicate with each other over the Internet and intranets. It is based on CORBA and extends the CORBA standard to the Web. Sun and Netscape both use JavaBeans to link Java to IIOP.

onto the server, and last, *what* component architecture will be used to develop components. Scalability requirements of most intranet data warehousing applications will demand distributing processing more evenly across the network. In order for JavaBeans or ActiveX to interoperate with components of other models *and* have them communicate with each other across the network, they must leverage an existing distributed component architecture (see the Sidebar "Distributed Component Architectures").

Selecting a component architecture is a pragmatic decision that is largely determined by the choice of a component API. Considering the competitive edge that Microsoft currently has in this area with ActiveX, we can expect DCOM to play a dominate role, whereas CORBA is likely to carve a significant niche in the high-end, where UNIX remains the dominant server operating system. Although intranet distributed computing standards are maturing rapidly, they are also constantly evolving. Because the distributed applications development aspects of the intranet are critical to building a scalable intranet data warehouse, it is an area that software developers must monitor very carefully.

CASE STUDY

Fidelity Investments Incorporated

Fidelity Investments is the largest privately held investment manager in the world, with more than $400 billion in assets under management and more than 20,000 employees worldwide. Throughout its history, Fidelity has focused on technology to enhance its services to institutional clients and individual investors; the company invests heavily in technology. In 1996 alone, Fidelity invested $500 million in hardware, software, and services to support research and analysis of virtually every publicly traded company in the world.

While Fidelity is widely recognized as the world's largest mutual fund company, it is also an enterprise of individual, tightly integrated smaller businesses. This diversified approach, combined with a significant investment in technology, keeps the company in touch with clients on an ongoing basis and helps it to maintain a leadership position in the financial industry.

With a strong push for commonality across all trading desks and a need for continuous monitoring of operations, funds, and fund manager perfor-

mance, Fidelity recognized a need to know more about how efficiently the business was running. To that end, management decided to centralize trade and holdings information in a data warehouse. Achieving commonality and analyzing trade activities such as trades, transactions that make up trades, and holdings information was the first step. As part of the infrastructure development, the company established dimensions such as markets, time periods, trade desks, traders, and various parameters of each trade. The structure provides levels within each dimension to allow trade controllers, for example, to look at trading activity from several views and to drill anywhere within the hierarchy to aggregate and analyze trading volumes by desk and number of trades completed by each broker.

Keeping the data warehouse information as close to the actual information sources across all trading systems was one design goal. "By using Information Advantage DecisionSuite and WebOLAP, our trading desks have consolidated analysis information at their fingertips 'near real time' so they can react very quickly to changes in the market," says Tim Davis, chief technologist and head of Data Warehousing at Fidelity. "Our goal is to keep the data warehouse to within 15 minutes of all trading systems."

To accomplish this, a lot of things must happen very quickly when information is loaded. There are four key steps: the load process, the index process, referential integrity checking, and aggregation maintenance. The automation and monitoring of these processes provides timely results. Davis continues: "To meet the goal of a 15-minute 'near real time' data warehouse, all processes must be finely tuned. For example, a complex report may run for two minutes, then the load and index processes are initiated, followed by referential integrity checking and aggregation maintenance of hundreds of gigabytes of data." As a result, an agent process can trigger reports to be automatically created and delivered to the decision makers, notifying them on a need-to-know basis. Within 15 minutes, managers have the knowledge they need to react and make decisions.

According to Davis, "The time factor associated with ad hoc analysis enables managers to continue their intuitive investigation. If, for example, a security that had not been trading for several years suddenly starts trading, an alert can notify managers, with more detailed ad hoc analysis generated from that point to look into the details of the trade. Intelligent agents act as a system of checks and balances. Because of the volumes, content, and complexity of the data, combined with the fact that all the businesspeople operate in a fast-paced environment, a proactive system is critical. If a risk limit is exceeded or there is a potential compliance violation, the appropriate departments are notified. Each person on the system is set up with hundreds of intelligent agents running continually in the background working on his or her behalf. The sophisticated approach to using agent technology goes beyond text- or report-based alerts by notifying managers of conditions via their pagers, the Internet and intranet."

Fidelity's long-term strategy relies heavily on the integration of the Web with the data warehouse. "Several initiatives are underway to deliver as much information as possible over the Web because it provides an efficient means for delivering cost-effective worldwide installation and support services, minimizes training, and facilitates data warehouse analysis anytime, anywhere by anyone," says Davis. "Now we can analyze structured data found in the warehouse combined with unstructured data found on the Web. The Web is a strong delivery mechanism for various types of reporting and solves problems at sites around the world."

With the company's most sensitive information contained in its data warehouse, Fidelity took security to a new level. In addition to operating system security and database security with encrypted passwords, the third level is metadata security. Using metadata inherent in the decision support software from Information Advantage is a good example of how direct access can be provided to the metadata environment and then controlled with data filters to determine who can access information down to specified levels of aggregation. A metadata registry was developed to drive functionality and direct access security for all facets of the data warehouse.

The company has also established stringent criteria for measuring the success of the data warehouse. For example, most analysis reports have to run in a subsecond to two-minute response range. And proactive reports initiated from intelligent agents must be created and delivered to desktops so that the recipient gets specific information whenever boundary conditions are exceeded. To report system activity and deliver the information to trading desks on a need-to-know basis, a series of agents continually monitor the system and produce reports based on complex calculations and automatic queries. "Producing such complex reports was not possible before we put the new analysis software in place," comments Davis. "With results like these, measuring the success of the data warehouse was not as difficult as we first thought."

Fidelity expects the trade and holdings information to expand the data *warehouse at a rate of 3 to 4 gigabytes each month, with 300 to 400 giga-bytes being analyzed this year. The company is currently extending the data warehouse and Web integration system to its offices throughout the world. Davis credits the system with increasing the speed at which the company reaches decisions and maximizing the potential of the Web in vital areas of the business.* ■

CHAPTER THREE

DATA WAREHOUSE DESIGN

The Internet has been successful, in part, because millions of people have participated in creating the largest information store on earth, piece by piece. Data warehousing for intranet access will result in a similar proliferation of databases, both internal and external to the enterprise. However, many organizations embark on their first data warehousing project as though it is going to be the single, all-inclusive "last warehouse" that they will ever need, when actually, taking a lesson from the Internet, organizations are very likely to build multiple data warehouses and data marts over time and to create numerous analytic caches. The alternative to creating a single, all-inclusive, "last warehouse" is to create an "organic" intranet data warehouse strategy, one in which the database continuously evolves to meet users' changing information requirements, and is likely to be a network of distributed data warehouses and data marts, all integrated with other information resources available to intranet users.

For the past several decades, corporations have strived to improve their on-line transaction processing (OLTP) systems. The by-product of these efforts is a vast store of data describing, in considerable detail, virtually every aspect of business operating performance. Information that can't be collected internally is often provided through independent sources in response to an ever-expanding need for market intelligence.

While the need to consolidate and organize such massive amounts of data for business analysis is not new, combining relational database management system (RDBMS) software with powerful server hardware does offer new solutions. Together, these technologies are removing many of the technical barriers to creating large databases (data warehouses) that can be shared by a broad range of business applications.

Early data warehousing applications enabled users to access the warehouse via PC tools that greatly simplified the process of generating SQL code for data retrieval. Once retrieved, the data was formatted for the user's PC and analyzed, often using spreadsheet software. Although this approach provided users with access to consistent data from a single, well-managed source, the burden of data analysis burden fell to the individual user.

As data access methods continue to improve, users' data analysis requirements also increase proportionally, not because of any new or previously unrecognized need for analysis, but because users expect to get fast, accurate answers to their questions. The demand for online analytic processing (OLAP) is based on the need for powerful analytical capabilities that can be performed on data stored in the warehouse. Sophisticated OLAP functions mandate careful attention to data warehouse design to ensure usability and to deliver optimal performance.

Because Intranets dramatically increase the number of users that can be efficiently supported by a data warehouse, the usability and performance issues associated with the data warehouse increase substantially. It is important to remember that although intranets offer an effective means for improving communications and collaborative decision making, much of the user community is likely to be unfamiliar with the data warehouse and OLAP functions. This emphasizes the need to insulate users from the technical sophistication of the intranet, the OLAP functions, and the data warehouse itself.

This chapter provides an overview of data warehouse design considerations and discusses a number of design alternatives. It is not intended to be an exhaustive discussion of all the issues involved in designing and building a data warehouse. Instead, it focuses on the major design considerations in an intranet data warehouse environment: flexibility, performance, and ease-of-use. Readers who are already familiar with data warehouse design topics may want to skip the design discussions and review the chapter to familiarize themselves with the basic concepts and terminology that are used throughout the remainder of the book. The chapter also explores the evolving role of metadata, which plays a key role in managing data that is distributed across multiple servers on the Internet and intranets. Finally, it introduces considerations involved with integrating the structured content of data warehouses with unstructured content (text, images, and audio data) common to an intranet environment.

What Is a Data Warehouse?

Recalling Bill Inmon's definition of a data warehouse as "a subject-oriented, integrated, time-variant, nonvolatile collection of data in support of management's decision-making process," the following terms can be explained:

- **Subject-oriented** refers to the way the data warehouse is organized to describe business performance. Operational databases built to support OLTP applications are business process-oriented.
- **Integrated** means data are organized to provide a single source.
- **Time-variant** recognizes that business performance is measured at points in time (such as month-end) and compared over time.
- **Nonvolatile** suggests that data, once entered into the warehouse, should not change. OLTP/operational databases change every time a transaction is processed.

In general, data warehouses are created to provide users with data access and to support online analytic processing necessary for decision support. Only a particular class of data warehouses, referred to as *operational data stores*, actually "warehouse" data, removing the nonvolatile criteria applied to a data warehouse for decision support. In this respect, operational data stores are one step closer to an OLTP database. In this chapter, we will focus on data warehouses that are nonvolatile and are intended for use with decision support applications.

What's Different about an Intranet Data Warehouse?

The creation of the Internet information warehouse was not planned; it is an organic process, which means the warehouse is constantly growing and evolving to better serve the interests of the users.

An organic intranet data warehouse strategy recognizes that data warehouses come online in stages to respond to changing user requirements. Data warehouses may even be temporary, existing only as long as they are needed to address a specific business issue. In many cases, a data archive may be required to centralize data administration and ensure data currency (accuracy, consistency, and timeliness) across multiple databases. Remember, an intranet data warehouse is highly distributed. Although it offers great potential as a business analysis tool, it does significantly complicate database administration and business applications delivery. Even though a primary advantage of the data warehouse is that it provides a single, integrated source of data, managing an intranet data warehouse necessarily involves inherent challenges in data synchronization and currency.

Online Transaction Processing and Operational Databases

An airline reservation system is a classic example of an online transaction processing (OLTP) application built on top of an operational database. For each scheduled flight, the OLTP system enables an agent to reserve seats, complete the ticket purchase, and ultimately record occupancy in an online operational database. The primary goal of the system is to avoid double-booking a seat, or worse, overbooking a flight. Once a scheduled flight has departed, the reservation system has completed the critical portion of its task.

The airline system illustrates that the single most distinguishing characteristic of OLTP applications is that the database is constantly being updated. For example, the passenger count for a specific flight between two cities changes continually—right up until the moment of departure; consequently, the reservation system is not useful for decision support. And because the reservation system is mission-critical, its design cannot be compromised to meet the unique demands of business analysis.

If a decision maker at the airline wants to analyze the profitability of providing service between two cities (say, Phoenix and Minneapolis), the analysis must include an assessment of each flight time, by day, and during various travel seasons. In general, the basic rule of analysis is the more historical data the better the analysis. More data provides more analytic flexibility and greater confidence in the conclusions drawn from the analysis. In contrast, OLTP applications focus on maintaining the current status of each transaction; therefore, historical information is largely irrelevant.

Online Analytic Processing and the Data Warehouse

The data warehouse places a premium on an accurate reflection of history at various points in time. Historical data shouldn't change! Every time a user asks, "What were sales for June 1995 in the Denver market?" the answer should be the same. Having accurate historical data about business operations is not a new requirement. For decades, information services organizations have produced monthly management reports that are deemed the "official" record of historical performance. What has changed in recent years is decision makers' increased demand for access to the data on a near real-time basis rather than hard-copy batch reports delivered weeks after the query.

Price/performance improvement for server hardware platforms has made large-scale data warehousing both practical and affordable. And the adoption of relational database management systems has provided an "open" solution. The assumption throughout this book is that data warehouses are built using relational database management systems, which execute queries based on the Structure Query Language (SQL) code. In essence, this is the technique that supports the claim of openness, even though each software vendor offers unique SQL extensions.

Ralph Kimball, author of *The Data Warehouse Toolkit* (John Wiley & Sons, Inc., 1996), differentiates between an entity data warehouse design and a dimensional data warehouse design. The entity model is a normalized relational database modeling approach that emphasizes the elimination of data redundancies in the design. It produces a database that is complete and easily maintained, making this approach suitable for a data warehouse that is intended for data archiving.

The dimensional modeling approach results in a database design that is consistent with the paths by which users wish to enter and navigate the data warehouse. Frequently requested aggregates, or calculated measures, are stored in the database, creating useful data redundancies that make it possible to avoid performance-inhibiting repetitive calculations every time a report is prepared.

Extending Inmon's original metaphor of a decision support system as a data warehouse, the entity data-modeling approach creates a warehouse that inventories the "raw materials." This type of data warehouse differs slightly from an operational data store in that it serves as a nonvolatile archive.

More recently, the term *data mart* has been introduced into the discussion of data warehousing. A data mart can be considered the distribution center, created to more efficiently serve a segment of the users. Data marts, like distribution centers, are supplied from a central warehouse of finished goods. Both the central warehouse and the distribution center (the data mart) are designed as dimensional databases.

Analytic caches, which are also referred to as multidimensional databases or data cubes, represent yet another type of database design. In some respects, these are more like application-specific workspaces than true databases, despite the fact that several OLAP software vendors describe their analytic caches as "multidimensional databases." All computationally intensive OLAP applications must have a means of enforcing strict database dependencies, and require a workspace for storing interim calculations. Sophisticated OLAP applications rely on analytic caches to overcome the limitations of SQL (SQL is an excellent database query language, but it is not a robust programming language for coding complex procedural logic).

An analytic cache may be created dynamically and stored temporarily, or it may be created as a routine database update and held as a persistent cache for repetitive use. The type of analytic caching strategy that a tool uses is one of the fundamental characteristics that differentiate OLAP software products. Chapter 4 details the various caching strategies, but the concept of caching is introduced here to explain the difference between vendor-specific databases that support OLAP and "open" data warehouses and data marts that are capable of supporting multiple business applications. Figure 3.1 illustrates four in-

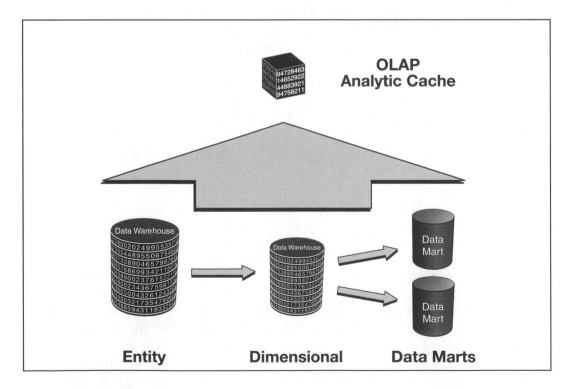

Figure 3.1   Four interrelated data warehouse database designs.

terrelated types of databases that are frequently discussed under the umbrella term data warehouse:

1. The entity model database that is the raw materials inventory.
2. The centralized finished goods warehouse based on a dimensional model.
3. The data marts or departmental distribution centers.
4. The analytic caches extracted for use by OLAP tools.

Entity Database Design and Applications

The entity data-modeling approach to data warehouse design is useful for creating a complete historical archive of data, a raw materials inventory. The entity model produces a design optimized to access data on a record-by-record (row-by-row) basis, at the lowest granular level—the transaction or occurrence level. In an entity model, the physical storage of the data is very important: Records are stored one after another for efficient extraction in contiguous bytes of information from the disk. Database design methodologies for this type of access are optimized for the efficient creation, update, and deletion of individual records. Figure 3.2 provides an example of the table structure that is typical of an entity model.

Organizations typically create an entity data warehouse to archive data, with the single most important goal to ensure that data is not lost. A data archive is also important if there is substantial transformation, cleansing, or integration of data sources. Query and reporting tools provide users with the ability to retrieve information from a data archive, but their analytical capabilities are limited by the database design, as are their reporting capabilities. In most cases, reporting is limited to generating a list of records.

Dimensional Database Design and Applications

In contrast to the entity model, data analysis requires data access on a field-by-field (column-by-column) basis. A dimensional database design meets flexibility, reusability, and performance requirements of a broad range of OLAP applications. For this reason, it is generally the focus of a data warehouse for intranet applications. For example, as in Figure 3.3, answering the question, What are the total sales of all red chairs in Minnesota for March? requires the selection of all rows that have Chair in them from the column *Product Type*;

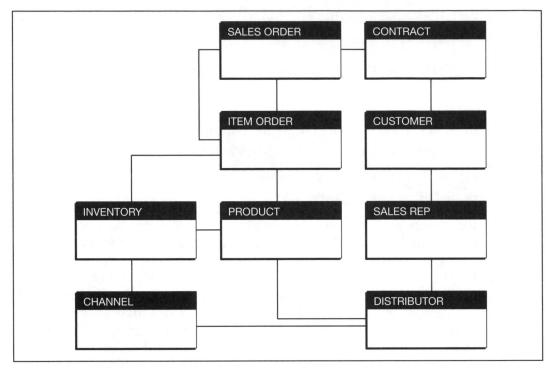

Figure 3.2 Logical design of an entity data model.

the selection of all rows that have Red in them from the column *Color*; the selection of all rows that have Minnesota in them from the column *State*; and the selection of all rows that have March in them from the column *Month*—returning the sum of the column *Sales Amount* for all rows matching these criteria.

In this situation, the data is analyzed by slices of time, rather than at the transaction or occurrence level, to produce meaningful comparisons. In the example, the "total sales of all red chairs in Minnesota for March" is most meaningful when sales are compared to the prior month or prior year, or if sales of chairs are ranked by color.

Dimensional modeling produces a database design that is consistent with the way the user enters and navigates the warehouse. The dimensional model is often referred to as the *star* schema because of the appearance of the logical database design.

Dimensional modeling combines fact tables that store time-series historical

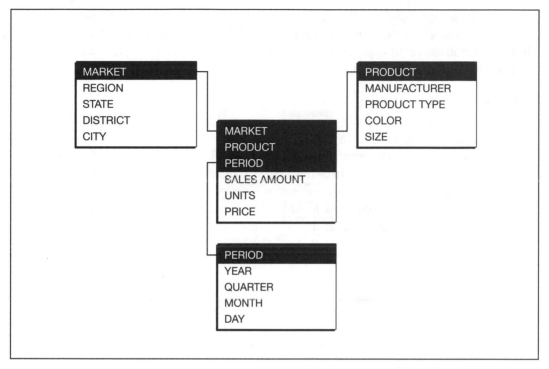

Figure 3.3   Logical design of a dimensional data model.

(usually numeric) data, indexed on dimensional keys, which are described in corresponding dimension tables, as shown in Figure 3.3. Dimension tables contain information such as time period, product, market, organization, accounts, vendors, and customers, and include descriptions and attributes of the dimension, as well as the structure of the dimension, such as groupings of products to brands to categories, cities to states to districts to regions, and so forth.

Fact tables include time-series data at the indicated structure levels. Thus, if the dimension table contains a structure reflecting the city, state, region, and total of a dimension, then the fact table also contains information at the city, state, region, and total levels. The lowest level of data is summarized to a slice in time, rather than at a transaction or occurrence level.

A query against this multidimensional model initially queries the dimension tables, translating filtering rules into keys, then accesses the larger fact table. This ensures precision data access via a complete key structure, eliminates table scans, and results in the highest performance possible from relational technology. The concept of storing the dimensions separately ensures that the database holds sparse arrays effectively (i.e., without storing gaps) and assures the most efficient access possible.

Fact Tables

The history of an organization's business metrics, or facts, are maintained as rows (rather than columns) in one or more historical fact tables. Each fact table has an indexed primary key composed of several columns, each of which logically corresponds to a major business dimension such as time period, product, or market. The time period dimension is always represented as part of the primary key. Figure 3.4 illustrates a fact table that contains sales, units, and inventory history. A single row of detail is retrieved by constraining on a unique time period key, product key, and market key.

Each dimension key must be represented and described in a corresponding

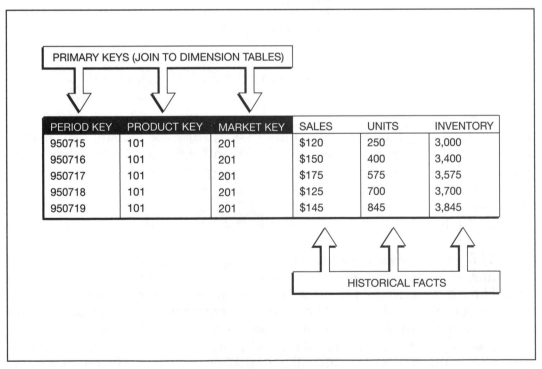

PERIOD KEY	PRODUCT KEY	MARKET KEY	SALES	UNITS	INVENTORY
950715	101	201	$120	250	3,000
950716	101	201	$150	400	3,400
950717	101	201	$175	575	3,575
950718	101	201	$125	700	3,700
950719	101	201	$145	845	3,845

PRIMARY KEYS (JOIN TO DIMENSION TABLES)

HISTORICAL FACTS

Figure 3.4 Fact table.

dimension table, which logically joins to the fact table(s) through identical primary key columns. As mentioned earlier, the time dimension is *always* one of the major business dimensions. Figure 3.5 demonstrates the logical join between a dimension table and a fact table using only the market dimension. Note that the joining keys are identically named, which greatly simplifies metadata definitions.

Logical join refers to the fact that these tables are accessible by a single SQL statement, physically joining the two tables; alternatively, they can be accessed sequentially, first translating dimension descriptions and attributes to keys, then accessing the fact table with a complete key structure.

A common error when creating a data warehouse from normalized, transaction information is that the meaningful key used to define an entity within the transaction system is also used as the primary key in the information system's fact and dimension tables, thereby restricting flexibility, lowering performance, and increasing maintenance. In contrast, the use of generated keys that

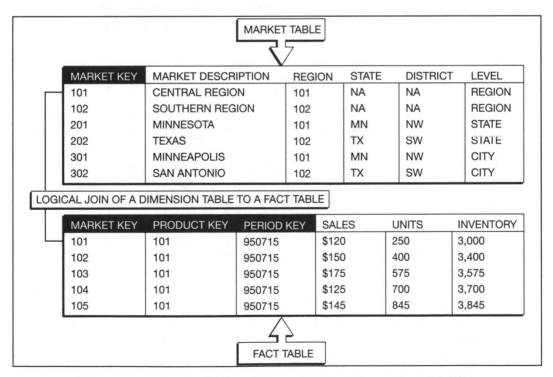

MARKET TABLE

MARKET KEY	MARKET DESCRIPTION	REGION	STATE	DISTRICT	LEVEL
101	CENTRAL REGION	101	NA	NA	REGION
102	SOUTHERN REGION	102	NA	NA	REGION
201	MINNESOTA	101	MN	NW	STATE
202	TEXAS	102	TX	SW	STATE
301	MINNEAPOLIS	101	MN	NW	CITY
302	SAN ANTONIO	102	TX	SW	CITY

LOGICAL JOIN OF A DIMENSION TABLE TO A FACT TABLE

MARKET KEY	PRODUCT KEY	PERIOD KEY	SALES	UNITS	INVENTORY
101	101	950715	$120	250	3,000
102	101	950715	$150	400	3,400
103	101	950715	$175	575	3,575
104	101	950715	$125	700	3,700
105	101	950715	$145	845	3,845

FACT TABLE

Figure 3.5 Logical join of fact tables to dimensional tables.

have no meaningful relation to the data they describe provides adequate flexibility for data warehouse maturity and higher performance.

The differences between meaningful keys and nonmeaningful keys exist on several levels. Through normalization of transactional data, meaningful keys are frequently represented by more than one column, depending on the level of summary they represent. In contrast, generated keys are always maintained in a single column per dimension. Using generated keys rather than meaningful keys provides three advantages:

- **Optimal flexibility:** A single metadata definition can be reused for any level of detail or summary that shares the generated key.

- **Consistent structure:** As the data warehouse matures (as new levels of summary are added or removed), the physical structure of the tables sharing the generated key does not change; only the content of the keys and the number of rows change.

- **Size:** Significant reduction in the size of the indexed primary key (because it has fewer columns in the index), results in a larger portion of the index being read at a single time, thereby increasing performance.

Two options exist to create single, generated-key columns. The first is to collapse multiple key columns per dimension into a single column per dimension by concatenating the content of each key. This approach achieves the first two benefits of generated keys, but falls short of improving performance, since it does not reduce the overall size of the index.

In the second method, the meaningful keys are dropped entirely and replaced with system-generated generic integers, which take up the smallest possible space in an index and permit a larger amount of data to be stored in memory. Note that this method does not necessitate the removal of the meaningful columns, therefore these columns can be used as additional attribute columns. Figure 3.6 demonstrates a dimension table containing normalized, or meaningful, key structures.

Figure 3.7 demonstrates a dimension table creating an artificial single primary key column by concatenating the contents of the three meaningful key columns. This type of key structure offers two advantages: It simplifies definitions of metadata, and eliminates the need to change the physical tables as the data warehouse matures. This approach does not achieve any performance gains, however, since the overall size of the index is not reduced.

REGION KEY	STATE KEY	DISTRICT KEY	MARKET DESCRIPTION		LEVEL
10	120	NA	CENTRAL REGION		REGION
20	210	NA	SOUTHERN REGION		REGION
10	120	NW01	MINNESOTA		STATE
20	210	SW03	TEXAS		STATE
10	120	NW01	MINNEAPOLIS		CITY
20	210	SW03	SAN ANTONIO		CITY

Figure 3.6   Using a normalized key structure.

Figure 3.8 demonstrates a dimension table using a system-generated key as its primary key column with the previous meaningful key columns as additional attribute columns. This type of key structure results in the highest flexibility of metadata, low maintenance as the data warehouse matures, and the highest possible performance from relational technology.

Aggregation is the process of summarizing granular, or detail, data and physically storing the aggregations in fact tables along common business hierarchies. Aggregating detail data in advance decreases access times, and speeds processes such as drilling. The example in Figure 3.9 illustrates the use of a market dimension and corresponding fact table containing physical levels of aggregation at city, state, region, and total.

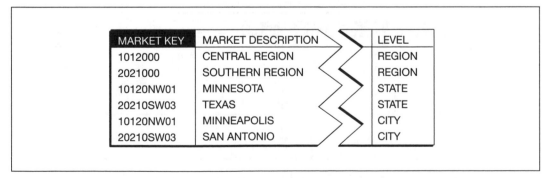

MARKET KEY	MARKET DESCRIPTION		LEVEL
1012000	CENTRAL REGION		REGION
2021000	SOUTHERN REGION		REGION
10120NW01	MINNESOTA		STATE
20210SW03	TEXAS		STATE
10120NW01	MINNEAPOLIS		CITY
20210SW03	SAN ANTONIO		CITY

Figure 3.7   Using the artificial key structure.

MARKET KEY	MARKET DESCRIPTION	REGION ID	DISTRICT ID	LEVEL
101	CENTRAL REGION	120	NA	REGION
102	SOUTHERN REGION	210	NA	REGION
103	MINNESOTA	120	NW01	STATE
104	TEXAS	210	SW03	STATE
105	MINNEAPOLIS	120	NW01	CITY
106	SAN ANTONIO	210	SW03	CITY

Figure 3.8 Using the system-generated key structure.

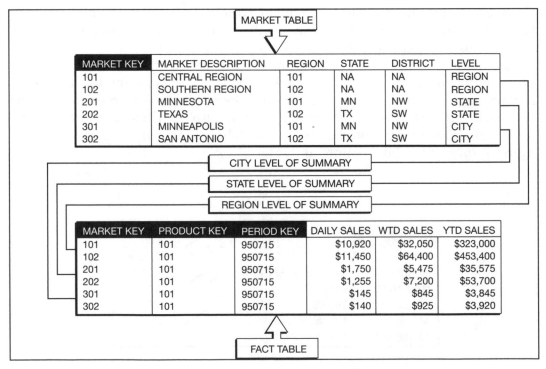

MARKET TABLE

MARKET KEY	MARKET DESCRIPTION	REGION	STATE	DISTRICT	LEVEL
101	CENTRAL REGION	101	NA	NA	REGION
102	SOUTHERN REGION	102	NA	NA	REGION
201	MINNESOTA	101	MN	NW	STATE
202	TEXAS	102	TX	SW	STATE
301	MINNEAPOLIS	101	MN	NW	CITY
302	SAN ANTONIO	102	TX	SW	CITY

CITY LEVEL OF SUMMARY

STATE LEVEL OF SUMMARY

REGION LEVEL OF SUMMARY

MARKET KEY	PRODUCT KEY	PERIOD KEY	DAILY SALES	WTD SALES	YTD SALES
101	101	950715	$10,920	$32,050	$323,000
102	101	950715	$11,450	$64,400	$453,400
201	101	950715	$1,750	$5,475	$35,575
202	101	950715	$1,255	$7,200	$53,700
301	101	950715	$145	$845	$3,845
302	101	950715	$140	$925	$3,920

FACT TABLE

Figure 3.9 Using dimension tables to identify aggregation levels.

The initial implementation of each new data warehouse should physically store all combinations of common business hierarchies. The challenge is to store data aggregations judiciously; a failure to do so can result in an explosion of the data warehouse size. For this reason, many OLAP tools incorporate aggregate-aware technology that effectively resolves the issues of determining when to retrieve a stored aggregate value or when to retrieve the detail data and perform an aggregate online.

Dimension Tables

As noted previously, dimension tables contain information about the dimensions of the data (time period, product, market, organization, accounts, and so forth). They should be designed from a user-centric perspective so that the description and attribute columns contain text descriptions that are meaningful to business users and appropriate for display in a report. It's never a good idea to compromise on dimension table design to save disk space.

Each dimension table should incorporate multiple attribute columns containing text and codes that further describe the key. Attribute columns are used to constrain or filter the contents of the dimension. Dimension tables should be heavily attributed to support the what-if questions required to derive decision-making information. Further, using integers as attributes when appropriate (for sizes, ages, salary, etc.) makes it possible to take advantage of dynamic filtering rules such as greater than, less than, and between.

As Figure 3.10 illustrates, the structure of the dimension also includes attributes to identify parent-child relationships for groupings of products to brands to categories, and cities to states to districts to regions, and so forth.

Each dimension table may also incorporate an additional attribute column with a text description of the level of summarization that each row represents. This column serves two primary purposes: It is an additional filtering attribute when selecting from that particular dimension ("select all cities"); and it serves as a mechanism to constrain parent, child, and attribute relationships when drilling up and down through hierarchies of data. Figure 3.11 illustrates the use of an additional attribute column in a dimension table.

Time Period Dimension

A time period dimension table is required to precisely identify the date of available data in fact tables. A time period table may seem unnecessary in a data warehouse since the time period key column in the fact tables uses a date-type

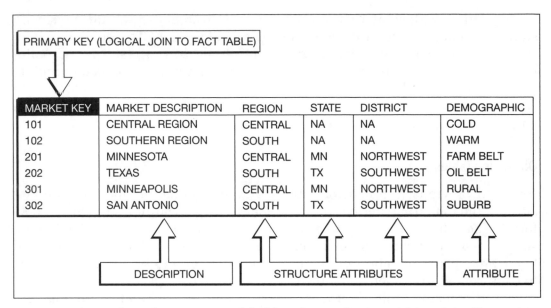

Figure 3.10 Identifying parent/child relationships within the dimension table.

format that identifies all valid dates, but this format is not a sufficient substitute for a time period table. Precision access to the fact table is lost when there is no dimension table describing time (i.e., identifying valid date keys before accessing the larger fact table). Also, intelligent filtering algorithms cannot be applied without the time period dimension table. From a user perspective, this is the most important reason for including a time period table.

MARKET KEY	MARKET DESCRIPTION	LEVEL
101	CENTRAL REGION	REGION
102	SOUTHERN REGION	REGION
201	MINNESOTA	STATE
202	TEXAS	STATE
301	MINNEAPOLIS	CITY
302	SAN ANTONIO	CITY

Figure 3.11 Adding level to define hierarchies within the dimension.

The time period table should contain a key column or columns that logically join two identical columns on one or more fact tables. As with any other dimension table, the time period dimension table must contain a unique description for each period as well as attribute column to provide filtering constraints on the table. Figure 3.12 provides an example of a period table with attribute fields.

Adding a "current" time period flag column to the time period dimension table offers a flexible mechanism that eliminates the need to update published reports prior to executing them against new data. This column might contain a Y or an N to indicate whether the time period in that row represents a date that is physically stored in a fact table. Figure 3.13 illustrates the use of a flag.

It is also possible to add a time period resolution column to the time period dimension table. This column, which is used to constrain the period list to the appropriate reporting level, operates identically to the level columns in other dimension tables. It is important to remember, though, that the current flag

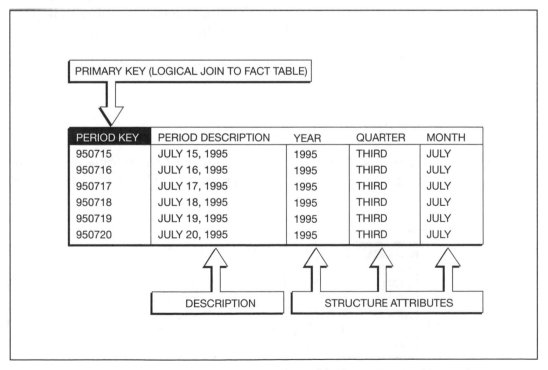

Figure 3.12 Example of a period dimension table.

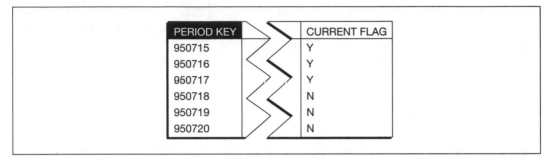

Figure 3.13 Current period flag in period dimension table.

column should be updated within each resolution. Figure 3.14 illustrates the inclusion of a time period resolution description.

Finally, the time period dimension table should incorporate a time period "sequence" column. This column, which contains a 1 to n sequence number in each time period resolution, identifies the relative order of each date. As Figure 3.15 illustrates, it is used to create multiple, reusable rolling time periods by itself or in conjunction with the current time period flag, such as:

> Current Four Weeks = Current Time Period through Current Time Period–4.

Categories within a Data Warehouse

The various data warehouse design options are described in some detail later in this chapter, but grouping the data into categories or subject areas is the first

PERIOD KEY	CURRENT FLAG	RESOLUTION
950715	Y	DAILY
950716	Y	DAILY
950717	N	DAILY
9505	Y	MONTHLY
9507	Y	MONTHLY
9508	N	MONTHLY

Figure 3.14 Time period resolution in period dimension table.

PERIOD KEY		CURRENT FLAG	RESOLUTION	SEQUENCE
950715		Y	DAILY	1
950716		Y	DAILY	2
950717		N	DAILY	3
9505		Y	MONTHLY	1
9507		Y	MONTHLY	2
9508		N	MONTHLY	3

Figure 3.15 Time period sequence in period dimension table.

step in determining which data warehouse design option is appropriate. These categories may consist of data that is logically separated; in other words, data that simply cannot be reported together. For example, sales information about products and markets may be logically separated from budget information on accounts and organization. Alternatively, the categories may be a logical definition of multiple views of the same data, either for a workgroup or to enforce security.

It is also possible to identify unique categories and to design separately for each unique combination of major business dimensions. Unique combinations of summary levels within a dimension are still considered part of the same category.

Figure 3.16 illustrates a data warehouse with two categories: a sales category organized by products, markets, and periods; and a financial category organized by accounts, organization, and periods. Categories may share common dimensions (in this example, the period dimension), but they should be identified and designed individually.

Data Warehouse Design Options

It's always a good idea to start slow—tackling a single challenge at a time—so organizations should focus on developing a data warehouse design model that offers the greatest possible performance and functional versatility before progressing to a model that provides higher data storage efficiency. Although the five data warehouse designs discussed here are suitable for use with a broad range of OLAP applications, a simple star schema is often the best starting point in the design process because it simplifies the database design and is

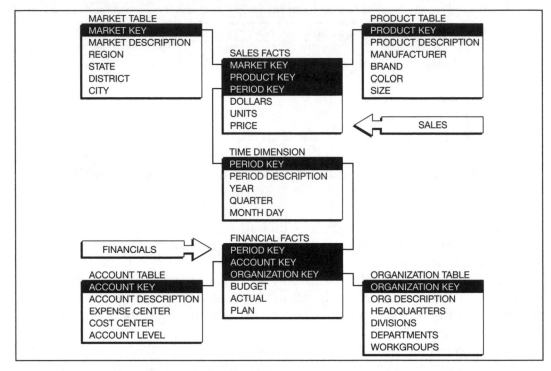

Figure 3.16   Logical database design consisting of two categories.

easily understood by nontechnical users. The design's flexibility also allows additional tables to be introduced to improve performance or to facilitate maintenance. The star schema is explained in more detail in Chapter 8, where a number of indexing techniques that maximize SQL query performance are presented.

Each of the five design options involves a unique set of advantages and considerations—from both a business and a technological perspective. The five warehouse design models are:

- Star
- Partial star
- Fact partitioning
- Dimension partitioning
- Snowflake

Star

The star warehouse design model has its roots in the consumer packaged goods and retail industries, both of which have traditionally analyzed their businesses by simple dimensions (products and markets) that are static in number and structure over time.

The star has four properties that differentiate it from the other data warehouse design models:

1. Within each category, a *single* historical fact table exists, containing detail and summary level data, stored at the structure levels indicated in each dimension table.
2. The fact table's primary key contains only one key column from each dimension.
3. Each key is a generated key.
4. Each dimension is represented by a single table, also using a generated key.

The example in Figure 3.17 illustrates a star schema with a single fact table storing a history of dollars, unit, and price. It is logically joined to a market dimension table, a product dimension table, and the time dimension table. The fact table contains summarized rows at the matrix of Region/State/District/City by Manufacturer/Brand/Item by Year/Quarter/Month/Day, resulting in 48 different aggregate combinations.

The star model offers a number of advantages, including higher performance through the use of generated keys that reduce the size of the index. In addition, the use of a single table per diminution and a single fact table per category ensures that metadata definitions can be reused, regardless of the level of summary or fact. Performance is also improved by issuing a single SQL statement to the fact table for each query—regardless of the content of the report.

When determining the feasibility of a star design, however, it is important to remember that single dimension tables may require redundant storage of description and attributes. Also, storing detail and summary information on the same table reduces query performance at higher levels.

Partial Star

The partial star data warehouse design model represents a variation of the star design in that multiple tables may exist for each fact and dimension, logically

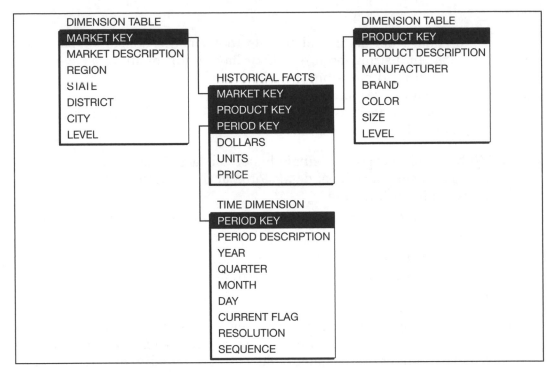

Figure 3.17 Logical database design of star database.

and physically separated by levels of summarization. This design expands the original consumer packaged goods and retail model into a model capable of supporting organizations that need to maintain a very large number of entities per level of aggregation. These organizations are typically found in the banking, pharmaceutical, catalog retail, and insurance industries, as well as other businesses that need to store information at a customer, account, or product level.

The partial star design creates multiple, overlaying stars, each uniquely representing a combination of levels of aggregation from each dimension. Thus, multiple fact tables exist within each category, physically separated by levels of summary. There is no logical join between the various fact tables or dimension tables, only between the dimension table and fact table within each group. The primary key contains only one key from each dimension, each of which is a generated key. Each dimension is represented by multiple tables, which are physically separated by levels of summary and keyed from a generated key. Facts that are common across levels of aggregation may have identical column names on each fact table, permitting metadata definitions to be reused across all levels of aggregation represented by the fact tables.

The example in Figure 3.18 illustrates the partial star model using only the market dimension and associated fact tables. This example partitions the data warehouse by hierarchical levels of summary, split by region and district. It also overlays two stars, the first representing the region level of summary, the second representing the district level of summary.

Adding this design to the other dimensions would create additional stars; for example, adding the product dimension summarized at the *Manufacturer* and *Brand* levels, the two upcoming models would expand to *Region/Manufacturer/Year, Region/Brand/Year, District/Manufacturer/Year, District/Brand/Year,* each combination represented in a separate, overlaying Star.

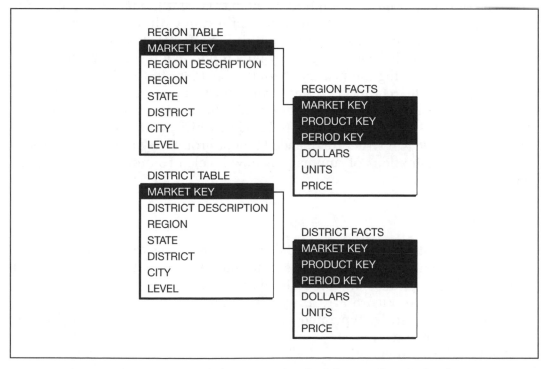

Figure 3.18 Logical database design of partial star database.

The partial star model is well suited for a number of applications. Partitioning tables by level of aggregation allows facts to exist uniquely at a particular level. For example, price is a fact that exists only at an item level within a product dimension. As fact tables increase in size, partitioning allows a higher degree of control over data load times, backup, and maintenance. And partitioning summary level information from detail information may increase performance on queries executed against those higher levels of detail. Primary advantages of the partial star model include high performance, due to the use of generated keys and reduced index size; the capability for facts to exist uniquely at a particular level because tables are partitioned by level of aggregation; and the existence of unique attributes at each level of aggregation due to support for multiple dimension tables per table. In addition, partitioning summary level information from detail information may increase performance on queries executed against the higher levels of detail. Further reduction in sparsity is possible by eliminating nonmeaningful columns at each level of summarization.

When considering implementation of the partial star model, it is important to remember that each star model requires definition within metadata, thereby increasing maintenance. Also, issuing multiple SQL statements when analyzing more than a single level of summary on a report can result in performance degradation. Measuring the market share (i.e., percent to total) of a city to its region, for example, requires accessing two tables and using two separate SQL statements. Finally, as with the use of meaningful keys, physically separating the data by levels of summarization reduces flexibility as the data warehouse matures. The physical structure of each table or group may require changes to reflect new combinations of summary as new levels of summary are added or removed.

Fact Partitioning

The fact partitioning data warehouse design represents a variation of the partial star model and applies principles from the star model. It is designed with a single table per dimension, joined to multiple fact tables partitioned by levels of summary. As Figure 3.19 illustrates, multiple fact tables exist within each category, physically separated by levels of summary and logically joined to a single dimension table.

Like the other design options, the fact partitioning model offers a number of benefits. Partitioning fact tables by level of aggregation allows *facts* to exist uniquely at a particular level, and partitioning summary level information

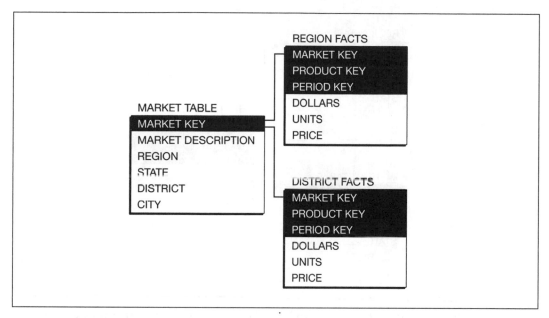

Figure 3.19 Logical database design of fact partitioning database.

from detail information can improve performance on queries that are executed against the higher levels of detail. But once again, it is important to consider that single dimension tables require redundant storage of description, and attributes and performance may be adversely affected when multiple SQL statements are issued to analyze more than a single level of summary on a report.

Dimension Partitioning

The dimension partitioning data warehouse model, like the fact partitioning model, is a variation of the star model that combines principles of the partial star model. This design has one fact table for each category, joined to multiple dimension tables that are partitioned by levels of summary. As Figure 3.20 illustrates, in the dimension partitioning design, a single fact table exists within each category, logically joined to multiple dimension tables that are physically separated by levels of summary.

The dimension partitioning design offers several advantages, including the ability to assign unique attributes for each level of aggregation and performance because only one SQL statement is issued to the fact table for each

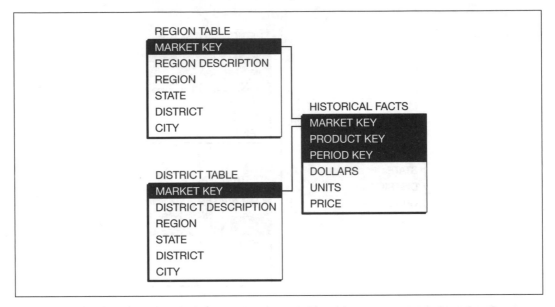

Figure 3.20 Logical database design of dimension partitioning database.

query, regardless of the content of the report. But, storing detail and summary information on the same table can reduce performance at higher levels.

Snowflake Models

The snowflake models employ a combination of database normalization to maintain data integrity and reduce redundantly stored data and denormalization to achieve higher performance. The snowflake models, which were originally developed for retail applications, support the ability to store product, market, and organization descriptions in a single location, thereby facilitating maintenance. Snowflake models have progressed into the banking and insurance industries as a means of maintaining customer information in a single lookup area. There are three primary types of designs in the snowflake family: lookup, chain, and attribute, described in this section. The snowflake design gets its name from the appearance of the logical database design diagram.

As Figure 3.21 indicates, the snowflake designs incorporate major dimension tables, which have a direct logical join into fact tables through their primary key, and minor outrigger tables, which are used to store descriptions and decodes for keys and codes on the major tables.

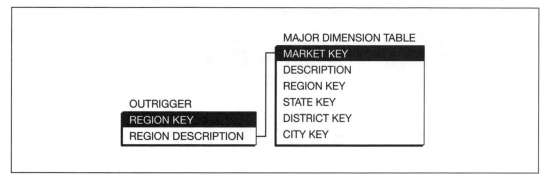

Figure 3.21 Logical database design of snowflake model.

Major dimension tables resemble star dimension tables, except that the attribute columns contain keys to the outrigger tables rather than text descriptions. Outrigger tables are linked to the major dimension table (or to other outrigger tables) through their primary key, and contain decode text and descriptions to coded or key values stored on the major dimension table.

Lookup

The lookup snowflake model employs outrigger tables as a source of decoded names and descriptions. This approach reduces the size of dimension tables by eliminating the redundancy of storing duplicate description names in many rows. Figure 3.22 uses the market dimension as an example. A major dimension table is logically joined to a single fact table. Four outrigger tables exist, acting as lookup tables to the key or coded values on the major dimension table. This allows each description name and decode value to be maintained once, allowing simplified storage and updating.

The lookup snowflake model offers a number of advantages. Maintaining decoded names and descriptions in a single location reduces the relative size of dimension tables and improves the integrity of the data. In addition, the use of lookup tables encourages the use of generated keys, providing higher performance, lower metadata maintenance, and flexibility for data warehouse maturity. Finally, the outrigger tables themselves provide a rich source of organizational data for simple queries.

However, performance may be adversely affected if multiple queries or joins are required to completely decode all key and code values to text for report creation; and outrigger tables require additional maintenance.

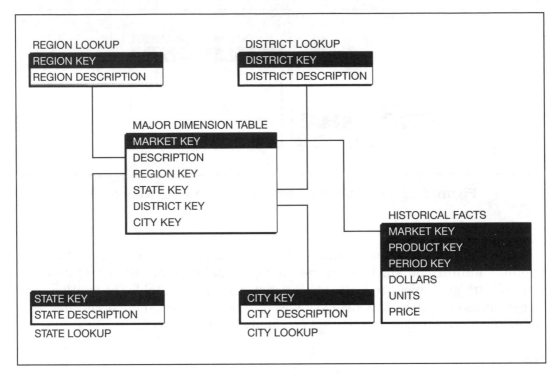

Figure 3.22   Logical database design of lookup snowflake database.

Chain

The chain snowflake model places outrigger tables end to end, beginning with the major dimension table, which is the entry point into the fact tables. In this design, the major dimension table contains the key to the first outrigger table (also called the root outrigger). The first or root outrigger table contains the information necessary to decode those keys, as well as the key to the next outrigger table, and so on, to the terminating outrigger.

Because the root outrigger defines only a single level of aggregation, the chain snowflake design is typically used when only the atomic, or lowest, level of detail is physically stored on the fact tables. This design is *not* recommended if there is a need to report on summary levels of information since it requires several steps to retrieve the correct keys and descriptions for summary levels, or requires multiple joins, which can significantly reduce performance.

Figure 3.23 uses the market dimension as an example. A major dimension table is logically joined to a single fact table. Four outrigger tables exist, the first acting as a lookup table to key or coded values on the major dimension table, the others serving as lookup tables to other outrigger tables.

The chain snowflake design offers a high degree of data integrity because decoded names and descriptions are maintained in a single location, thereby reducing the relative size of dimension tables. But performance can be adversely affected by the multiple queries or joins that are required to completely decode all key and code values to text for report creation. Also, because the root outrigger table defines only a single level of aggregation, the chain snowflake model is typically used only when the atomic (the lowest) level of detail is physically stored on the fact tables, reducing the ability to report on and drill through levels of hierarchy. Finally, the design also requires a relatively high level of outrigger table maintenance.

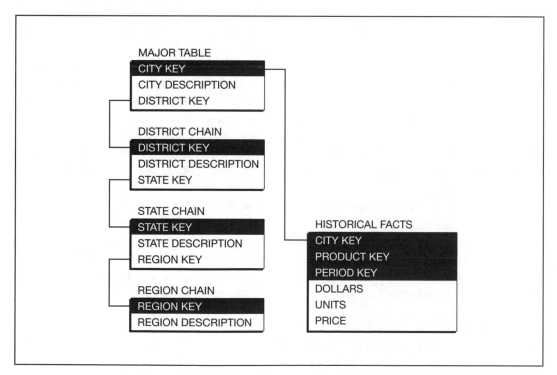

Figure 3.23   Logical database design of chain snowflake database.

Attribute

The attribute snowflake model makes it possible to construct a dimension from several disparate attribute groups that are not associated with any other dimension. It also supports combining a number of infrequently used dimensions into a single artificial dimension for simplified reporting. The attribute snowflake design is particularly effective for reducing the number of dimensions in a database. It is commonly used by banks and insurance companies as well as other organizations with large marketing databases that are very heavily attributed and contain eight or more dimensions. Reducing the number of dimensions improves the usability of the reporting application and reduces the overall size of the index, as well as the complexity of generated SQL. This, in turn, improves performance and eliminates nonprimary key entry points into fact tables.

The major dimension table, which is artificially created in the attribute snowflake model, contains the foreign keys from all disparate attribute or dimension tables. The table's primary key is a generated key, and a unique row is added for every valid combination of all attributes or dimensions. Each attribute outrigger table has a primary key linking it back to the artificial major table, as well as a description or decode field.

The example in Figure 3.24 uses size, color, form, and scent as nondimension associated attributes of dimensions. Without this type of model, each of these attributes or dimensions would typically be maintained as a foreign key on a fact table, resulting in a nonprimary (and most likely nonindexed) key entry point into the fact tables—a situation that should be avoided. An additional dimension table would contain a row for each valid combination of size and color, allowing a single, indexed entry point into fact tables for multiple, disparate attributes.

Advantages of the attribute snowflake model include reductions in the relative size of dimension tables and improvements in data integrity. Multiple, nondimension-associated attributes or infrequently used dimensions can be joined together to share a single entry point into fact tables through a primary key instead of foreign keys. This approach minimizes the complexity of generated SQL and reduces the overall index size, affording significant improvements in performance.

Performance can be adversely affected if multiple queries or joins are required to completely decode all key and code values to text for report creation. And, because no common description exists for each unique combination of attributes, the description to be placed on reports must be created using the

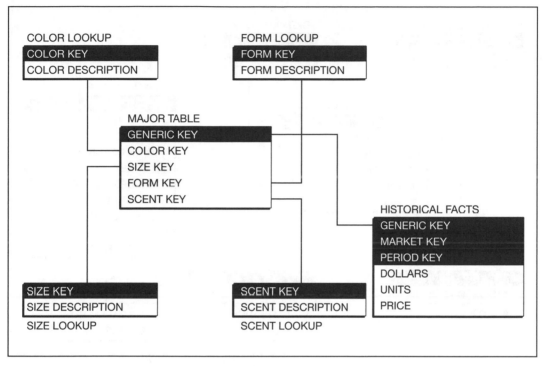

Figure 3.24   Logical database design of attribute snowflake database.

data mart approach. Figure 3.25 illustrates this approach—creating a data mart dimension table above a snowflake lookup schema. The data mart dimension table can exist physically or through a view, but a physical table offers higher performance gains due to the reduction of run-time joins.

Additional Database Strategy Issues

Equally important to database design is database integrity. Proper database design ensures usability and optimal performance, but users must also be able to trust the answers that are generated by analyzing the data in the data warehouse. Operational databases are often the primary source of such data. Operational data must be transformed, validated, cleansed, and integrated to achieve optimal value. The real benefit of data warehousing can be achieved

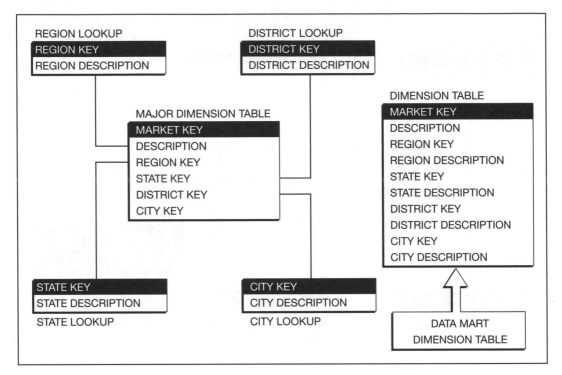

Figure 3.25 Data mart approach to snowflake and star designs.

only by creating a reliable source of historical performance measures. Since every enterprise's data-cleansing requirements are unique, there are few short-cuts for validating data warehouse content.

It is important to remember that the data warehouse design can (and should!) evolve to continually improve usability and performance. If users lose confidence in the information that is generated from a warehouse, it is very difficult (or impossible) to regain that confidence. A lack of data integrity can be a major setback to the success of a data warehouse project.

Data Archive or Data Mart?

Many industry experts believe that the processes of transforming, validating, cleansing, and integrating data sources are so critically important that it is necessary to create an operational data store (an entity database model) to serve as a central data archive type of warehouse. This archive can be used to populate central data warehouses or data marts. Proponents of this strategy place a premium on centralizing the data processing steps necessary to guarantee database integrity and efficiently administrate database management. Unfortunately, this approach is both costly and time-consuming, and users, impatient by nature, will not realize immediate benefits from the data warehouse effort.

The high costs involved with data warehousing, as well as the long lead times required for planning and implementing, have created a backlash of sorts. Some industry "experts" advocate creating data marts (single subject area/dimensional database designs) to more quickly address decision-makers' needs. Although data marts require the same processes of data transformation, validation, cleansing, and integration to ensure database integrity, they do offer a more immediate solution to decision support requirements and involve a smaller financial commitment. The scope of a data mart is more narrow than that of a data warehouse; a data mart focuses on the needs of a specific segment of the user community and, therefore, a relatively limited set of decision support requirements.

The term data mart can be misleading, however. The databases associated with data marts need not be limited in size. In fact, for many applications, data marts can exceed 50 gigabytes and may even approach several hundred gigabytes. Size is largely dependent on the frequency of the database update cycle. Daily updates create a database that is 30 times larger than one that is updated on a monthly basis.

The disadvantages of a data mart become apparent when an enterprise needs to create and maintain several data marts; the difficulties are particularly acute if some data elements are common across data marts. Database synchronization issues are likely to result in a database management challenge that, over time, becomes more costly than maintaining an integrated central data warehouse (dimensional model).

If there is risk of historical data being lost, or if the transformation, validation, cleansing, and integration requirements are significant, a data archive should be created (an entity model), then a dimensional database (a central warehouse or several data marts) created from the archive data warehouse. In all cases, it is important to remember that the primary goal of the data warehousing project is to deliver required information to decision makers as quickly as possible. A data mart may offer a good means for satisfying decision makers immediate needs while planning and developing a more integrated data warehouse strategy.

The Expanding Role of Metadata

The definition of metadata is "data about data." We're all somewhat familiar with metadata, even if we're not aware of what it is. For example, television programming schedules, library card catalogues, and telephone directories are all common types of metadata. Metadata is absolutely critical in data warehousing and OLAP applications since it describes the data that is contained in the warehouse. For example:

- When was the data last updated?
- Which transformation rules were applied in processing the data?
- What is the database schema?
- What are the data aggregation rules?
- Which aggregations (i.e., data redundancies) exist within the data warehouse?
- What are the reporting hierarchies (i.e., territories, districts, regions, country, etc.) within each dimension?

The software used to manage the warehouse (to extract, process, and update the warehouse) and the associated OLAP functions require various types of metadata to establish the links to different types of data warehouses. Even though all applications rely on some form of metadata, there are few widely supported standards that facilitate sharing metadata, although most data warehouse/OLAP tool software vendors use a proprietary metadata layer. The lack of standardization results in a proliferation of metadata tables and an administrative burden caused by the need to synchronize metadata.

Administering metadata for multiple warehouses employing a variety of OLAP tools for a range of business applications is particularly challenging. The Metadata Council, which is supported by many of the data warehouse/OLAP software vendors, was established specifically to create minimum standards for shareable metadata.

The intranet introduces still another definition of metadata; that is, "data about data *on the Net.*" The Internet depends on a host of powerful metadata search engines such as Yahoo, Lycos, and Excite—all of which attempt to describe all available information sources. Once again the Internet provides a useful model for the way corporations should organize internal information resources. Search engines used in conjunction with an intranet browser provide a new form of metadata for data warehouse and OLAP applications and offer the opportunity to integrate structured content (data warehouse) and unstructured content (text, images, and audio data types). A user who enters "Fourth of July promotion" into an intranet search engine should be able to select from among the marketing plans associated with the promotion (text), the promotional advertisement (image), or a report comparing sales pre/postpromotion (numeric report generated from data contained in the warehouse).

This expanded view of metadata is particularly relevant to intranet data warehousing since it is likely to result in the creation of multiple warehouses and a growing need to integrate structured and unstructured content. Common metadata standards are likely evolve in the short term in response to intranet integration requirements.

Chapter 4 provides further detail on the OLAP functions designed to aid management in designing intranet data warehouses and to facilitate the decision-making and decision implementation processes. While it is necessary to build the data warehouse prior to delivering applications to the user community, ultimately, it is the users' analytic requirements that define the content and design of the data warehouse.

CASE STUDY

A.C. Nielsen

Mention the name A.C. Nielsen to most people and they immediately think of their favorite TV show. But measuring television viewing patterns is a small part of this $1.3 billion market research company's business. A.C. Nielsen also delivers market research information and analysis to the consumer products and services industries; the company tracks market activity in more than 90 countries, measuring anything from toothpaste market share in Tokyo to household purchases in London.

A.C. Nielsen is an information company. It gathers data from a variety of sources. Its Retail Measurement Group uploads scanner data from supermarkets, mass merchandisers, and drug stores, while the Consumer Panel Group collects data from households that individually scan their purchases and transmit the data back to A.C. Nielsen via modem. The Media Measurement Group features a "People Meter" that sits on top of television sets and transmits viewing behavior back to central collection systems, and the customized Research Group uses CATI (computer-assisted telephone interview-

ing) systems to survey respondents and enter data directly into the data warehouse.

Traditional businesses take raw materials and turn them into finished products. For information companies, data is the raw material. Value is added to the data by cleansing it and combining it with other data sources. Additional value is created by overlaying intelligent software that turns the data into information. The final step in the refining process is turning information into insight. Today this is achieved primarily through human intervention. An analyst drives a software tool through an iterative set of analysis until a conclusion is reached. In the future, techniques like data mining, neutral networking, and intelligent agents promise to automate some of the investigatory labor.

Once a business creates its finished product, its next challenge is getting it to market. Traditional businesses use transmodal means (ships, rail, and trucks) to deliver goods to local retailers. Traditional information providers rely on similar means to transport the printed word (for example, shipping bound documents like this book). More progressive information providers deliver information over electronic networks. While most of these companies use commercial service providers like CompuServe or America Online, A.C. Nielsen has traditionally relied upon its own private network. Tomorrow's information providers are likely to rely almost exclusively on the Internet and intranets to deliver their information products.

A.C. Nielsen defines an intranet as a limited-access, secured version of the Internet, and views it, along with the Internet, as the ultimate distribution channel for information. For that reason, the company has aggressively embraced Internet technologies. Its Internet activities currently extend into three areas: Web market research, Web site measurement, and Web delivery. Web delivery focuses on integrating the Web with the data warehouse for market research and information delivery.

A.C. Nielsen's SalesNET uses Internet technologies to eliminate obstacles between the company and its customers. This subscription-based service is available to consumer packaged-goods producers and retailers. It offers Internet access to thousands of specialized databases containing information from more than 800 retailers, as well as information on the buying habits of 40,000 U.S. households. SalesNET provides fast, simple access to strategic and tactical information for remote and brokered salesforce users. Salespeople from A.C. Nielsen's 600 U.S. clients and more than 9,000 international clients in 93 countries can access the service via the Internet.

A.C. Nielsen plans to extend its use of Internet technologies with Global-NET, a service that will assist packaged-goods manufacturers to identify market trends across countries. In 1997, the company intends to offer the first of many country-specific local warehouses, providing real-time OLAP queries against its data warehouses. GlobalNET's local warehouses will be run by each A.C. Nielsen country office, allowing worldwide access to centralized information originating from decentralized knowledge centers. ■

CHAPTER FOUR

Online Analytic Processing: From Data to Information

OLAP is a label, rather than a technology. It applies to all analytic functions (i.e., generating a database query, performing mathematical calculations and data formatting) required to create useful information from data stored in data warehouses. OLAP enables users to perform data analysis functions while freely traversing the many dimensions of the data warehouse. It also provides the dynamic document creation for linking structured content (i.e., alpha/numeric data) to the intranet's store of unstructured content—predominantly text and image information. This chapter introduces the concepts of OLAP and differentiates the various categories of OLAP applications.

Using OLAP to Transform Content into Information

The Internet and intranets are well suited to retrieve "static" documents that are stored and updated on a server, and OLAP is essential for transforming data warehouse content into a useful form of information that can be delivered to a large number of users. OLAP documents—reports and graphic data representations—are created "dynamically" (which is the online aspect of OLAP) to meet a user's request for information.

In an intranet data warehouse, the OLAP functions reside between the Web browser and the data warehouse, transforming the raw data from the data warehouse into usable information that can be returned to the client via the Web browser. In general, OLAP application software products integrate five basic functions:

- **Interface:** The screens and methods used to issue internal instructions to other functions based on user selections.
- **Query:** The application logic used to generate SQL code.
- **Process:** The application logic that performs data analysis on the result set returned from the database query.
- **Format:** The application logic required to properly label rows and columns of data and create a standard file (i.e., an HTML file).
- **Display:** The presentation of the formatted file, as a report or graph, for viewing on the user's PC.

Figure 4.1 illustrates the relationship of the five functions to the data warehouse. With point-and-click ease (interface), a user executes the generation of SQL code (query), which is submitted to the data warehouse and returns a result set. The query result set is enhanced by performing computations (process) and organized into a file structure (format) so that the data can be represented as a report or graph (display).

Within the context of an intranet data warehouse, the interface and display functions are presented within the Web browser. The query, process, and format functions can be performed on the user PC, but are more appropriately maintained as server-resident functions, thereby supporting the "thin-client" architecture of the Internet or intranet. Partitioning and distributing OLAP functions are two of the distinguishing characteristics of the intranet data warehouse.

The Evolution of OLAP

In his 1993 white paper, E.F. Codd outlined 12 rules for OLAP to differentiate simple database query and reporting tools from a sophisticated form of information analysis. In describing a technology, Codd reserved the OLAP label for sophisticated "multidimensional" analysis. It represents an attempt to segment (some would say fragment) an already confusing array of products designed to retrieve and add informational value to the raw facts stored in a data warehouse. Before Codd introduced the term OLAP, software vendors used a multitude of other phrases including decision support systems (DSS), execu-

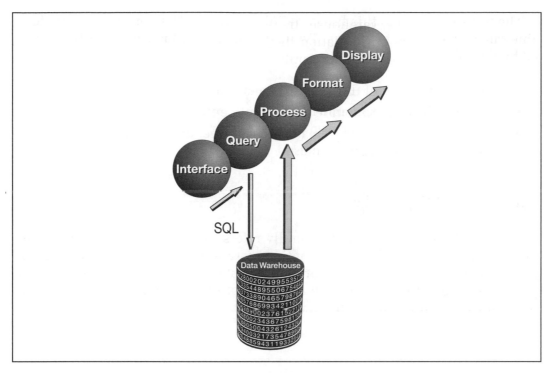

Figure 4.1　OLAP applications perform five basic functions.

tive information systems (EIS), data interpretation systems (DIS), and business intelligence systems (BIS) to describe the high-level process of retrieving, analyzing, and interpreting raw data. Despite this wide-ranging terminology, however, the goal of data analysis and reporting software has always been the same: to provide decision makers with more and better-timed information with which to reach business decisions.

OLAP, like OLTP, is rapidly becoming a general classification. Today most vendors of data warehouse access and analysis tools use the OLAP label and adhere to a simplified definition of OLAP capabilities. Throughout this book we use the OLAP acronym to describe any software tool that facilitates the generation of a database query (simple OLAP) or that supports more complex forms of data analysis. This broad definition views OLAP as the analytic extension of the data warehouse. As discussed in Chapter 3, data warehouses and data marts should be designed using dimensional modeling techniques to best support OLAP applications.

The tools that fit into this broad definition of OLAP incorporate a considerable range of analytic functions. Typically, OLAP products can be differentiated by the following factors:

- The sophistication of the computational functions.
- The application architecture (Is it client-centric or server-centric?).
- The way OLAP functions create and manage an analytic data cache (persistent or temporary cache).

Computational Capabilities

The broad definition of OLAP generally refers to four analytical capabilities. Vendors of OLAP products are continuously enhancing their products and adding analytic functions that blur the lines of classification among OLAP applications. Nevertheless, each OLAP application vendors focuses on one of the application areas shown in Figure 4.2:

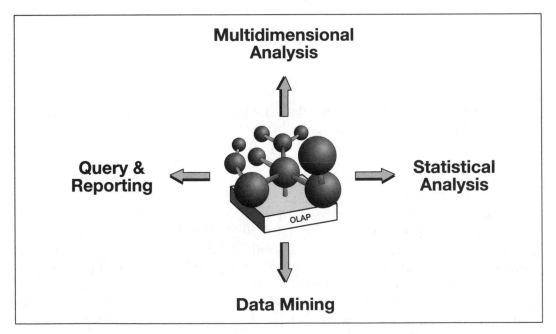

Figure 4.2   Four types of OLAP analysis.

- Query and Reporting
- Multidimensional analysis
- Statistical analysis (user-directed)
- Data mining (agent processing)

Query and Reporting Tools

Query and reporting applications provide the most basic type of OLAP data analysis, with computational capabilities that are typically limited to those that are readily supported by relational database management systems. These tools are designed to facilitate the ad hoc specification of a query (i.e., to generate SQL code) and to provide rich report formatting and graphical presentation capabilities that can be executed on the user's PC. Such applications generally conform to the Microsoft Windows model for an easy-to-use interface, and most are increasing their computational flexibility with each new release in order to move up in the OLAP "food chain." Query and reporting applications generate SQL code on the user client PC and often use Microsoft's open database connection (ODBC) to provide a common interface to data warehouses developed in any of the leading relational database management systems.

Query and reporting applications are useful for addressing users' requests for lists, counts, or status updates for which the computational requirements are relatively simple. For example, query and reporting applications are ideally suited for responding to such queries as:

- **Status reporting:** What were XYZ product sales last month?
- **Count:** How many customers used the XYZ credit card in restaurants during the month?
- **List:** Which customers have negative account balances?

Although these applications provide only limited analytic capabilities, most users' business questions can—at least initially—be satisfied through the basic data response. The responses to the initial questions, in turn, often trigger true analytical processing. Users' insatiable appetite for information then leads to the need for more comprehensive data analysis applications.

Multidimensional Analysis

More complex OLAP computational functions involve multidimensional data analysis, emanating from the rapid-fire questioning sequence that users employ to retrieve specific information from the data warehouse. A robust set of data computational and navigational capabilities distinguish multidimensional analysis applications from query and reporting applications. Multidimensional analysis applications enable users to enter the data warehouse along any single dimension and to navigate freely to all other dimensions. For example, a user may initiate an analysis at the region level (in the geographic dimension), then drill down the product detail hierarchy (in the product dimension) to isolate a specific product performance issue, then return to the geographic dimension to continue the analysis at the district or territory level. The ability to move up and down all dimensional hierarchies while maintaining the integrity of the computational aspects of the user's analysis request represents the true strength of multidimensional analysis.

Multidimensional analysis provides the analytic flexibility to answer such questions as:

- How have advertising expenditures affected sales?
- Where are competitors making inroads?
- Which products should be discontinued?
- Which customers are most loyal?

Answers to these types of questions require a computational layer of software because the information that is needed to respond is not usually stored in the data warehouse; the information is derived as calculated measures from the raw facts in the data warehouse. Because it is virtually impossible to predict the data requests and analysis path that a user will select to answer such questions, multidimensional OLAP applications are designed to let users create reports containing calculations and multiple layers of subtotals. Such computational layers generate up to four to five times more calculations and aggregations than the basic facts that are stored in the data warehouse.

Of course, users must also be able to navigate within the report shell (to drill up, down, and across) and to change report parameters to isolate the specific information needed to resolve the question, without having to respecify computational formulas or aggregation rules. As additional questions surface, the analysis becomes even more mathematically complex.

Statistical Analysis

Statistical data analysis represents the next higher level of OLAP complexity. It is designed to reduce a large amount of data to a simple relationship or formula, such as calculating an average or mean. An average income calculation, for example, is a single number that may represent thousands of data points.

Calculating an average is the most common form of statistical analysis. More sophisticated statistical analyses include regression, correlation, factoring, and clustering. Statistical analysis techniques are typically used to generate the types of models used in sales forecasting and market segmentation applications. Such models are essential for answering what-if questions. For example, regression analysis identifies, in mathematical terms, the possible relationship of a dependent variable (e.g., product sales) to independent variables (e.g., product price, distribution, and weather). The regression model (a mathematical formula) can be used to establish an expected value for the dependent variable, given new values for the independent variables. Once the statistical model has been created, the user can insert variables to answer such questions as: What if we lower price by 10 percent?

When talking about using statistical analysis to enhance decision support capabilities, it is important to draw a distinction between the analysts who develop the models using statistical analysis products and the business users of the models. In general, there are far more users of the models than there are analysts responsible for creating and validating them. This is fortunate because the statistical analysis process is relatively complex and requires precision in order to produce valid models. Business users, who frequently employ the models to assess and predict outcomes based on various scenarios, can usually be shielded from the complexity of model development. In a typical data warehouse environment, a user should be able to retrieve a model, substitute data retrieved from the warehouse, and view the output of the model. This process is commonly used, for example, to update a sales forecast with the most recent data available. In this way, the statistically derived models become another computational option that can be applied in multidimensional analysis.

SAS Institute and SPSS, Inc. currently lead the market for statistical analysis applications.

Data Mining

Data mining uses many of the same techniques as statistical analysis, and adds more complex functions such as neural networking to identify patterns and relationships within an analyzed data set. Data mining uses sophisticated pattern recognition and learning algorithms to generate predictive models. It is particularly useful for modeling nonlinear problems with large numbers of variables (i.e., automated multivariate analysis).

Whereas statistical analysis is user-directed, data mining applications are implemented as agents working on behalf of users to discover hidden insights that might otherwise go unrecognized. One of the best examples of a data-mining application is the determination of factors associated with credit card fraud and risk assessment. In this case, the data-mining application identifies a combination of user profile and behavioral characteristics that are associated with credit card misuse. These associated data elements are often difficult to discern with other analytical methods because they involve a large number of possible combinations and variables.

Although the data-mining applications market is relatively new (at least relative to data warehousing technology), it is developing rapidly. Major competitors in this arena include IBM, with its Intelligent Miner product, as well as HNC Software Inc., DataMind Corp., Neo Vista Solutions Inc., and Information Discovery Inc.

Application Architecture

The second means of differentiating OLAP products is based on the application architecture. Query and reporting tools, for example, emphasize an easy-to-use interface and rich display options—both intended to isolate the user from the difficulties of coding SQL. These tools generally rely on a two-tier application architecture in which the data tier (the data warehouse) is partitioned from the presentation/logic tier (the OLAP functions, including the interface and display components of the application). Figure 4.3 illustrates the application architecture of a typical query and reporting tool.

This application architecture presents some problems, however, when faced with the demand to analyze large query result sets. The difficulties are magnified because SQL is not a general-purpose programming language designed to code complex analytical procedures. The Sidebar "SQL Procedure for Data Analysis Computation" provides an example of this situation.

Most OLAP tool vendors recognize the limitations of a two-tier architecture with respect to coding complex analytic functions, and consequently use higher-level programming languages such as C and C++ rather than SQL for coding complex procedural logic for multistep analytic routines (the process component of an OLAP application). This creates a three-tier applications architecture in which the presentation tier (the interface and display components) is partitioned from the analytic logic tier (the query, process, and format functions) and the data tier.

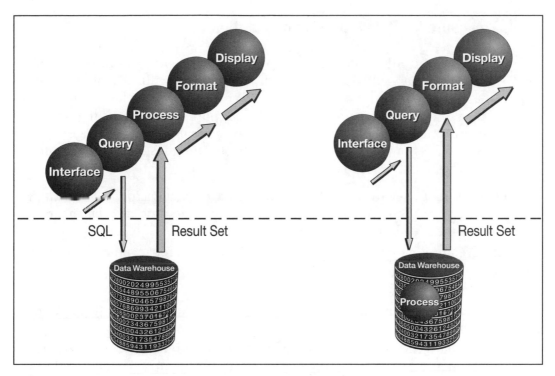

Figure 4.3 Two-tier application architecture.

(It is important to note that application partitioning is not the same as distributed computing, although application partitioning facilitates distributed computing. Application partitioning is a component software development model that emphasizes selecting the appropriate software development tool for each tier and the application programming interfaces (API) that facilitate communications between tiers. All software tiers can, in fact, reside on a single platform; in practice, however, the data warehouse and, increasingly, the analytic logic tiers are distributed to one or more servers, as shown in Figure 4.4.)

Application partitioning is particularly important in deploying intranet data warehouses. As Sun Microsystems' Java and Microsoft's ActiveX programming languages continue to gain momentum, more vendors are likely to use them to develop their presentation tiers. The presentation tiers incorporate a series of components or applets that can be downloaded to the user PC on demand. With this approach (see Figure 4.5) the browser functions as a

SQL Procedure for Data Analysis Computation

A simple example illustrates the complex SQL procedure required to per-form a simple data analysis computation. The user's request is an example of a "share" type of analytic calculation: "Show me how each customer of a population of customers compares to the total population." Relying on SQL and SQL structures alone, the question can be answered only through a very complex and inefficient process. The answer to the question would require the following steps:

1. Initiate query to the data warehouse to retrieve a row for each cus-tomer in the population. For this example, assume a thousand rows are retrieved (database I/O #1).
2. Create a temporary table (I/O #2), and insert the retrieved rows (I/O #3).
3. Query the temporary table and summarize the rows to calculate the "total population" (I/O #4).
4. Create a second temporary table (I/O #5), and insert the summarized total (I/O #6).
5. Execute the query, join the two temporary tables, dividing each row in the first temporary table with the second temporary table (I/O #7) to create the "share" calculation.
6. Create a third temporary table (I/O #8), and insert the new computed rows (I/O #9).
7. Read the third temporary table and return the computed rows to the user (I/O #10); assume return of a thousand rows.
8. Drop each of the three temporary tables (I/Os #10, #11, and #12).

The net result for this simple computation is the creation of three tempo-rary database tables and a total of 12 database I/Os. Some relational database management systems may offer more efficient ways to perform this query, but this example illustrates the complexity of SQL procedures. Many ana-lytic queries require a minimum of seven temporary tables and as many as 50 to process complex requests. Certainly, most relational database manage-ment systems can support this type of load for single users, but concurrent usage exacerbates the problem. Few, if any, database products can handle the creation, insertion, query, and deletion of hundreds of temporary tables and thousands of I/O procedures, as often happens in an intranet deploy-ment of data warehouse access.

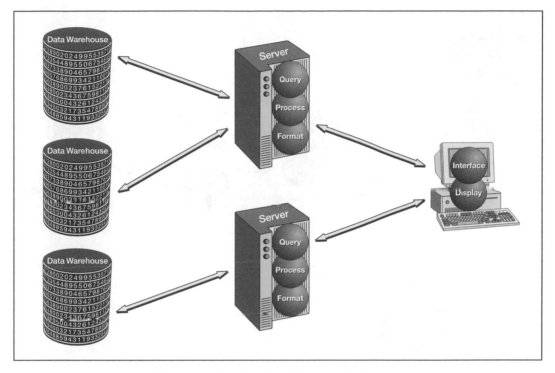

Figure 4.4   Application partitioning.

shell for the creation of highly adaptable user interfaces and information displays, and the logic tier is accessible from a Web server using a popular protocol like the Internet Inter-ORB Protocol (IIOP) or the Common Gateway Interface (CGI). (Refer to Chapters 6 and 7 for additional information on the use of advanced standards for Internet and intranet distributed computing communications in the Microsoft and Sun/Netscape environments, respectively.)

As mentioned in Chapter 2, a true three-tier architecture (one that separates the data access logic from the application logic and the presentation logic) offers three distinct advantages: performance, flexibility, and scalability. Performance and scalability are both enhanced by the ability to apply the appropriate hardware and software solution at each of the three tiers; flexibility is optimized by the fact that development can occur independently at the data, application, and presentation layers. In fact, a three-tier architecture is advisable

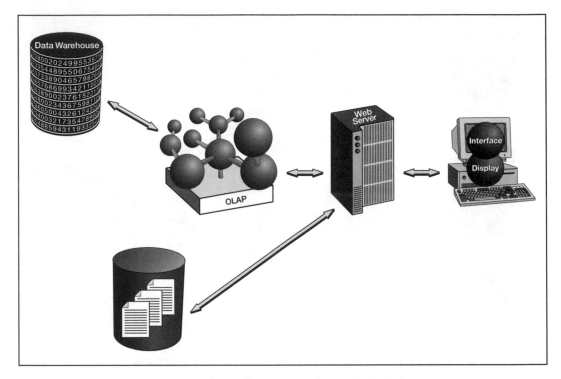

Figure 4.5 Distributed computing model of the intranet.

for any large data warehouse and user community, and is absolutely essential for intranet deployment.

A three-tier application architecture allows the same application logic to be shared by either a Microsoft Windows or Web browser presentation tier. In this way, the Windows and Web browser interfaces become deployment options rather than separate applications.

Analytic Cache

OLAP applications that provide data computational functions (multidimensional analysis, statistical analysis, and data mining) require a temporary workspace (a cache) to enforce strict database dependencies. In addition, the applications may use the cache to store interim computational results. Query and reporting applications are the exception because they offer very limited analytic functionality. The way the computationally intensive OLAP applications create and manage their analytic caches is the third notable feature of OLAP tools. This factor is most important in distinguishing among the approaches for providing multidimensional analysis capabilities.

All of the leading multidimensional analysis software vendors use one of the following three techniques to provide caching and database recognition capabilities in their products. Figure 4.6 illustrates the various analytic caching strategies.

- **Temporary Database Cache:** This technique uses temporary tables as the caching strategy, performing all calculations within the relational database management system. A database caching technique is not

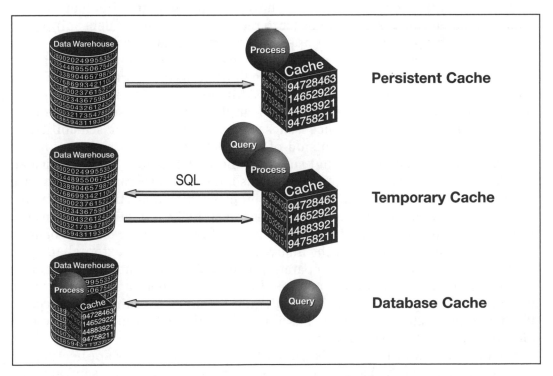

Figure 4.6   Analytic caching strategies.

generally recommended for any type of large-scale OLAP application.

- **Temporary External Cache:** This technique dynamically extracts data from the relational database management system and temporarily caches the analytic data set in memory to perform OLAP functions.

- **Persistent External Cache:** This technique, which is sometimes referred to as a "data cube" for multidimensional analysis, routinely updates a separate cache and ensures that the cache is constantly available for the execution of OLAP functions in memory. A persistent cache may be server-resident (to support user sharing) or PC-resident, which permits users to be disconnected from the network while performing analysis.

A temporary database caching strategy is essentially a two-tier application partitioning approach that transfers the computational requirements to the database management system in order to reduce the amount of data shipped to the user's PC for processing. This approach relies on complex SQL code to generate temporary tables, which serve as the analytic cache. Unfortunately, it does not overcome the procedural programming limitations of SQL, and must rely on database tuning to improve performance. Although experienced SQL programmers can quickly create new applications employing a database caching strategy, maintenance and performance issues represent challenges in scalability.

Creating a separate cache outside of the relational database (i.e., external temporary or persistent caching) supports the development of sophisticated applications since it allows developers to use powerful programming language such as C or C++ rather than SQL to develop complex analytic requirements. Using a more robust programming language to code the analytic logic does not limit the developers' ability to take advantage of SQL features for load balancing between the database and the analytic engine. Persistent external analytic caches are often updated as a separate process. Vendors that create a temporary external cache rely on the analytic logic tier to generate an SQL query to populate the temporary cache. The SQL query strategy is optimized to accomplish as much data reduction as possible within the database in order to efficiently populate the temporary cache.

A temporary external cache is generally the best choice for applications in which the data warehouse is updated daily or weekly and the users' analytic requirements are unpredictable. Because each user can create multiple caches, maintaining data in a persistent cache is not a practical option in this type of environment. It is important to note that while temporary caching imposes no artificial constraints on ad hoc analysis of the data warehouse, the increase in flexibility may have an adverse affect on performance. Marketing and behavioral decision support applications are well suited for temporary caching. In both cases, the databases are large and frequently updated, and the users' analytical requirements are rarely predictable.

A persistent external cache usually provides the best solution for applications in which the data warehouse is updated on a monthly basis and user requirements are relatively predictable. Although persistent caching offers some performance advantages, it limits true ad hoc analysis of a large data warehouse (e.g., 50-plus gigabytes). Financial decision support applications are particularly well suited for a persistent caching strategy.

Information Advantage, Inc.'s DecisionSuite is one example of a multidimensional analysis application that uses a temporary analytic cache, while Arbor Software Corp.'s Essbase and Oracle Corporation's Oracle Express Server are examples of multidimensional analysis products that employ a persistent external cache.

Although each type of product addresses a specific aspect of an organizations' analytic requirements, some combination of OLAP applications is usually necessary to meet the full range of decision support requirements. This is one reason why data warehousing is a particularly attractive option: Multiple OLAP functions maintain data consistency by accessing common data warehouses.

Applying OLAP Functions to an Intranet

There are several ways to provide intranet users with information that is derived from data stored in the data warehouse. The easiest way is to create and store reports or graphic output as "static" HTML pages accessible from a browser. This is essentially OLAP without the online aspect: The data warehouse is not really being accessed by users; it is simply the data source used for batch reporting. This method requires periodic analytic processing to create static reports, which can then be retrieved and displayed as HTML pages, the same way that other documents are retrieved from a Web server. The advantage here is that the batch reporting system creates digital, rather than paper, reports that can be displayed in a Web browser. By using HTTP, users navigate along predefined paths to find "pages" in large reports, thereby enhancing their ability to locate specific types of information. Figure 4.7 illustrates this type of intranet data warehouse information distribution.

Static reporting of data warehouse content is often the most efficient way to distribute routine reports, such as those providing status or performance information required by a large numbers of users. In most organizations, however, this approach addresses only a very small proportion of users' decision support requirements. Static reporting provides the lowest common denominator of information that can be disseminated to a large number of users, but it does not address the need for dynamic information retrieval by users who need access to a specific segment of the data in the warehouse.

A second class of applications facilitate dynamic data warehouse access, but provide virtually no analytic processing capability. This type of application is often encountered when accessing data on the World Wide Web. The

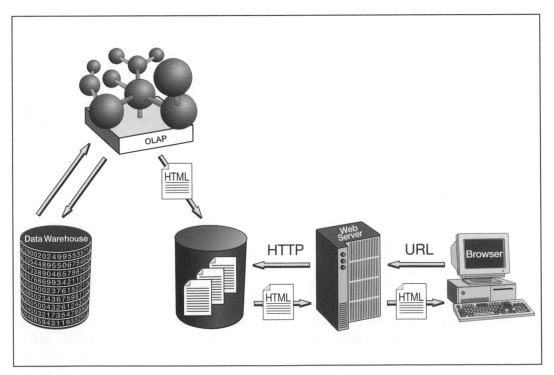

Figure 4.7 Static reports and graphics produced from data warehouse content.

type of function provided is actually online access without the application processing or, in this case, OLAP without the analytic processing aspect. The reporting application simply retrieves data stored in the data warehouse and displays it. Because most of these applications retrieve only a single record from the database, there is no need for report formatting. It is possible, for example, to retrieve a credit card balance (a single number) from a central database merely by entering a credit card number and an assigned password. Although this type of application constitutes dynamic access to the data, the query itself is always the same (i.e., static). There are several ways to embed and send a query from a Web browser application or to trigger a database-stored procedure from the data warehouse. This type of query application is covered in detail in Chapters 6 and 7; here, it's important to understand that an SQL query (e.g., a single select statement) can be passed through a Web server gateway (i.e., CGI, ISAPI, or NSAPI) to retrieve online data from the data warehouse. Figure 4.8 illustrates this type of online access to the data warehouse.

A third approach to using intranets to provide access to data in the data warehouse is to employ the network to more effectively distribute OLAP software. Since the intranet is based on the enterprise's TCP/IP network, the same communications infrastructure is shared by traditional client/server applications and intranet browser-enabled applications. The intranet browser can be used to download OLAP software to the user PC. The application code may (depending on the user's requirements) remain cached on the PC, simplifying software distribution and user support. Several vendors of query and reporting applications provide this level of integration with the intranet architecture. The applications continue to provide robust report formatting and graph-

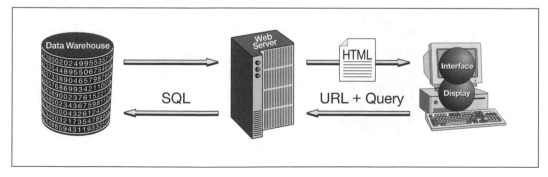

Figure 4.8 Static query updating an HTML page.

ic display with dynamic data warehouse access. Although this approach offers some advantages for software distribution (see Figure 4.9), the applications do not fully realize the performance advantages available from distributing data processing across the network.

Providing a large number of intranet users with access to the data warehouse and using PC tools that can potentially return large query result sets to the user PC raises the very real possibility of network bottlenecks. The solution to the problem is to relocate the data-intensive OLAP functions—specifically, query, process, and format functions—to the server. While the Web browser manages the interface and display functions, the query, process, and format functions move behind the Web server, closer to the data warehouse. The formatting function is responsible for producing an HTML document on-line, based on the request sent from the Web browser.

Figure 4.10 illustrates the steps necessary to dynamically create a report in the form of an HTML document based on instructions passed to an external program called by the Web server. In this type of application, the user locates the information resource via a URL, and once access is granted, downloads the interface components used to formulate an information request. The request is then sent to the Web server and passed to an external program to execute the query, process, and formatting functions. The formatted document is then returned to the browser for display. Figure 4.10 outlines a high-level view of the flow of the requests for OLAP functions residing on a server. Chapters 6 and 7 also cover the ways external programs, such as server-based OLAP functions, are supported as distributed intranet applications.

The most advanced forms of OLAP—statistical analysis and data mining—

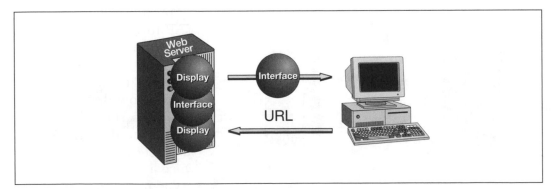

Figure 4.9 Software distribution over the intranet.

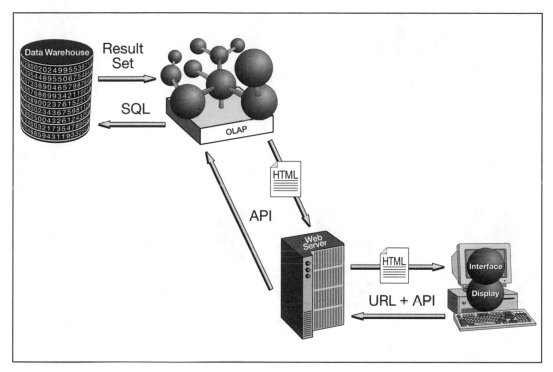

Figure 4.10   Dynamic document creation using intranet to distribute computing.

are typically used to construct models based on the results of data analysis. The models themselves are widely used to simulate or predict outcomes based on alternative scenarios. Integrating this level of OLAP functionality with an intranet is likely to entail downloading the models, as applets, to the user PC, thereby permitting the user to perform what-if analysis.

Figure 4.11 illustrates how these advanced forms of OLAP can be integrated into business analysis. In this example, a bank loan officer downloads a model from the intranet Web server. The manager then answers a series of model-generated questions to determine whether the applicant qualifies for a loan. The model itself is based on a data-mining model constructed from a thorough analysis of the factors that predict low credit risk. Once again, in this type of application, there is no need to provide users with dynamic access to the intranet data warehouse.

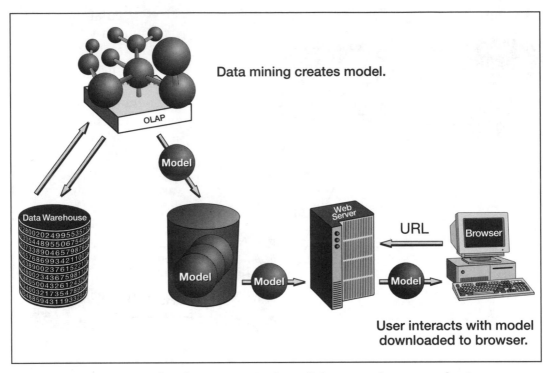

Figure 4.11 Downloading statistical models as applets over the intranet.

The balance of this chapter focuses on integrating server-resident multidimensional analysis functions with an intranet. Multidimensional analysis functions—sometimes described as "a spreadsheet on steroids"—are the basis for most computationally intense intranet data warehousing applications.

Multidimensional Analysis Applications

As discussed earlier, a data warehouse stores facts, such as unit sales, price, occupancy, expenses, and so forth, and permits users to calculate relevant measures from those facts. A user can, for example, calculate the measure "volume change" by subtracting a prior period volume from the current period volume. This measure, when divided by the prior period volume, yields a second measure, "percent change."

The "fact" that sales were 240,000 units during the most recent month, for instance, has minimal information value. In contrast, the "calculation" that indicates that sales declined 10 percent in the most recent month versus a year ago raises many management questions. As each question is answered, new questions emerge. This type of online analysis model is significantly different from a hypertext search used to "follow a thread" in reviewing textural documents. Textural documents are linked to one another by common themes. The type of exploration that is required within the data warehouse has no predefined path. Instead, each analysis process generates its own unique path.

The goal of multidimensional analysis OLAP functions is to dynamically create and display documents containing computed values. Providing useful multidimensional analysis capabilities to intranet users requires that they have the ability to direct the path of their analysis. One difficulty of creating a robust multidimensional analysis OLAP application lies in the need to maintain the integrity of the analysis as users add computed fields and navigate data warehouse dimensions. The following description highlights the challenges inherent in providing flexible user-directed online analysis, and focuses on the capabilities that must be supported in the logic tier of a multidimensional analysis OLAP application.

In the intranet data warehouse, facts are reported and measures are computed over time. Time, the one database dimension that is common to every data warehouse, is difficult for multidimensional analysis tools to handle because of the infinite number of time period combinations. Time periods may be expressed as days, weeks, months, or accounting periods. In addition, users often aggregate data for nonstandard time periods such as the Christmas season or the current six weeks.

A single dimension analysis allows users to retrieve facts and calculated measures for one or more time periods, including the total for a group of periods. If, for example, unit sales is a fact that is stored in the data warehouse each week, the information can be used to calculate a comparison of the percent change in unit sales for the current six-week period and the prior six-week period. In this type of comparison, the unit sales for each six-week summary period (i.e., the current and prior periods) are totaled and a volume change measure is computed, from which a percent change measure is calculated. This is not a difficult process, but data warehouses are seldom limited to a single dimension.

Additional database dimensions define the business characteristics that are unique to each enterprise. A package goods manufacturer, for example, is likely to want to include both product and market dimensions, which may include sales territories, distribution centers, and sales representatives. An insurance company is likely to track customers as a key dimension, while retailers typically include store and vendor dimensions. Databases commonly contain three or four dimensions, and it is not uncommon to encounter many more.

The unique requirements of multidimensional analysis begin to emerge when a user requires the capability to subtotal facts and measures along multiple dimensions, including the time dimension. Many facts and most calculated measures are "nonadditive." These include facts such as price, which must be computed at the time of the request using a weighted average function; and percent change, which must be computed on the fly at each level. Figure 4.12 provides an example of a typical multidimensional analysis report, one that is based entirely on computed measures.

In order to understand the challenges in developing flexible multidimensional analysis applications, it is useful to draw a parallel with the spread-

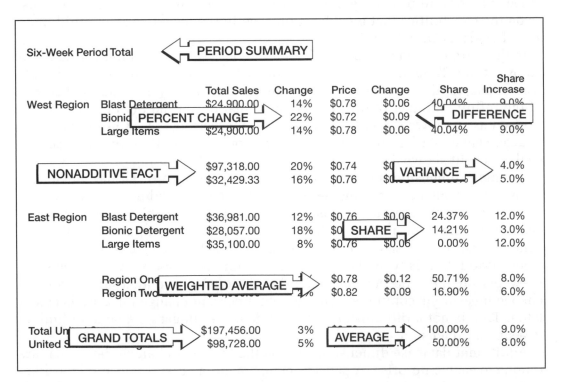

Figure 4.12 Typical multidimensional report.

sheet application. The spreadsheet is the most pervasive type of data analysis, and it is extremely useful as long as the data set being analyzed is very small.

Most spreadsheet users are accustomed to a spatial model in which formulas are defined by referencing cell location. In fact, a spreadsheet actually has two dimensions: the letters (A, B, C, etc.) and the numbers (1, 2, 3, etc.). The specific value in a cell is unimportant in defining the formula; only the cell reference is important. We've all encountered problems caused by a misplaced parenthesis in a spreadsheet formula; a calculation error occurs without any warning, and may proliferate rapidly if the computed cell is referenced in other formulas.

Multidimensional analysis is like a spreadsheet in several ways: It uses the location of data in the database to specify a formula to calculate a measure and allows the use of calculated measures in the definition of other calculated measures. In a spreadsheet, if prior period sales data is located in cell A1 and current period sales are in B1, then sales volume change is expressed simply as A1-B1. In multidimensional analysis, however, the formula requires the location of two facts defined by the database dimensions. So, to compute sales volume change, we subtract prior period sales from current period sales for a given product and market set of dimensions. The power of multidimensional analysis lies in the fact that the formula does not change regardless of which product, markets, or periods are specified. At least in theory, users can navigate any combination of dimensions while the logic to calculate the required measure is maintained.

In addition to defining calculated measures by referencing the location of facts within the database dimensions, users need to be able to drill down/up/across any dimension, pivot a report (i.e., alter the column/row formula), and modify the constraints of any dimension—all while maintaining the integrity of the computed measures and embedded subtotals. The following example of a typical multidimensional analysis session demonstrates the power of these tools.

Figure 4.13 shows a report that includes facts stored in the data warehouse (e.g., unit sales and unit price) for a series of products sold in the U.S. market. For the sake of simplicity, the data warehouse in this example is limited to three dimensions: period, product, and market.

If the user adds several subtotals to the product dimension, the software must compute measures on the fly in order to satisfy the request. It is important to note that the subtotals are not derived simply by summing values. As

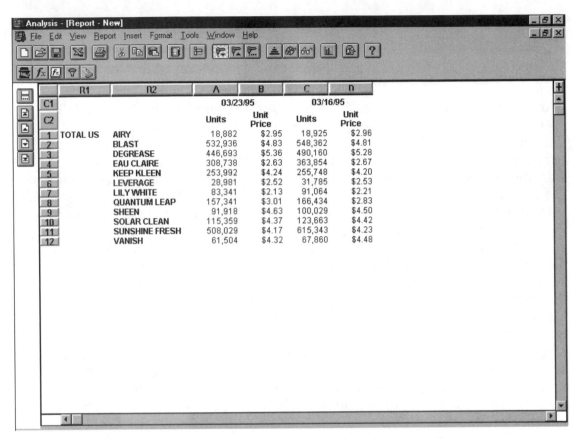

Figure 4.13   Simple OLAP report example.

in Figure 4.14, the subtotal of product price is determined by a weighted average calculation using product sales volume.

As Figure 4.15 shows, when the user drills down on the market dimension, the software displays the sales regions within the total U.S. market definition, maintaining the embedded subtotals for products as the drilling logic is invoked. In Figure 4.16, we see what happens when the user pivots the report format to display regions as column headings.

Finally, Figure 4.17 illustrates the result when the user simplifies the report format by specifying that only period totals be displayed. In each case, unlike the spreadsheet in which computational logic is linked to cells, multidimen-

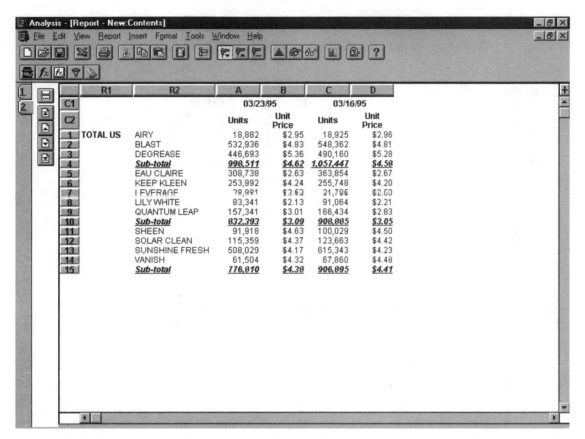

Figure 4.14 Subtotaling rules are different for additive and nonadditive facts.

sional analysis references data in a multidimensional analytic cache. The power of both the spreadsheet and multidimensional analysis is that the data references are maintained during the analysis process.

Although this simple example illustrates the use of multidimensional analysis, it is important to note that users often need to report data based on multiple exception criteria, to, for example, "report only those product and region combinations in which unit sales declined during the current month and where price remained unchanged."

One characteristic that differs widely among multidimensional tools is the extent to which a user can author and publish new calculations and filters,

		03/23/95		03/16/95	
		Units	Unit Price	Units	Unit Price
CENTRAL REGION	AIRY	2,650	$2.68	3,306	$2.72
	BLAST	89,726	$5.18	94,781	$4.97
	DEGREASE	74,353	$5.80	78,920	$5.65
	Sub-total	*166,729*	*$4.95*	*177,007*	*$4.80*
	EAU CLAIRE	64,062	$2.60	66,994	$2.67
	KEEP KLEEN	31,084	$4.57	29,769	$4.40
	LEVERAGE	10,942	$2.20	11,792	$2.19
	LILY WHITE	26,308	$2.52	36,353	$2.61
	QUANTUM LEAP	22,542	$3.43	22,865	$2.84
	Sub-total	*154,938*	*$3.30*	*167,773*	*$3.14*
	SHEEN	9,637	$5.32	10,143	$4.93
	SOLAR CLEAN	18,774	$4.40	21,663	$4.59
	SUNSHINE FRESH	82,592	$4.19	85,551	$4.33
	VANISH	17,065	$4.85	17,135	$5.05
	Sub-total	*128,068*	*$4.73*	*134,492*	*$4.74*
EASTERN REGION	AIRY	4,802	$1.59	5,124	$1.87
	BLAST	85,195	$4.77	84,270	$4.66
	DEGREASE	193,644	$5.23	224,359	$5.13
	Sub-total	*283,641*	*$4.54*	*313,753*	*$4.42*
	EAU CLAIRE	117,879	$2.55	129,306	$2.71
	KEEP KLEEN	95,911	$4.30	94,127	$4.45
	LEVERAGE	1,014	$2.68	1,315	$2.64
	LILY WHITE	21,731	$1.95	21,235	$1.95
	QUANTUM LEAP	4,880	$2.90	5,304	$2.81
	Sub-total	*241,415*	*$3.09*	*251,287*	*$3.15*
	SHEEN	21,402	$4.65	23,033	$4.33
	SOLAR CLEAN	37,676	$3.99	39,094	$3.87
	SUNSHINE FRESH	258,170	$3.88	353,398	$3.89
	VANISH	27,137	$4.45	30,349	$4.54

Figure 4.15 Computational logic is maintained as user navigates data warehouse dimensions.

and/or easily add subtotals to an analysis. The power of a spreadsheet lies in its ability to define a calculation or replicate the calculation down a row or across a column. The power of multidimensional analysis is similarly enhanced by the ability users have to author calculations and filters based on database dimensions, distribute them across analyses, and share the analyses with another user, workgroup, or the enterprise.

This simple example illustrates some analyses that are common to a product manufacturer, but the concept is essentially the same for banks, insurance companies, and airlines, as well as any other industry that must analyze data across multiple dimensions.

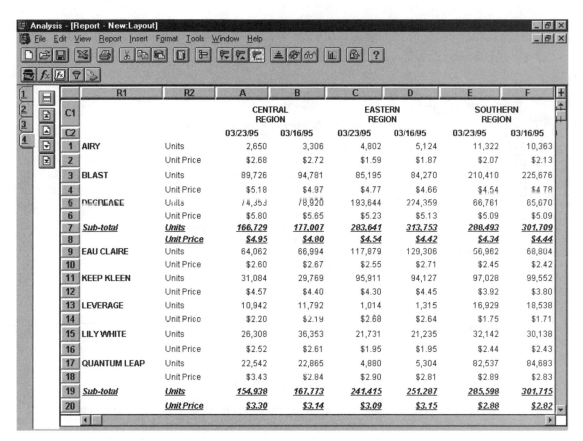

Figure 4.16   Computational logic is maintained as report is pivoted.

The Database Link

Returning to the spreadsheet analogy, we recognize that A1, B1, and C3 are co-ordinates in a two-dimensional space. A1 provides a row and column coordinate for data stored in the spreadsheet cell. The coordinate is used to locate cell contents (i.e., facts or measures derived via formulas) that can be referenced in the creation of another formula. The numeric value contained in the cell is substituted for the coordinate used in specifying the formula when the spreadsheet logic is executed.

Database dimensions are much like the number and letter dimensions of the spreadsheet. The period, market, and product dimensions in the preceding ex-

Analysis - [Report - New:Contents]

File Edit View Report Insert Format Tools Window Help

	R1	R2	A	B	C	D
S1	**Two Week Total**					
C1			CENTRAL REGION	EASTERN REGION	SOUTHERN REGION	WESTERN REGION
1	AIRY	Units	5,956	9,926	21,685	240
2		Unit Price	$2.70	$1.74	$2.10	$5.29
3	BLAST	Units	184,507	169,465	436,086	291,240
4		Unit Price	$5.08	$4.72	$4.66	$4.83
5	DEGREASE	Units	153,273	418,003	132,431	233,146
6		Unit Price	$5.73	$5.18	$5.09	$5.28
7	*Sub-total*	*Units*	*343,736*	*597,394*	*590,202*	*524,626*
8		*Unit Price*	*$4.88*	*$4.48*	*$4.39*	*$5.14*
9	EAU CLAIRE	Units	131,056	247,185	125,766	168,585
10		Unit Price	$2.64	$2.63	$2.44	$2.89
11	KEEP KLEEN	Units	60,853	190,038	196,580	62,269
12		Unit Price	$4.49	$4.38	$3.86	$4.15
13	LEVERAGE	Units	22,734	2,329	35,467	236
14		Unit Price	$2.20	$2.66	$1.73	$3.52
15	LILY WHITE	Units	62,661	42,966	62,280	6,498
16		Unit Price	$2.57	$1.95	$2.44	$1.74
17	QUANTUM LEAP	Units	45,407	10,184	167,220	100,964
18		Unit Price	$3.16	$2.86	$2.86	$2.82
19	*Sub-total*	*Units*	*322,711*	*492,702*	*587,313*	*338,552*
20		*Unit Price*	*$3.22*	*$3.12*	*$2.85*	*$3.24*

Figure 4.17 Computational logic references the analytic cache of the multidimensional tool.

ample support the definition of coordinates in the data warehouse. By constraining a combination of database dimensions (for example, where product = Blast, and where market = Eastern Region), facts can be easily located within the data warehouse. In multidimensional analysis, we use database coordinates to specify formulas. Multidimensional software, like spreadsheet software, substitutes actual numeric values for the coordinates and continually modifies the coordinates to correspond with changes entered by the user. In a spreadsheet, the user changes the value in a cell and recomputes all of the formulas. In multidimensional analysis, however, the user changes the constraints on one or more dimensions. For example, the user can modify the "where market" constraint from Eastern Region to Central Region. Such changes are, however, somewhat more complex in multidimensional analysis than in a spreadsheet, because a data warehouse has many more dimensions than can be displayed in a two-dimensional array.

Selecting the Appropriate OLAP Tools

Increasingly, multidimensional analysis functions are being viewed as the core OLAP component needed to extend the analytic capabilities of the data warehouse. For this reason, many query and reporting applications are adding multidimensional analysis capabilities and/or are offering links to other vendors' multidimensional analysis products. Multidimensional analysis provides a powerful set of analytic capabilities that are needed to respond to the rapid-fire questioning sequence that is a standard requirement for effective business analysis. At a fundamental level, multidimensional analysis supports the ad hoc creation of calculated measures, warehouse navigation (i.e., drilling, pivoting, and aggregation,) and presentation (formatting and exporting to a PC tool or Web browser environment). These functions can be combined with query and reporting, statistical analysis, and/or data mining to provide full-featured OLAP capabilities.

Tool selection for client/server data warehousing typically focus on the ease-of-use characteristics of the interface component and the "richness" of the display options, with a panel of user representatives often casting the deciding vote. In an Internet or intranet environment, however, ease-of-use criteria are largely irrelevant given the adaptable nature of the interface and display components that can be delivered via Web browser presentation. This is not to say that the interface and display components are unimportant in the Internet and intranet environments, only that users can adapt these components to their particular needs. In an intranet data warehouse environment, architectural considerations outweigh the interface and display option characteristics in tool selection. Specifically, the tool selection process for the intranet data warehouse must emphasize scalability and security. These issues are explained in more depth in later chapters, but for now it is important to understand that the tools that support the intranet data warehouse, including multidimensional functions, must adhere to the same secure, scalable architecture as the data warehouse itself.

Selecting an appropriate multidimensional analysis tool is not a simple decision given the widening choice of products and capabilities and the ever-changing cast of players competing in the market. The 15 characteristics described in the following pages differentiate multidimensional analysis tools from one another and are useful in selecting an appropriate tool. Consider these keys as the minimum requirements of a multidimensional analysis application.

- **Multidimensional View:** The tool should provide a multidimensional view of the data warehouse, which shields users and developers alike from the complexities of the underlying data structures and query algorithms. It should allow them to pose questions from their business perspective. Each dimension should define standard hierarchies, including multiple hierarchies within a single dimension.

- **Pivot/Rotation:** The tool should permit users to point and click at any time to dynamically cast and recast dimensions into any report layout of columns, rows, and section breaks. This capability enables users to view and present analytic results from an unlimited number of perspectives.

- **Drilling:** The tool should permit users to dynamically explore their business at any level of detail by drilling down, drilling up, or skipping multiple hierarchy levels on any dimension at any time without predefining drill paths.

- **Cross-Dimension Calculations:** Users should be able to dynamically create, save, and share simple and complex custom calculations without writing stored procedures. Calculations affecting one dimension should operate correctly when applied across other dimensions during analysis.

- **Dynamic Sets:** Users should be able to dynamically create, save, and share custom item groupings and summaries across any dimension. Users should also be able to define a hierarchy of custom groupings and to immediately drill up and down through the hierarchy. This permits users to define and analyze unforeseen or temporary business occurrences when necessary.

- **Filters:** Users should be able to define report content by dragging and dropping filters that constrain the data appearing on the report to items meeting specific criteria. It should be possible to combine filters associated with one dimension with filters from other dimensions at any time. Users should be able to create, save, and share filters.

- **Decision Groupware Capabilities:** Users should be able to create and share any decision support information objects (e.g., reports, analyses, sets, calculations, filters, templates, intelligent agents, alerts, and triggers) across workgroups or the entire enterprise. To be completely effective, groupware should contain "live information." For example, a workgroup user should be able to create a report, perform analysis, and share the report with others in the group who receive an intelligent "live" report so that workgroup members can immediately drill, analyze, rerun, and resend the report. Live reports contain not only the text, but the calculations and assumptions supporting the analyses. Just sharing the text of the report is not decision groupware. Shared information objects must also incorporate appropriate security to prevent unauthorized access.

- **Collapsible Browsing:** Users should be able to easily define report content by browsing a list of all valid choices in the data warehouse and selecting from the list items for inclusion. Available lists of items should "collapse" as users constrain dimension attributes. For example, a 100,000-item listing of soft drinks may collapse to 25 items when the user selects "diet, 12-oz., can, caffeine-free, cherry, cola." Users should be able to expand and collapse browse lists by pointing and clicking.

- **Flexible Period Definitions:** Multidimensional analysis logic should support multiple noncontiguous periods, period ranges, period calculations, and period variables, including "most recent." Support for nonstandard time period analysis is critical (e.g., "compare fiscal year 1996 to calendar year 1995"). Users should be able to create period calculations and define nonstandard time period analysis without storing the computed values in advance.

- **Access to Data Warehouse:** Multidimensional analysis relies on an analytic cache that is extracted from the data warehouse. There are a number of approaches to providing an analytic cache: It may be generated on demand and maintained temporarily to support a single analysis session; it may be updated periodically and maintained as a persistent cache; a third alternative, a database caching strategy that relies on the construction of temporary database tables, is not recommended for large-scale implementations with large numbers of concurrent users.

- **Metadata:** Metadata, a data directory that describes the data warehouse to the application, can (and should) be used as more than a card catalog. It should function as an architectural component that reduces development time and user support requirements by providing a dynamic layer between the data warehouse and application logic. Metadata should transparently manage business rules to allow instant drill-up/drill-down, user-created calculations and custom groupings. Changing the database structure should not require altering the business application.

- **Sparse Matrix Schema Support:** Multidimensional analysis logic should support sparse matrix schemas, which are often encountered with large, highly granular database dimensions. For example, the matrix formed by daily time period and individual dimensions results in a matrix in which fact values would not be expected at every intersection. The database design should not require the storage of N/As or zeros where dimensions intersect but data doesn't exist (e.g., "July sales of snow shovels in Phoenix"). Products requiring the storage of nonexistent data points can cause the size of the database to increase dramatically.

- **Read and Write:** Users and applications should be able to read and write to the data warehouse. Many decision support applications require this capability, including forecasting, budgeting, and salesforce automation.

- **Query Generation:** The multidimensional analysis logic should dynamically generate efficient SQL at runtime based on user requests and applications requirements. This capability provides users with unlimited interactive exploration of the data warehouse.

- **Openness:** Multidimensional analysis logic should be able to directly access standard local or distributed relational databases. Multidimensional logic should be accessible by any PC development and productivity tool.

OLAP Market Trends

Data warehousing is accelerating interest in data analysis products that can effectively support decision making. Further, intranet data warehousing is prompting many organizations to alter their deployment strategies for providing users with access to robust online analysis capabilities as well as the data warehouse itself. As Figure 4.18 illustrates, two classes of OLAP applications are beginning to emerge as the current classification of OLAP tools (based on computational capabilities) becomes less relevant with each new release of vendor software. Based on the belief Intranets will redefine distributed computing as we know it, the two segments of the OLAP market that will emerge are likely to be:

- OLAP applications that focus on the computational processing requirements of business analysis. These applications typically reside on the server and are executed via a published API.
- OLAP applications that focus on information presentation, including report formatting and graphical information display. These applications generally reside on the user PC or are downloaded on demand in the form of applets and call the computational OLAP functions by

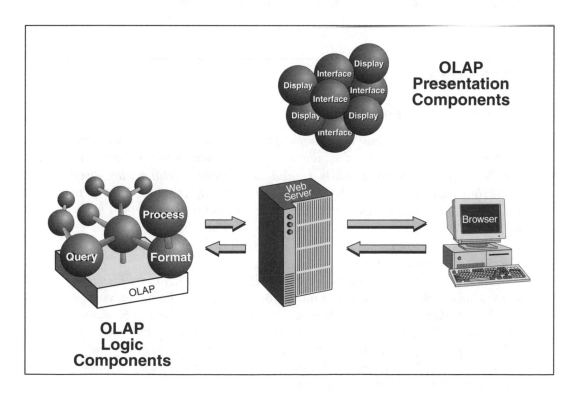

Figure 4.18 OLAP functions evolve into two classes of software objects.

linking to the API. In other words, presentation-tier objects (chunks of code) interface with computation-tier objects to form a highly adaptable OLAP solution.

As the products evolve, the presentation tier (the user interface and information display) are likely to adapt to meet the requirements of specific market segments. In addition to computational capabilities, server-based OLAP products can be expected to manage data access security, metadata, automated agent processing, and other services that are required in a robust computing environment.

Because intranet data warehousing is more similar in structure to mainframe/terminal computing than it is to PC-centric client/server computing, corporate information services managers are likely to play a dominant role in building decision support systems for use throughout the next decade. The next chapter outlines some of the issues that management is likely to face in planning and implementing an intranet data warehouse.

CASE STUDY

Dayton Hudson's Use of OLAP

Success in retail merchandising increasingly depends on timely, accurate understanding of customer preferences, combined with swift responses to market shifts and product trends. Leading mass market retailers are discovering that sophisticated database techniques can help them to improve performance in both areas. Data warehouses combined with analytical tools enable merchants to gain insights into their customer base, manage inventories more tightly, and keep the right products in front of the right people at the right place and time.

"The merchants and store managers in all our operating units face the same kinds of decisions, day in and day out," says Mike Peterson, vice president of Marketing at Target Stores, a $25 billion unit of Dayton Hudson Corporation. "Experience and good instincts count for a lot, but nothing takes the place of accurate, timely information that's easy to get to and work with. People who are making million-dollar decisions on a regular basis deserve the best decision support systems we can give them."

Dayton Hudson decided to standardize its decision support systems across three key operating units: Target Stores, a 752-discount store chain headquartered in Minneapolis, Minnesota; Mervyn's, a 300-unit moderate department store chain headquartered in Fremont, CA; and the Dayton Hudson Department Store Division. "Our overall objective from an IS perspective was to standardize our IS environment on the best practices, applications, and products that had been developed or implemented by our major operating units," explains Dayton Hudson Senior Vice President and CIO Vivian Stephenson.

At Target Stores, more than 1,000 marketing and merchandising professionals use applications based on DecisionSuite a multidimensional analysis tool from Information Advantage to create 50,000 reports each month. The most widely used applications are:

- Info Retriever, which provides "drill-anywhere" access and analysis to sales, profitability, and other financial data by location and time.
- Instocks, which assists merchandisers to identify their top-priority buying and stocking issues at a click of a button.

The applications, known collectively as the Decision Maker's Workbench, are used to analyze nearly a terabyte of raw data stored in the warehouse. The data warehouse is managed on a Tandem Himalaya running Tandem's Non-Stop SQL. The Multidimensional OLAP functions are distributed across six processors on a Hewlett-Packard HP T-500 UNIX server.

With the data warehouse and server-based multidimensional analysis capabilities in place, Target was able to create a Web browser application that gives vendors access to portions of the data warehouse so that they can monitor the sales performance of their products. In this way, retailers and vendors can collaborate on how best to stock, price, and merchandise products. A retailer has limited shelf space; the goal is to optimize the return on that space.

"Web deployment gives us a simple, flexible, cost-effective way to take advantage of the World Wide Web," says Maria Bogakos, Dayton Hudson's group leader for Decision Support. "Users benefit because they can work with the browser they know best on whatever computer platform they have. We benefit because we greatly expand our data access and analysis capabilities with minimal cost in infrastructure and training. Our vendors love it because they get timely performance information when they need it."

"A big reason for Target's rapid growth in a competitive market has been our customer-focused merchandising," says Peterson. "Instead of a one-

size-fits-all approach, we are now able to more accurately stock the products that appeal to our customers on a regional or local basis."

Dayton Hudson is creating business applications to analyze direct product profitability (DPP), inventory control, and store management. In addition to targeted marketing efforts in retail operations, the company employs multidimensional analysis for customer analysis in its credit card operations. Dayton Hudson is one of the largest U.S. issuers of credit cards, a business that places a premium on identifying and keeping customers who have the right financial histories, purchasing power, and credit habits. Dayton Hudson expects to complete standardization of its DSS environment across the three operating units during 1998.

"In the future, web deployment will provide a simple, flexible, cost-effective way to leverage decision support technology," said Maggi Keith, Dayton Hudson IS Director of Corporate Services. "Organizations will be enabled to greatly expand their data access and analysis capabilities with minimal cost in infrastructure and training using whatever browser and computer hardware platforms they have installed." ■

CHAPTER FIVE

PLANNING THE INTRANET DATA WAREHOUSE

In planning the intranet data warehouse, management should view the effort as a long-term commitment to accelerating information-rich communications and collaboration throughout the enterprise. An intranet data warehouse is not, and should not be viewed as a fixed-term "project." It warrants permanent "departmental" status, fully staffed and capable of managing the ongoing evolutionary process.

Change is a constant factor in planning and managing an intranet data warehouse. Unlike traditional OLTP applications in which users are trained to record or process transactions repetitively, in an OLAP intranet data warehouse environment, users "train" the system by communicating their rapidly evolving information needs. When organizations decide to deploy data warehousing and OLAP applications across an intranet, they significantly increase their need for a planning process that readily adapts to change. The intranet data warehouse planning process must consider:

1. The diversity of users' roles and responsibilities.
2. The rapid growth of the user population, especially nontechnical (casual) users.
3. Constant improvement in the technical skill set of users.
4. Evolving decision-making processes that are based on extensive communications and collaboration.

Planning an intranet data warehouse requires an approach that can deal effectively with constant change and shifting priorities. This chapter introduces an evolutionary planning process that recognizes that users are the driving force in the design of the intranet data warehouse and the delivery of effective decision support applications. Users' decision support requirements—and users' perceptions of their requirements—are influenced by many factors, including competition, government regulation, and the popular press. Although performance is always important to the success of any system (the topic is discussed in some detail in later chapters), the primary design goal of an intranet data warehouse is flexibility, where the ability to continuously evolve to meet changing user needs is even more crucial than efficiency.

One challenge of building an intranet data warehouse in a rapidly changing business environment is compressing the time needed to meet user requirements while maintaining the flexibility to refocus the development effort if necessary. Meeting this challenge requires cooperation from both information technology (IT) management and business users throughout the organization. The two groups must cooperate to identify the appropriate scope of a pilot project, recognizing that the initial work must establish a foundation capable of supporting ongoing change. The intranet data warehouse planning process that we describe in this chapter facilitates iterative evolution and concurrent development.

In many ways, building an intranet data warehouse is much like building a city. The starting point is the foundation of the first building. As the effort progresses, construction begins to occur in many places concurrently. Figure 5.1 reflects a fundamental principle of building an intranet data warehouse: Start small and grow.

Business Requirements Planning

Because the evolutionary design of an intranet data warehouse must be consistent with the strategic direction of the organization, the planning process should begin at the senior management level with a thorough definition of business requirements. Figure 5.2 illustrates the business requirements layers that must be defined in order to decompose the corporate mission into technology plans that, when implemented, can support the necessary decision-making processes. The four layers of business requirements definition—mis-

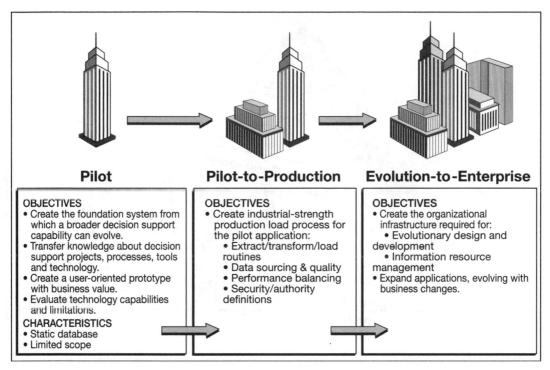

Figure 5.1 Evolutionary design and development.

sion, decisions, users, and information requirements—identify the business issues in greater detail at each step of the planning process.

Determining the Corporate Mission and Stating Goals

Although documenting a mission statement is one of the most important steps in the planning process for any major development effort, it is often the one step that organizations omit. The corporate mission statement should define the goals of the enterprise in business terms and, in doing so, also define a clear purpose for investing in an intranet data warehouse. In addition, documenting the mission statement is essential for ensuring that the implementation process adheres to the general tenets of the plan as well as to the goals of the organization.

The mission statement for the business should set specific goals for helping

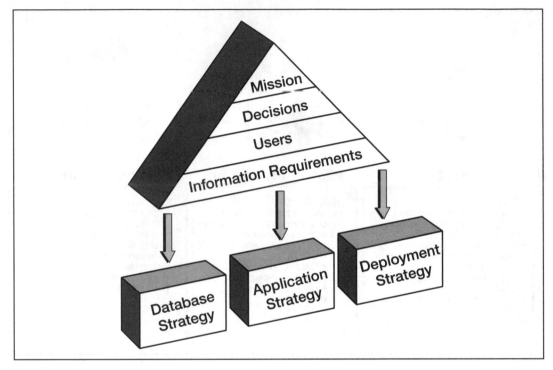

Figure 5.2 Planning model for an intranet data warehouse.

to achieve business growth, spelling out the implications of achieving those goals in financial terms. At the highest level, most corporations are pursuing one or more of the following goals to increase revenue and income:

- Become the low-cost producer.
- Expand the market geographically.
- Expand the market size.
- Enter new markets.
- Build share of market.

The key question in formulating a mission statement is: What are the critical success factors for achieving revenue and income growth? In translating the mission statement into goals, the key question is: How will we know if we are successful?

Senior management must be involved in developing and documenting the mission statement business goals and establishing priorities. While the mission statement itself can be stated rather simply (e.g., accelerate international expansion), the business goals that support the statement should be quantifiable. For example, the mission to expand geographically might translate into a specific goal of increasing revenue from international operations by 25 percent. The more clearly and succinctly the business mission and goals are stated, the easier it will be to align the intranet data warehouse design and applications with the organization's mission.

Identifying Necessary Questions and Decision Points

Identifying the types of decisions that are necessary to accomplish the goals stated in the mission statement is a radical departure from the structured analysis and design techniques used to build transaction systems. Users typically find it difficult to describe their information needs. They frequently alternate between "All I want is this one report" and "Just give me access to everything; I'll find what I need." Neither answer provides sufficient information to properly design a data warehouse or to determine how best to meet users' data analysis needs. A useful approach to defining users' needs is to start by defining the decisions they are tasked with making.

An intranet data warehouse should be designed to support three types of decisions: operational, tactical, and strategic; however, the intranet data warehouse is ideally suited to operational and tactical decisions.

- Operational decisions are made every day, generally by first-line managers. These decisions tend to rely on repetitive analysis of new data and usually require reporting and data analysis systems that are highly targeted for a specific business issue. Decision-makers needing to make operational decisions want information as content, already processed to aid in making the appropriate decision. Because intranet applications place content in front of the application logic, users request and receive information rather than an analytic tool that can be used to generate content (structure a query and execute analytic routines).

- Tactical decisions require greater flexibility than operational decisions in terms of data access and the analytical capabilities provided to users. Although still very much focusing on efficiently delivering content to users, tactical decision support applications also provide users with analytic capabilities associated with the content. For example, a tactical decision support application might provide the user with a report that allows him or her to drill down on key report dimensions or to add elements to the dimension.

- Strategic decisions require ad hoc analysis of data contained in the warehouse, as well as data resources that are not managed as part of the data warehouse. Strategic decision support focuses on providing users with powerful tools that can be used to create content. Satisfying the needs of users for strategic decision support has been the primary focus of client/server data warehouse application deployment. In fact, the client/server model will continue to meet a large portion of strategic decision support requirements. However, as organizations create multiple data warehouses and data marts and users seek access to both structured and unstructured content, the intranet data warehouse will begin to play a larger role in strategic decision support. Strategic decision making also benefits from an open exchange of ideas and experience—the type of collaboration that can be facilitated on an intranet.

Focusing on users' questions is an effective means for determining what decisions need to be made; in other words, what questions do the users, who are charged with making operational, tactical, and strategic decisions, ask when discussing the organization's business goals? All too often, the individuals responsible for planning intranet data warehouses focus on users' data and reporting needs rather than trying to understand the questions that users are asking or the problems they are attempting to solve. Only by understanding the users' questions can data warehouse developers establish an insight into their information needs.

The decision-making process is generally based on information gathered as a result of users posing a rapid-fire series of questions, starting with relatively simple queries and growing in complexity as each preceding question is answered. A single report often is the catalyst that triggers a multitude of questions about an identified problem or opportunity, such as What is going on? followed by Why? One way to effectively isolate user requirements is to invite users to role-play. For example, given the corporate objectives, which questions need to be answered? Assuming that we get the answers to the questions of what and why, we can proceed to the next steps in decision making:

1. Generating alternatives.
2. Performing a cost-benefit analysis of alternatives.
3. Choosing among the alternatives (making the decision).
4. Implementing the decision.

Throughout the decision-making process, we need to constantly reassess our information needs: Do we have sufficient information to make a decision or recommend a course of action? If not, what additional information do we need?

The approval process typically begins after all of the clearly identifiable questions have been answered. Depending on the approval process, a new round of questions may begin at this point, drilling even further into the available information, or taking a top-down approach to ensure that the recommended decision complies with overall policies and procedures. And once the decision is approved, yet another series of questions may be needed to implement it, to, for example, ensure that the approved course of action does not conflict with other decisions.

Identifying the Users

The next step in planning the intranet data warehouse is to identify the various user groups responsible for operational, tactical and strategic decisions. The term "users" suggests that there is a single group of decision makers that need to access the data warehouse and the analytic tools to retrieve information and/or perform data analysis, when actually there are commonly four classes of data warehouse users:

- **Administrators:** Members of the support staff who perform both technical and business-related management tasks such as ensuring the quality of the warehouse contents and the applications that access it; maintaining security authorization (both internal and external to the Net); and maintaining the metadata to inform the other users about changes in the data warehouse or applications.

- **Authors:** The power users who develop business applications. Authors typically seek the most powerful and functionally rich ad hoc data analysis tools available and often have the technical skills to use these tools proficiently.

- **Active Users:** Somewhat less technically skilled than authors, active users generally spend a great deal of time seeking information from the data warehouse and analyzing the responses. This group typically includes the line decision makers who don't want to embark on intensive, aimless fact-finding excursions; they want fast, accurate answers to business issues. This group tends to be the most impatient class of users.

- **Casual Users:** The least technical group, casual users are also the least frequent users of the data warehouse system. This group usually includes senior executive-level managers and first-line managers, but often spans all levels of an organization's management structure, from executives to field sales representatives. It often represents the largest user community to be served and the user group that is most starved for timely information access. Because casual users, by definition, infrequently sign on to the data warehousing system, simplicity is a primary design requirement for this group. They need commands and controls that are both easy to use and easy to remember; casual users are easily frustrated and often very vocal.

The three-dimensional grid in Figure 5.3 illustrates the wide diversity of decision support requirements that exist within most corporations. One dimension represents the classes of users, the second dimension lists the types of decisions users are likely to face, and the third represents business functions. This grid, which defines specific decisions and business questions for each cell, can be modified to reflect the functional areas of any particular enterprise. It is particularly useful for organizing and presenting user requirements. Recognizing a broad diversity of requirements is key in designing the data warehouse and selecting OLAP products.

The next step in the planning process is to identify the specific data and data analysis requirements that are necessary to resolve the questions and implement the decisions that users identified. At this stage, additional input is required from the user community, but some caveats apply here. First, it is essential to obtain a representative sampling of users in order to fairly represent the requirements of all user classes—administrators, authors, active, and casual users. Too often, the requirements of the most technically proficient users are considered at the expense of less sophisticated casual users. Second, the plan must accommodate growth and continuous change of the user population, as rapid growth in the number and type of users can be expected.

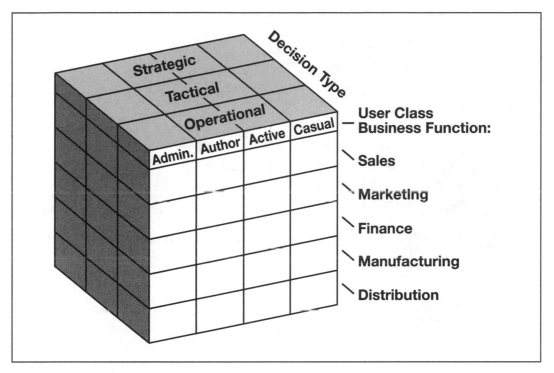

Figure 5.3 Decisions classified by user class, decision type, and business function.

Information Requirements

Once the necessary questions and decisions are identified, the next step is to specify the content of the data warehouse and the data analysis (i.e., OLAP) requirements. The planning team must determine what data sources are required—and available—to answer decision-makers' questions. The team must then determine what types of OLAP analysis functions are required by users. The information requirements will vary by class of user and functional responsibility. Figure 5.4 isolates an element of the grid in Figure 5.3 that further limits the scope of the user requirements definition.

Well-defined information requirements are essential to building a solid foundation for the intranet data warehouse, for it is at this stage in the planning process that the scope of the pilot project begins to take shape. The scope

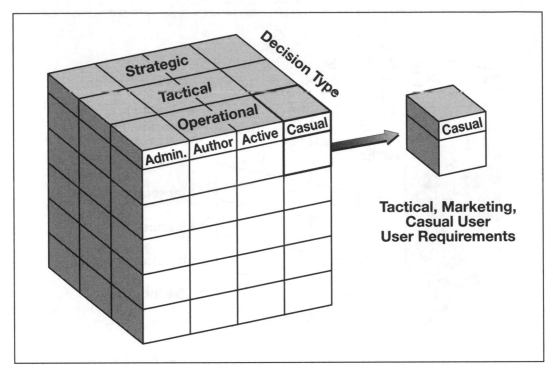

Figure 5.4 Information requirements scope limited by identifying user class and business function.

of the pilot project is defined within the context of the broad data warehouse content and OLAP analysis requirements, but is limited by time and budget constraints. The pilot project is likely to support a single department or class of user, yet it establishes the foundation to support decision making at all levels throughout the enterprise. Because of the evolutionary nature of an intranet data warehouse, it is critical to establish the processes to identify user needs during the initial planning and implementation phases. Users should be encouraged to view the intranet data warehouse as an evolutionary effort that is responsive to their needs and ideas.

At this point in the planning process, it is possible to translate the conceptual model of user needs into logical and physical information system models. It is important to remember that this conceptual model is unlike any found in transaction systems; it is designed to bridge the communication gap between human information processing needs and IT planning and design processes.

Technology Planning

After the business objectives and information requirements are identified, the intranet data warehouse technology-planning process can proceed on three interrelated tracts:

- **Database Strategy:** How will the data warehouse be created and integrated with the intranet?
- **Application Strategy:** How will OLAP functions support the operational, tactical, and strategic decision making?
- **Deployment Strategy:** How will various classes of users access applications?

Database Strategy

The database strategy deals with creating the data warehouse and integrating data warehouse access with other information resources available to intranet users. At a summary level, the key components of the database strategy include

- **Content:** What data are required to address users questions?
- **Source:** What are the sources of the data?
- **Extract:** How will the data be extracted and periodically updated to the warehouse?
- **Preparation:** What steps are required to cleanse and validate source data?
- **Design:** What is the appropriate database design?
- **Tuning:** How will performance issues be integrated into the design?
- **Platform:** Where will the data warehouse reside (network, hardware, and software)?
- **Administration:** What is required to manage the data warehouse in terms of security, update process, metadata management, quality assurance, and related issues such as human resources and management structure?

Central Data Warehouse or Distributed Data Marts?

The key decision in the database strategy is to determine whether it is most effective to build multiple data marts, thereby creating a *distributed* warehouse, or to build a *central* warehouse. A third approach is to create a distributed data warehouse using multiple data marts that are fed by a central warehouse. Figure 5.5 illustrates a data warehousing strategy that employs a data warehouse and several data marts. The advantage of this approach is that the source data is integrated and cleansed one time; subsets of the data are then distributed to appropriate user groups.

The demand for low-cost, quick solutions is driving many companies to build data marts to support department-level decision making, bypassing the creation of a central data warehouse that serves as an archive. If there is little risk in losing historical data from operational systems—or, more important, if there is no need for consistent decision support above the departmental level—eliminating the central data warehouse (the archive of historical data integrated across departments, divisions, etc.) may decrease the amount of time required to meet departmental users' information needs. But it is important to

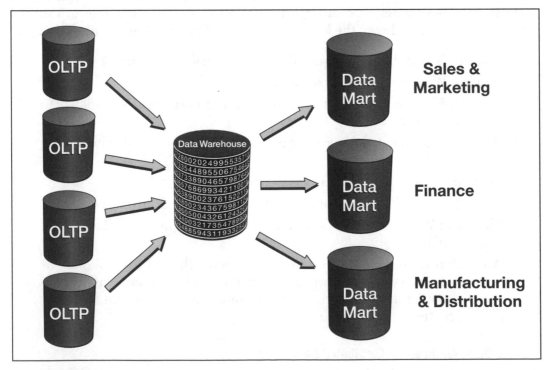

Figure 5.5   Employing a single warehouse and multiple data marts.

point out that all of the steps involved in building a data warehouse apply to building data marts. Any savings in time and cost result only from the more limited scope of the data mart.

Information Warehouse

The intranet data warehouse strategy should span users' needs for both structured (data warehouse) and unstructured information. While the term data warehouse is currently used only to describe alphanumeric data resources, the broader view is the creation of a warehouse that includes *all* information that is necessary for decision making.

The concept of an "information" warehouse introduces additional strategic decisions to the planning and implementation processes. As mentioned in Chapter 3, several relational database management system vendors now offer "universal" servers that combine object-oriented database management functions and relational database management functions to create a hybrid system capable of managing access to all data types. Clearly, these vendors view the integration of data types as the province of the database management system.

The alternative view, one that is effectively demonstrated every day on the World Wide Web, is that data integration can occur at the application level. The Internet provides access to millions of separately managed information resources by adhering to a relatively small number of standards. Metadata, in the form of Internet search engines, perform valuable services in locating information. The search engine provides a relatively simple mechanism for accessing unstructured information. Similarly, to fully integrate the data warehouse with intranet technologies, search engines must be able to locate all of the data warehouse's information resources. The role of search engines in managing the broader information warehouse is one that is likely to evolve as intranets mature, as addressed in more detail in Chapter 11.

To a certain degree, data warehousing technology is moving in two distinctly different directions. On one hand, organizations are creating data marts to expedite the process of meeting users' information needs; but, at the same time, the scope of data warehousing is expanding significantly as we begin to integrate other information resources. The implication is that the database strategy must be extremely flexible to accommodate the technologies' "organic" nature. An intranet data warehouse is not based on a single warehouse or data mart, but rather is a combination of information resources. The key to developing an appropriate database strategy is to manage the process in well-planned stages.

Applications Strategy

The applications strategy identifies the data analysis functions that are needed to meet user requirements. More specifically, the strategy identifies which OLAP capabilities are required and the extent to which these capabilities are integrated to address specific business management problems.

- **Access:** Which users should have access to the data?
- **Analysis:** Which data analysis functions are necessary?
- **Modeling:** Is there a requirement for statistical data analysis, data mining, or other mathematical modeling support?
- **Applications:** Is there a need for specific business applications?
- **Process:** How will the decision-making process be improved?
- **Support:** How will users receive training and ongoing support?

The application strategy deals with the technology at two points: the analytic logic tier and the presentation tier. Identifying data access and analysis requirements defines the set of basic user requirements. Some user questions can be answered simply by retrieving data from the warehouse, but many more questions require some type of analytic routine to be performed on the raw data. These analytic routines can range from something as simple as calculating a sales volume percent change to creating a complex mathematical model.

The key to developing an applications strategy is to provide users with the general-purpose tool and/or the business applications that best meet their specific requirements. Authors, for example, generally seek a robust set of analytic tools, while active users are often more interested in solutions to specific business problems; and casual users are usually satisfied with a set of reports and graphic output if they can navigate within the boundaries of the report (i.e., drill down on various dimensions to elicit more detailed information). And authors need the ability to generate reports for use by active and casual users. In short, in developing the applications strategy, planners must consider a wide range of users and information requirements, as well as general business issues.

It is also important to remember that the applications strategy must correspond with the overall implementation plan for the intranet data warehouse. Because applications are usually implemented in stages over some period of time, it is critical to establish priorities for the rollout early in the planning and implementation process.

Deployment Strategy

The intranet offers organizations a low-cost means for providing large numbers of users with access to the data warehouse and OLAP applications. Certainly, the needs of casual users are particularly well served by an intranet browser type of interface, whose simplicity makes it easy to deploy applications. The active and the author user classes benefit from the enhanced communications and collaboration capabilities of intranet applications. As intranet application development tools mature, more functionally rich business applications will migrate to the intranet. The following are some of the key issues that must be considered in determining a deployment strategy.

- **Interface:** Which users should be provided with intranet browser and/or Windows applications interfaces?
- **Collaboration:** How will user collaboration be encouraged?
- **Agents:** How will the reporting and analysis process be automated?
- **Search Engine:** How will the information resources of the intranet data warehouse be registered with the intranet search engines?
- **Security:** How will database security be maintained?

There is little doubt that PC-centric Windows applications will continue to meet the needs of authors and active users for a while longer, but the intranet is becoming the primary delivery vehicle for information destined for casual users, particularly as organizations begin to understand the potential for creating a higher degree of communications and collaboration among decision makers.

In planning a deployment strategy, it may be practical to initially provide intranet browser applications to the casual user group, although some applications are well suited to intranet deployment, regardless of the target user. The key to an effective deployment strategy is to manage the process in well-planned stages. Figure 5.6 illustrates how the database strategy, application strategy, and deployment strategy occur in parallel.

Unique Technological Challenges of the Intranet Data Warehouse

An intranet data warehouse introduces a number of additional challenges to the process of building and maintaining a data warehouse, specifically:

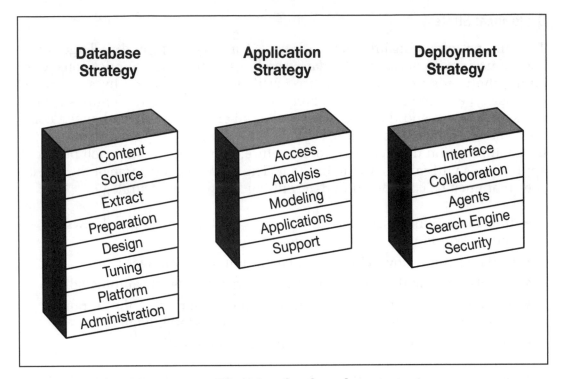

Figure 5.6 Planning the three key strategies.

- An Intranet data warehouse is likely to result in a larger number of distributed databases, hence the term the organic warehouse, introduced at the beginning of the book.

- The number of users that must be supported by an intranet data warehouse can be expected to grow exponentially.

- The intranet requires a server-centric distributed computing applications architecture, discussed in the upcoming section on application objectware.

The Organic Warehouse

The term organic warehouse is derived from lessons learned from the Internet. The information resources available on the Internet are created and evolve organically, and without a master plan, to meet users' demands. An integrated information warehouse for the intranet is likely to evolve in a similar fashion.

In many organizations, the goal of creating a single, integrated, and complete data warehouse is gradually yielding to the realization that multiple data warehouses (or data marts) may be needed to respond to the diverse set of changing user requirements. Data warehouses also are being developed for public and syndicated data sources, providing online access to information through the Internet. Unfortunately, the proliferation of data warehouses may well cause the very problems associated with data accuracy, validity, consistency, and currency that centralizing data in warehouses was intended to resolve.

The need to integrate the structured content of the data warehouse with unstructured content that is typical of an intranet further complicates data warehouse planning issues. To deal effectively with these issues, organizations need a comprehensive strategy for managing the "universal" information resources of the enterprise. If the data warehouse is not centralized, then the administration must be centrally organized to ensure that users can locate information and that the information is accurate and current. Metadata plays a critical role in a distributed database environment. Defining metadata requirements and establishing effective data management are key topics in planning for the organic warehouse.

Application Objectware

Because the user interface for accessing the World Wide Web changes within the application shell defined by the Web browser each time a new site is accessed, Internet users have come to expect their desktop to adapt to their needs and to the structure of the information resource. In much the same way, the intranet user interface can be adapted to suit the needs of the various classes of users. In fact, this is one of its major attributes as an applications development platform.

The applications development model of the intranet is distributed *objectware*. On the client side, the Web browser provides a standard shell for managing the presentation tier. The presentation tier becomes highly adaptive as the application controls, information display, and portions of application logic are developed as Java or ActiveX applets. The presentation portion of the application, presented as a library of applets, enables users to retrieve only those components of an application that are useful. On the server side, analytic functions become shareable objects.

As vendors concentrate on developing analytic functions in the server-centric architecture of the intranet, distributed computing standards and metadata standards become increasingly important. Organizations require an adaptable interface to a broad range of OLAP and data visualization tools. Increasingly, those tools will be provided by multiple vendors. Figure 5.7 provides an example of how client and server objects might be distributed.

The architecture of the intranet poses some major challenges to applications software vendors in a data warehouse development project. In an intranet environment, the selection of appropriate OLAP tools focuses on scalability issues and analytic capabilities rather than on user interface components. This is particularly true as the user interface becomes more adaptable; and, as more vendors migrate their products to the intranet environment, there is an increasing emphasis on compliance with distributed object computing standards.

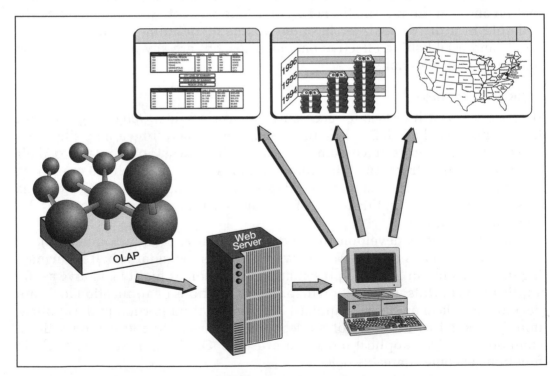

Figure 5.7 Application objectware components.

Organizational Planning

Of course, planning the intranet data warehouse and determining the design requirements must occur within the context of organizational change. Typically, the organizational planning effort must address three aspects: structure, skill sets, and processes that support evolutionary design and implementation.

Organizational Structure

It can not be said often enough: Building an intranet data warehouse is a long-term commitment to increasing the intellectual capital of the enterprise. As the data warehouse evolves to meet user needs, so too must the design evolve, undergoing continual review and update to accommodate new data sources. Data analysis requirements also will change in response to new business management issues, so as the intranet data warehouse matures, the business applications will expand from the need for better *reporting* (i.e., supporting management's information requests) to *action* (i.e., enabling faster decision implementation). An intranet accelerates information-rich communications and collaboration and can substantially change the way information is used to support decision making.

As already stated, too often, organizations view building a data warehouse as a project. To that end, they appoint a project team to design and build the data warehouse, and even select the OLAP tools. Typically, the team adheres to an implementation plan and establishes a short-term, goal-oriented project management methodology. And they usually succeed in that goal, completing the assigned task by the target date.

In contrast, viewing the process of building an intranet data warehouse as an organizational commitment rather than as a project results in a *mission-oriented* approach to staffing and managing the effort. Rather than appointing a temporary project team, savvy organizations establish a permanent data warehouse group as part of an organizational structure that bridges information services and the business community. The long-term charter of the data warehouse group is to accelerate management's ability to make highly informed decisions. Progress is measured in terms of business stages, and there are no clearly defined start and end dates for the overall process.

When data warehousing is integrated with online analytic processing and intranet technology, a new type of information infrastructure emerges. To accomplish this, however, organizations need to manage the implementation effort in a way that ensures the long-term commitment to meeting corporate business objectives. This involves assembling a staff, developing clear-cut goals for each stage of the process, and gaining the understanding and support of top-level management. While this chapter discusses those requirements and helps to identify the issues that make planning the intranet data warehouse unique, it does not give advice on managing the implementation of an intranet data warehouse. It does, however, incorporate an example of a departmental organization chart to identify crucial management roles.

Staffing the Intranet Data Warehouse Group

The functional organization chart in Figure 5.8 delineates the many, varied talents that should be assembled in an intranet data warehouse group. Note that some of these positions are the very ones that were eliminated during the efficiency-oriented downsizing of the '80s and early '90s! In this hypothetical

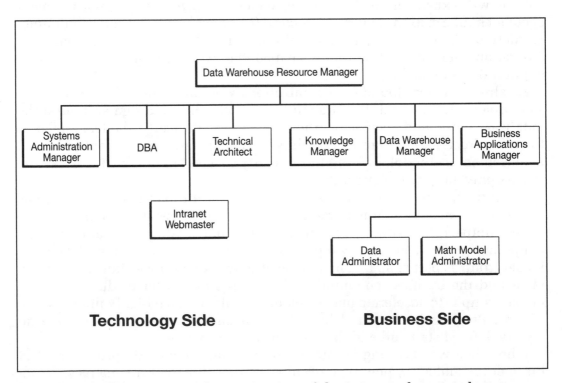

Figure 5.8 Functional organization of the intranet data warehouse.

organization, the department manager is responsible for the evolutionary design and development, starting with establishing new processes directed at managing constantly changing development priorities, defining the scope of each phase of development, and ensuring that development activities are aligned with the business management objectives.

Business-Side Functions

The information resource manager (or data warehouse administration manager) has overall responsibility for managing the content of the data warehouse. The staff that reports to the information resource manager is charged with maintaining the data warehouses and distributed data marts, as well as the related data dictionary and other forms of required metadata. Database security and management of mathematical models also falls under the responsibilities of this manager.

The business applications manager is the primary link to the various user communities. This individual is generally responsible for providing user support and applications development resources.

The intranet Webmaster has overall responsibility for determining what content is made available over the intranet and for ensuring that the information is organized for easy retrieval. This function is closely related to that of both the information resource manager and the business applications manager.

Bridging the business and technology sides of this organizational entity is the knowledge manager, who is responsible for the education and knowledge transfer of both technological and business aspects of the intranet data warehouse.

Technology-Side Functions

The technical architect is responsible for engineering the system to ensure the proper integration of hardware and software, including server hardware and operating systems, network hardware and software, data extract and load software, database management system software, and OLAP tool selection.

The systems administration manager is responsible for the network and server hardware and software environment, as well as for meeting the ongoing challenge of providing optimal system performance.

The intranet Webmaster manages the Web environment.

Certainly, the broad range of functions depicted in this organization, along with the necessary support staffs in each branch, require a very substantial investment in personnel hiring and training. These costs, combined with the considerable financial outlay required for the hardware and software products necessary to build the intranet data warehouse, clearly indicate why top-level management must actively support the concept of an intranet data warehouse, both during the initial implementation phase and thereafter to ensure that the system continues to evolve to meet user needs.

Maximizing Intranet Data Warehouse Rewards

Operational databases and OLTP applications are typically designed to improve the efficiency of mission-critical business processes. Data warehouses and OLAP applications, on the other hand, are designed to provide corporate management with accurate, timely information to support effective decision making. The measure of success for an OLTP application is often stated in terms of cost savings that result from greater operational efficiencies. The measures of success for the data warehouse and OLAP applications are revenue growth and/or expense reduction that result from management decisions.

To maximize the rewards of an intranet data warehouse, it is important to focus the creative talents of the enterprise on finding new ways to truly improve the decision-making and decision implementation processes. Data warehousing, OLAP tools, and the intranet eliminate many of the technology barriers that frustrate decision makers. Users accustomed to using spreadsheets to meet their data analysis requirements find that the ability to "surf the Web" for additional information resources is a mixed blessing. Having too much information to analyze can make the analysis and resolution processes more rather than less difficult.

Although users often find that it is actually easier to retrieve public domain information from the Web than it is to obtain corporate information from the enterprise data stores, having access to reams of data is not in itself a means for improving decision making. Users must also have the ability to analyze the data to convert it to meaningful information for their specific needs, and of course, they must be able to communicate that information. The Internet and the World Wide Web do, however, serve as examples of how an intranet data warehouse can help the enterprise to achieve simple access to an ever-changing information store; and coupled with an effective means of communication, it can help to create a highly collaborative culture and a constantly evolving application development platform.

The Internet and intranets share more than technology. Both provide users with simple access to information; and as the technologies continue to evolve, the information will transcend enterprise borders, enabling manufacturers to share product information with retailers or credit card companies or to share customer credit information with banks. Some of the oft-noted benefits of an intranet include:

- The ability to accelerate decision making and decision implementation to provide the competitive advantage of speed.
- The ability to provide information-rich communications and collaboration among decision makers.
- The ability to offer a highly adaptable applications development platform that can evolve rapidly to keep pace with changing user requirements.

Monitoring progress in meeting the mission and business goals provides the feedback necessary to continuously evolve the intranet data warehouse as a reliable and responsive decision support tool. Unfortunately, it is often difficult to link the contribution of information to a management decision and then to the financial impact of the decision. In successful implementations, the intranet data warehouse plays a support role in hundreds of decisions that are made each day.

The executive managers and users who provide early input into the design and requirements planning phase of the intranet data warehouse are in an excellent position to review progress and determine when it is appropriate to modify or extend the scope of the effort. Users need to be assured that the intranet data warehouse is *their* system and that information services maintains it on their behalf. The most successful intranet data warehouse initiatives should result in an organizational cultural change from better reporting to faster action.

Moving Ahead with the Intranet Data Warehouse Implementation Process

At this point it should be clear how an intranet data warehouse contributes to raising the intellectual capital of an enterprise. I've discussed some of the factors that should be considered in planning an intranet data warehouse system, and summarized the three technologies—data warehousing, OLAP, and the intranet—that comprise an intranet data warehouse system. The remainder of the book explores some of the underlying technologies and products that you'll want to consider when you begin to build an intranet data warehouse. It covers implementation issues such as scalability, security, and performance in greater detail.

CASE STUDY

Tyson Foods

Tyson Foods has long been synonymous with quality chicken products—and with good reason. With an annual chicken production equal to that of Japan and Great Britain combined, the company is the largest producer of poultry products in the world. More than 55 plants process nearly 35 million chickens each week, providing more than 6.5 billion pounds of poultry annually to its demanding customers. Tyson helps satisfy the food service needs of 97 of the top 100 restaurant chains; it exports products to more than 60 foreign countries; and it provides quality products to an ever-expanding retail market.

The $5.5 billion poultry, beef, seafood, and frozen foods producer relies on timely accurate business information to develop sales and operational plans. But company management realized that sending reports to the field salesforce via the traditional mail service was no longer efficient. By the time the reports reached the hands of the decision makers, the information was often more than a week old. Tyson management decided to migrate to a solution that could support timely, collaborative analysis and remote access, while leveraging the existing data warehouse. Providing a scalable enterprisewide solution that could be integrated with the World Wide Web was a key part of the decision criteria.

Tyson conducted an extensive search with strict evaluation criteria including architecture, Web integration, report authoring, agent technology, scalability, open APIs, and mass-distribution capabilities. It eventually selected a thin-client, server-centric approach that provided a natural migration for integration with the Web. Using intelligent agents and open APIs, reports are scheduled and run in the background on the server. Results are dynamically converted to Microsoft Excel, then e-mailed to users at Tyson and to non-Tyson employees, including vendors and distributors, without charge.

"The goal of our retail data warehouse is to deliver information to the right people when they need it," says Rick Brattin, MIS project leader at Tyson Foods. "By implementing the new solution, we are able to efficiently

provide our field salesforce with timely sales information to support more accurate decision making. We are also leveraging intelligent agents and alerts to automate report delivery to our business partners via e-mail and fax." Other factors that were considered in the planning process include the ability to analyze large amounts of complex data on the fly, securely and over the World Wide Web. The company updates the centralized data warehouse on a weekly basis, except for orders, which are updated daily. Updated information is immediately accessible by both Windows and Web users for review and/or further analysis. Applications are available to the local sales staff and users at 30 remote offices.

Integrating the Web into the data warehouse strategy provides an economic means for disseminating information directly to the people who make the decisions that are critical to the business—without incurring the cost of training users on a new front end. Integrating the existing data warehouse with the Web ensures that information is also accessible to executives, managers, and analysts within Tyson, as well as to vendors and distributors outside the company—all without the need for additional Web server hardware or software. ∎

CHAPTER SIX

The Microsoft Intranet Data Warehouse: Architecture and Tools

In the last year or so, Microsoft has released an unprecedented number of new products and technologies for the Internet and intranet markets. Microsoft now offers a complete set of tools for building and deploying Web-based applications, including data warehousing solutions. The rapid pace of new product releases and the sheer number of products available make it difficult to keep the big picture strategy in view. This chapter is intended to provide that view, then drill down to the technologies that are most applicable to the intranet data warehouse.

Blending the New with the Old

Before jumping into specifics, it is important to note an overriding philosophy of the Microsoft strategy. The software giant is consciously approaching the Internet from two angles: *extending* existing products and tools to incorporate Internet technology, and creating *new* technologies where appropriate. There are many advantages to this approach, the most important of which is that developers already familiar with Microsoft tools can leverage these skills effectively on Internet development efforts since many of the new Internet concepts fit well into existing frameworks. This reduces the learning curve and lessens implementation time. A related advantage is the pool of talent, resources, and tools that come with mature technology.

Some of the existing products that now offer Internet functionality include developer tools such as Visual Basic and Visual C++; the Microsoft Office development platform, which includes Excel, Access, Word, PowerPoint, Project, Team Manager, Outlook, and the common Visual Basic for Applications language; and Microsoft's BackOffice server suite, which includes Windows NT, SQL Server, and Exchange. Microsoft has also introduced new tools for Web authoring (FrontPage), an Internet development environment (Visual InterDev), scripting languages (VBScript and Jscript), a Java development tool (Visual J++), and a Web server (Internet Information Server), as well as a host of other server products too numerous to cover here.

The ActiveX Platform

ActiveX is the critical technology that weaves throughout all of these tools. ActiveX is becoming an industry buzzword, and as such there are many misconceptions about its meaning and scope. Before defining it, let's dispel some of the more common misinterpretations of ActiveX. First and foremost, ActiveX is not in any way a programming language. It is not valid, for example, to directly compare Java and ActiveX (I'll explain why in a minute). Second, ActiveX is not a specific product (although it manifests itself as features in almost all products). Third, ActiveX is not limited to the domain of Internet and intranet applications; it is equally applicable to typical desktop and LAN-based client/server applications as well. And last, ActiveX is not exclusively controlled by Microsoft; the company turned over control of many of its core elements to an industry standards group in 1996.

ActiveX is really a set of *integration* technologies. It helps applications and components communicate and coordinate with one another, whether on one machine, across a LAN, or over the Internet. ActiveX is language-neutral, meaning that many languages can, and do, create and interact with ActiveX components. It is also platform-independent, meaning it is not intrinsically tied to the Windows platform. It is convenient to think of ActiveX as an umbrella for many technologies that help to implement applications. Some of the more common ActiveX technologies include ActiveX Controls, ActiveX Automation, and ActiveX Scripting.

Controls are packaged chunks of functionality that can easily be incorporated into an application regardless of the development tool being used to develop it. Controls have a history of names at Microsoft: They started as VBXs (or VB custom controls), grew and matured into OCXs (or OLE controls), and then were renamed as ActiveX Controls (where they gained a set of optional Internet-specific functionality). Today, these controls can be incorporated into applications built with tools ranging from Visual Basic, Visual C++, and Power-Builder to Microsoft Excel and Access to HTML-based applications running in a browser. There are literally thousands of controls for sale on the market, and many tools available to build them from scratch.

The second ActiveX technology, ActiveX automation is the ability to expose the functionality of an application to developers through what is called an *object model*. Microsoft Office is the best example of the power of automation. There are literally hundreds of objects available to the developer, providing everything from charting, data analysis, and complex calculations to report formatting, production, and printing to messaging and group scheduling. By exposing this functionality through an object model, developers can build applications on top of existing applications, thereby focusing effort on the unique aspects of the problem, not those that have been solved previously.

Scripting, which is closely related to automation, is the implementation of languages that can manipulate automation objects to tie them together, coordinate their actions, and act as the "glue" in an application. Visual Basic can serve as a scripting language in any of its many forms.

ActiveX, OLE, COM, and DCOM

The terms OLE, COM, and DCOM are often mentioned in the same context as ActiveX, so it may be useful to define each of these terms at this point as well.

OLE, which has a long history, has been effectively replaced by the term ActiveX. At its beginning, OLE was the technology that enabled documents to be embedded within and linked to one another. It was extended to incorporate a whole set of integration and operating system services including controls, automation, scripting, and a host of other services. When the Internet became the focus of the industry, Microsoft replaced OLE with ActiveX (hence the progression from OLE Controls to ActiveX Controls). Today, OLE has retreated to its original meaning, referring only to the mechanisms for embedding and linking documents. In other words, it is now a subset of ActiveX.

COM (the Component Object Model) is the low-level foundation on which ActiveX (and OLE) is built. It is an object-based programming model designed to allow components written by different vendors to interoperate in a well-known and consistent manner. It is a binary standard, meaning that it can operate across platforms and can be implemented using any programming language.

DCOM (the Distributed Component Object Model) is COM extended to work over a network. DCOM allows components to communicate directly with one another, regardless of their physical location. Using DCOM, applications can be implemented as a collection of components that reside on different machines connected through a LAN, WAN, or even the Internet.

ActiveX Controls, automation, and scripting are really just a higher-level implementation of the foundation provided by COM and DCOM. Building on this solid base, ActiveX offers a language- and platform-independent means of constructing applications from a mixture of off-the-shelf and custom parts, then running them in a local or distributed manner. ActiveX and DCOM provide the essential foundation for constructing intranet data warehouse applications that require communications among distributed application components to query, process, and format data for presentation in a browser.

The Microsoft Internet Tool Suite

With the Microsoft philosophy and the ActiveX platform as a backdrop, let's examine the major categories of tools that are covered in this chapter. This discussion is by no means all-encompassing; it focuses on the tools that are most applicable to data warehousing applications. Microsoft's tools can be loosely grouped into the following categories:

- Internet Information Server with Active Server Pages
- Internet Explorer with Client-Side Components/Scripting
- FrontPage
- Visual Studio
- Microsoft Office
- SQL Server
- Transaction Server

Microsoft's tools provide the developers with the means to develop an intranet data warehouse, from managing the warehouse to creating the user interface and providing the browser.

Internet Information Server with Active Server Pages

Internet Information Server (IIS) is Microsoft's Internet server product; it provides standard Web, FTP, and Gopher services. More interesting, however, is its implementation of Active Server Pages (ASP), a server-side scripting environment where complex code can be built directly into HTML documents. This code can interact with databases through a facility called Active Data Objects (ADO) and communicate with other components residing on the server. All script code execution takes place on the server. The result of the script is always "straight" HTML, meaning that any browser will be able to interact with an application written using ASP.

Internet Explorer with Client-Side Components/Scripting

Internet Explorer (IE), Microsoft's entry into the browser market, incorporates a set of unique features that make it an effective application platform. In addition to supporting all standard HTML and popular extensions, it has the ability to host controls or components—both ActiveX components (written in any language) and Java applets. It also supports client-side scripting (i.e., code to automate and coordinate embedded objects that run in the browser). It natively supports VBScript and JScript, with hooks to support other languages that may arise.

IE also supports another ActiveX technology called ActiveX Documents, which is the technical term for in-place activation of non-HTML documents in the browser window. With IE, users can open and interact with Excel spreadsheets, Word documents, and third-party document formats whose application supports the ActiveX Document interface. Finally, IE supports full SSL 3.0 security technology, making it a secure platform for delivering sensitive data.

Visual Studio

Microsoft offers a number of development tools to build applications, controls, and components and plug them into a complete solution. These tools, which ship as the Visual Studio suite, include Visual C++, Visual Basic, Visual J++ (Microsoft's Java implementation), and Visual InterDev (a tool for HTML-hosted applications). The suite also includes Visual SourceSafe, a version control tool, and a variety of other tools.

FrontPage

Microsoft's main entry into the HTML document authoring market, FrontPage creates not only individual documents, but also manages the structure of an entire Web site. In addition to FrontPage, all Microsoft Office products can serve as HTML editors.

Microsoft Office

Always a key part of Microsoft strategy for leveraging the functionality of its desktop applications in custom application development efforts, the current version (Office 97) incorporates a host of Internet and intranet features. When used in conjunction with the embedded VBA development environment, these features enable developers to build a variety of serious business applications.

Excel is probably of most interest to data warehouse application developers. It incorporates numerous built-in OLAP features, including PivotTables, which is an interactive n-dimensional analysis tool, as well as advanced charting features. Excel can be programmed to receive data into its PivotTable cache via HTML streams, to implement hyperlinks and drill downs, and to automatically chart data. This makes it an attractive option for a front end to many data warehouses, a capability covered in more detail later in this chapter.

SQL Server

SQL Server, Microsoft's database server product, can serve as the repository for a data warehouse. In addition to a host of standard database server features, it provides several Internet-specific and data warehouse-specific features discussed in detail later in this chapter.

Transaction Server

Microsoft also offers a host of other server-based products for implementing Web site applications. Perhaps the most important of these is Transaction Server, a platform for building distributed object-based applications that combine the functions of a TP monitor and an object manager. In a data warehousing environment, the object manager functions of Transaction Server can help applications scale as concurrent user load increases.

Using Tools in an Intranet Data Warehouse

I'll frame the detailed discussion of these tools in the context of a typical data warehousing solution built using Microsoft technology. First, assume that the solution is implemented in three distinct and well-defined tiers: user services, business services, and data services.

- **User Services:** This layer is the graphical interface with which the user interacts. It presents data and captures user input (e.g., a request to drill down on a particular value).
- **Business Services:** This layer is a set of components that perform analysis on the data. This analysis may be very computing intensive in that it requires multiple passes through the database and the application of unique business rules. This layer has no user interface.
- **Data Services:** This layer consists of one or more relational databases.

Figure 6.1 illustrates the relationship among these layers, showing how a data warehousing application can be built using Internet Explorer at the User Services layer, Active Server Pages and COM Objects at the Business Services layer, and SQL Server as the Data Services data repository.

An application with this type of architecture works in the following manner:

1. The user views an HTML page in Internet Explorer, which provides a mechanism to construct a query of some kind. The page may have embedded controls to prompt for the data, and may use client-side script code to gather the input and pass it along to the server.
2. User inputs are packaged into a string of parameters, concatenated onto the end of a URL requesting an Active Server Page, and sent to the server via HTTP.
3. An Active Server Page receives those parameters, then instantiates COM objects to perform complex analysis. These objects may reside on the Web server (in which case they are communicated via COM) or on another server (in which case they are communicated via DCOM).
4. The COM objects communicate with one or more databases via Microsoft's Open Database Connectivity (ODBC) protocol or other means,

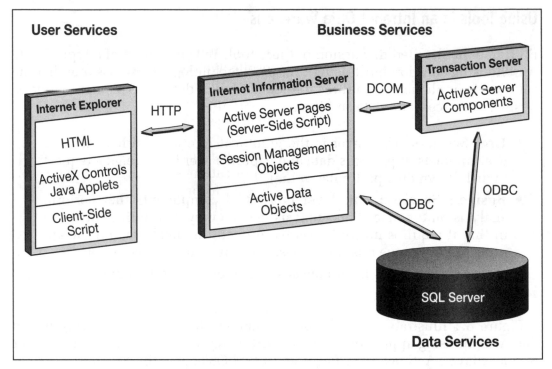

Figure 6.1 The three-tier Internet data warehouse application.

as appropriate, and perform whatever logic is pertinent to their function.

5. The resulting data is dynamically published as HTML documents and sent back to the browser for viewing. The data may also be viewed in embedded controls and further manipulated at the client through additional script code.

There are a number of variations that can be applied to this same procedure. For example, the state of users' input can be retained between pages by using the session object, which is a feature of the ASP environment. Alternatively, the server-side COM objects may be deployed onto the Microsoft Transaction Server to help them scale to a large number of users. It is also possible to achieve direct access to the database for simple queries through Active Data Objects, yet another feature of the ASP environment. This architecture is examined in greater depth in the following sections.

User Services Layer

Starting at the user services layer, the user interacts with the application through the Internet Explorer (IE), Microsoft's Web browser. Using IE gives the advantages of a single point of entry, cross-platform support on the client (Windows NT, Windows 95, Windows 3.x, Apple Mac, and UNIX), and the popular Web navigation metaphor that many users are comfortable with.

IE's interface consists of HTML-based Web pages with embedded ActiveX controls and/or Java applets ("controls" is used here to refer to both). HTML typically provides the framework of the application—a consistent shell within which the user navigates. It can also be used to present data, particularly in tabular form; as shown later, any data presented in HTML will be dynamically generated on the server at runtime.

Embedded Controls

Embedded controls are used to provide functionality that is not possible in straight HTML. For example, a charting control can be used to present data in a graphical format. Using a control rather than a static image of a chart generated on the server adds to the interactive potential of the application. A chart control can, for example, enable the user to select from different chart types and formats as shown in Figure 6.2. This manipulation can occur on the client side (i.e., in the browser) without communicating with the server. In the figure, the Web page consists of an HTML document with three embedded ActiveX controls: a charting control and two slider controls. Visual Basic Script code is attached to the "change" events of each slider to alter the rotation and elevation of the chart.

Embedding controls in HTML requires the use of special tags; the OBJECT tag is used for ActiveX Controls, and the APPLET tag is used for Java applets. The following HTML fragment of the page illustrated in Figure 6.2 shows how the chart and slider controls were embedded:

```
<h3>Sensitivity Analysis</h3>The following chart summarizes how the value of the op-
tion is affected by changes in the price of the underlying asset and for non-U.S.
Dollar investors, changes in the exchange rate.<p>

<OBJECT ID="chtSensitivity"
WIDTH=400
HEIGHT=300 CLASSID="CLSID:31291E80-728C-11CF-93D5-0020AF99504A"
CODEBASE="MSChart.OCX" ></OBJECT>
<OBJECT ID="sldElevation"
WIDTH=28
```

```
HEIGHT=300 CLASSID="CLSID:373FF7F0-EB8B-11CD-8820-08002B2F4F5A"></OBJECT><p>
<OBJECT ID="sldRotation"
WIDTH=400
HEIGHT=28 CLASSID="CLSID:373FF7F0-EB8B-11CD-8820-08002B2F4F5A">
</OBJECT>
```

The most important attributes of the OBJECT tag are ID, CLASSID, and CODEBASE. ID establishes a name for the control that can be referenced in script code. CLASSID is the GUID (globally unique identifier) for the particular control; it tells the browser which control to display. CODEBASE tells the

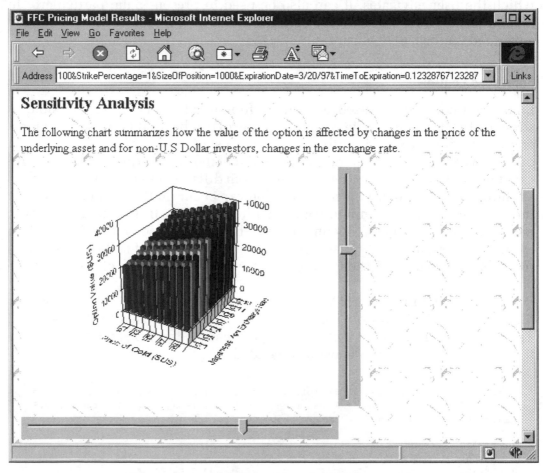

Figure 6.2 HTML with embedded controls.

browser where to get a copy of the control if it is not yet installed on the user's machine. This allows the browser to dynamically install and configure controls for use as they are encountered. This capability is often referred to as *Internet component download*.

Client-Side Scripts

Closely related to embedded controls are client-side scripts. Scripts are used to "connect" embedded controls. IE supports both Visual Basic Script and JScript (Microsoft's implementation of JavaScript). Both of these languages are scaled down versions of their parent languages (VB and Java, respectively) in that they have a limited number of data types, cannot perform file I/O, and are otherwise purposely restricted from being used as a means of writing destructive or malicious code. What they can do, however, is manipulate the properties and methods of embedded controls, respond to these controls' events, and exploit IE's own object model.

Continuing the charting example, scripts can be used to let the user change the view of the chart interactively. The following VBScript routines are embedded directly into the Web page shown in Figure 6.2. Each reacts to a "change" event on a slider control and changes the elevation or rotation of the chart control accordingly:

```
<SCRIPT Language="VBSCRIPT">

Sub sldElevation_Change()
  chtSensitivity.Plot.View3D.Elevation = sldElevation.Value
End Sub

Sub sldRotation_Change()
  chtSensitivity.Plot.View3D.Rotation = sldRotation.Value
End Sub

</SCRIPT>
```

Communicating with the Server

Thus far, we have been examining the user service layer in isolation. In a data warehousing application, users need to be able to specify the data they are interested in, pass that request on to a server, and receive the results back. Let's take a look at how those user requests are passed along to the business services layer on the server.

The first step is to gather the user's input from a page running in the browser. This input can be gathered either directly from an HTML-based form or from an embedded control written specifically to capture input unique to the application. In either case, the input is packaged as a string of parameters that are appended onto the end of a URL representing a component that we want to run on the server. This string is then sent to the server via standard HTTP protocol. The form shown in Figure 6.3, for example, prompts the user for parameters to run a query on the server. The list boxes are embedded ActiveX controls, and their values are passed to the server by a routine written in VBScript.

The form depicted in Figure 6.3 would pass its request to the server with a string similar to:

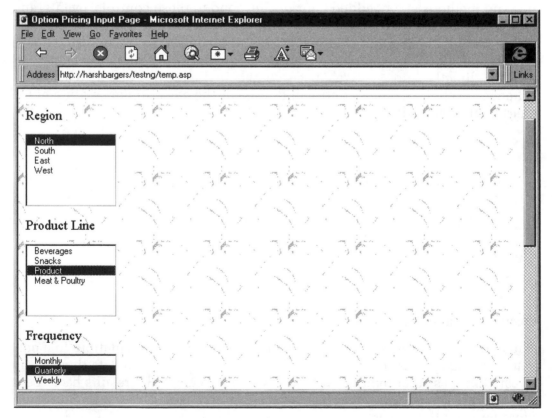

Figure 6.3 Gathering user input.

```
http://www.xyzcorp.com/Analyze.asp?Region=North&ProductLine=Beverages&Frequency=
Monthly
```

Breaking this URL down into its components, note the following:

http://	HTTP protocol
	Site name
/Analyze.asp	The name of an Active Server Page to run (more on this in the next section)
?	Denotes that parameters are about to follow
Region=North	The name (Region) and value (North) of the first parameter
&	Denotes the end of the first parameter
ProductLine=Beverages	The name (ProductLine) and value (Beverages) of the second parameter
&	Denotes the end of the second parameter
Frequency=Monthly	The name (Frequency) and value (Monthly) of the third parameter

This approach, while relatively simple, works very well for most data warehousing applications. The number of variables is usually small and can therefore be packaged and sent along as URL parameters quite efficiently. The next section demonstrates that the facility for receiving the parameters on the server end is also very straightforward.

Script code is often used to create this URL from the user input and send it along to the server. For example, the following code fragment could be attached to a button to package the parameters gathered by the page in Figure 6.3 and pass them along to the server:

```
Sub cmdSubmit_Click()
  sParams = ""
  sParams = sParams & "Region=" & lstRegions.Text & "&"
  sParams = sParams & "ProductLine=" & lstProductLines.Text & "&"
  sParams = sParams & "Frequency=" & lstFrequencies.Text
  Location.HRef = "Analyze.asp?" & sParams
End Sub
```

Business Services Layer

Moving from the user services layer, which is concerned with the capture of user selections and display of results, we next encounter the business services layer. This layer is responsible for the heavy number crunching and business analysis that is most appropriately performed on a powerful, centralized server. It is implicitly assumed that this layer is necessary for data warehousing applications; in other words, a direct connection between the user services and data services layers would not be of any value because a significant amount of summarization and analysis has to happen in between—more than would be practical with stored procedures. Microsoft's strategy for implementing this layer is straightforward: Build your business services as COM objects and automate them with Active Server Pages.

As discussed earlier, COM objects are packaged chunks of functionality with a well-defined set of interfaces (properties, methods, and events). They can be built with any number of development tools including Visual Basic, Visual C++, and Visual J++ (Java). When used on a server to implement business services, COM objects go by the name ActiveX Server Components. An ActiveX Server Component has no user interface and is primarily, although not always, implemented to run in process as a DLL.

Active Server Pages (ASP) are HTML documents with embedded server-side script code. You can recognize these documents by their .ASP extension; ASP applications are created using Visual InterDev, the newest member of Microsoft's development tool family.

Like its client-side cousin, ASP can use either VBScript or JScript. The basic idea behind ASP is as follows:

1. Parameters can be received easily from the browser.
2. Work can be performed on the server by calling ActiveX Server Components.
3. Results can be returned to the browser as native HTML.

The most important concept to understand about ASP is that although HTML and server-side script code are stored in the same document, the script is executed on the server, then straight HTML is sent to the browser. This lets users do quite a bit of work on the server while making sure the output is browser- and platform-neutral HTML.

Two other features of ASP are important to this discussion: session management and Active Data Objects. Session management refers to the ability to maintain information about the state of a particular user between pages (or interactions with the server). The "cookies" technique is often applied to solve this problem. ASP offers another alternative: the session object, an intrinsic object that can be used to store and retrieve virtually any state information about a user. Although the session object does use cookies behind the scenes, it shields the developer from that technique and uses a simpler programming model.

Active Data Objects (ADOs) comprise a set of objects that let ASP scripts communicate directly with a database. They are similar in form and syntax to Data Access Objects (DAO) and Remote Data Objects (RDO). Although data warehousing applications generally require a middle tier of custom COM objects to communicate with the database, ADO can play a role where a simple SELECT of data is required.

All of these technologies rely on Microsoft's Internet Information Server (IIS) running under Windows NT Server for their implementation. In this sense, Microsoft's server strategy is platform specific, while preserving a multiplatform client. The balance of this section provides more detail about the way these technologies can be implemented in a data warehousing solution.

Receiving User Requests from the Browser

Recall the earlier example on user services in which a user request was packaged as a URL with a parameter string appended to the end. That request looked something like this:

```
http://www.xyzcorp.com/Analyze.asp?Region=North&ProductLine=Beverages&Frequency=
Monthly
```

This is a request to run an Active Server Page (Analyze.asp) with the indicated parameters. So what happens next? When IIS receives a request for an ASP file, it first parses and runs an embedded server-side script code. This code is differentiated from the HTML with special delimiters (<% and %>).

The code we're interested in at this point is that which determines the parameters being passed in. To do that, ASP gives us an object called Request that represents the stream of data coming in from a browser. To determine the values of parameters, we simply reference the Request object and ask for the parameters by name, as in Figure 6.4. The embedded server-side script code in

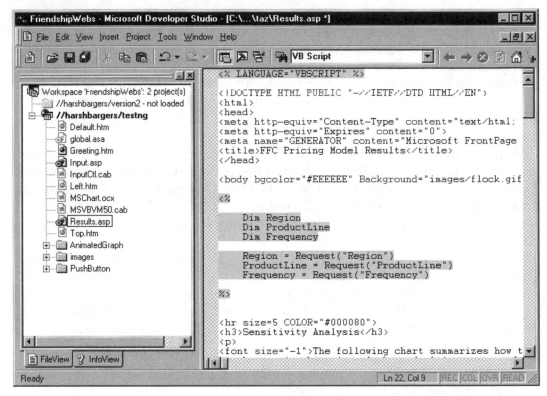

Figure 6.4 Getting user parameters through the Request object.

the ASP document is denoted by <%/%> pairs, and is highlighted by the visual InterDev development environment.

Automating ActiveX Server Components

Once the user parameters are retrieved from the Request object, ActiveX Server Components (COM objects) residing on the server (or another server) can perform analysis and number crunching. This is achieved in ASP code via simple automation—an instance of the component is instantiated using a CreateObject command, then its properties and methods are manipulated by name. "Under the hood" the component is being communicated with via COM (if it is on the same server as IIS) or DCOM (if it resides on a different server). That distinction is transparent to the ASP developer, however; therefore, this leaves it to a system architect to deploy components on whatever machines are necessary to optimize for performance, and to change the configuration at will without affecting the application code.

The following code fragment shows how a component would be instantiated and automated using ASP script code:

```
<%
Dim objAnalysisEngine

Set objAnalysisEngine =
Server.CreateObject("DataWarehouse.AnalysisEngine")

objAnalysisEngine.Region = Request("Region")
objAnalysisEngine.ProductLine = Request("ProductLine")
objAnalysisEngine.Frequency = Request("Frequency")

objAnalysisEngine.PerformRollup

%>
```

Clearly, integrating COM objects into ASP applications is very straightforward. The objects themselves may be very complex to implement and may do very difficult work, but once written they can be integrated with minimal effort.

Returning Results to the Browser

Once the ActiveX Server Components have done their work, the remaining task is to return data to the browser. Data can be returned as HTML or it can be displayed in controls embedded in the HTML. We'll take a look at an example of each.

Returning Data as HTML

To return data as HTML, the ASP code retrieves it from one or more ActiveX Server Components, then uses the intrinsic Response object to send it back to the browser as a dynamically generated HTML stream. The interesting thing here is that dynamic HTML can be mixed freely with static HTML, much like a mail merge fills variable data into a template.

The following code fragment shows how a page similar to the one depicted in Figure 6.5 can be generated. It creates a table with one row for every state in the requested region and one column for every product in the requested product line. Note the use of the <%= syntax: This literally means "insert into the HTML the value of the following script expression."

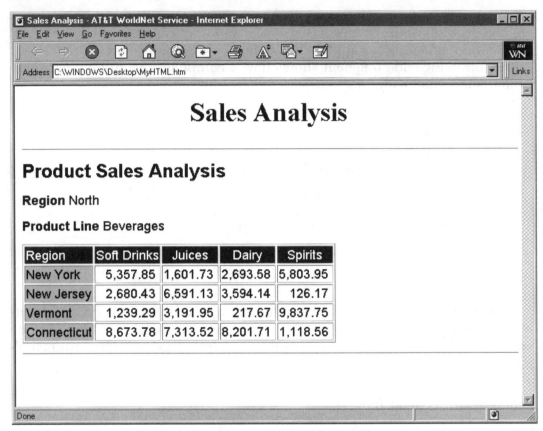

Figure 6.5   Dynamically generated HTML.

```
<TABLE BORDER>
<%For x = 1 to objAnalysisEngine.NumStates%>
  <TR>
  <TD><%=objAnalysisEngine.State(x)%></TD>
  <%For y = 1 to objAnalysisEngine.NumProducts%>
      <TD><%=objAnalysisEngine.Sales(x,y)%></TD>
  <%Next%>
  </TR>
<%Next%>
</TABLE>
```

After this script runs, the following HTML is generated and sent to the browser:

```
<TABLE BORDER>
  <TR>
      <TD>New York</TD>
      <TD>5357.85</TD>
      <TD>1601.73</TD>
      <TD>2693.58</TD>
      <TD>5803.95</TD>
  </TR>
  <TR>
      <TD>New Jersey</TD>
      <TD>2680.43</TD>
      <TD>6591.13</TD>
      .
      .
      .
</TABLE>
```

Figure 6.5 illustrates how the completed HTML document (which is generated from more complex code than is shown here) would look.

Returning Data into Embedded Controls

Using a similar technique, data can be loaded into controls that are embedded into the HTML document. The difference here is that embedded controls are not instantiated at the server, but are instead created by the browser on the client machine. This means that the server cannot load them directly; it must pass instructions to the browser telling it to load the controls after it creates them. This is done by dynamically generating client-side script code on the server. The client will be run by the browser with the data generated by the server-side code. This technique is very powerful, but it is somewhat difficult to visualize in the ASP documents since server, client, and HTML code are all intermixed.

The following code fragment could, for example, be used to generate a page similar to that in Figure 6.2, which as you recall is an embedded chart control. This example generates a Window_OnLoad routine, which happens to be the routine which IE runs when a new page is loaded.

```
<SCRIPT LANGUAGE="VBSCRIPT">Sub Window_OnLoad
<%For x = 1 to objAnalysisEngine.NumStates For y = 1 to
objAnalysisEngine.NumProducts %>Chart.DataGrid.SetData
<%=x%>, <%=y%>, <%=objAnalysisEngine.Sales(x,y)%><%nextnext%>End
Sub

</SCRIPT>
```

After this script runs on the server, the browser receives a routine that looks like this:

```
<SCRIPT LANGUAGE="VBSCRIPT">Sub Window_OnLoad
  Chart.DataGrid.SetData 1, 1, 5357.85Chart.DataGrid.SetData 1, 2,
  1601.73Chart.DataGrid.SetData 1, 3, 2693.58
  Chart.DataGrid.SetData 1, 4, 5803.95Chart.DataGrid.SetData 2, 1,
  2680.43Chart.DataGrid.SetData 2, 1, 6591.13
 .

 .

.End Sub

</SCRIPT>
```

Maintaining State with the Session Object

A common need in Web applications—data warehousing and others—is to maintain data specific to a user throughout an entire session. Since HTTP is a connectionless protocol, each time a user requests a new page, he or she is effectively starting over in terms of input supplied, choices made, or results received. Of course, a well-written application will "remember" values a user supplied previously to eliminate the need for rekeying them.

ASP uses the Session object to retain data throughout a session. The Session object represents a user, and can be referenced across all ASP pages in a web. Developers can store data in this object by name and retrieve it later using the same name. To put this in concrete terms, consider the following example. Suppose a user fills out the page depicted in Figure 6.3 to form a query (call this the input page), then views the results in the page depicted in Figure 6.5 (call this the results page). When the user navigates back to the input page, the previous choices should be retained. To ensure this, we would write server-side script in the results page ASP file to store the user's choices in the session object, as in the following example:

```
<%
Session("Region") = Request("Region")
Session("ProductLine") = Request("ProductLine")
Session("Frequency") = Request("Frequency")
%>
```

Then we would write server-side script in the input page that, in turn, generates client-side script to initialize the controls on the page with their latest values:

```
<SCRIPT Language="VBScript">
Sub Window_OnLoad()
  lstRegions.Text="<%Session("Region")%>"
```

```
lstProductLines.Text="<%Session("ProductLine")%>"
lstFrequencies.Text="<%=Session("Frequency")%>"
End Sub
</SCRIPT>
```

Writing ActiveX Server Components

While an in-depth discussion of writing components is outside the scope of this book, we can certainly discuss some of the features of these components and tools that can be used to write them. As already defined, an ActiveX Server Component is merely a COM object written specifically to implement business logic and run on the server. The complexity of each object is encapsulated behind a well-defined interface of properties and methods. The objects themselves communicate with the database via ODBC (or other methods if appropriate). The internal workings of the objects are then implemented using any and all capabilities of the tool used to develop them.

Since COM is a binary object standard, any language can, in theory, be used to develop COM objects. Microsoft offers two main choices, Visual C++ and Visual Basic, both of which ship as part the Visual Studio developer suite. Visual C++ has always been able to author COM objects, but this capability is relatively new in Visual Basic. The choice of tool depends on several factors including: (1) ability of the language to express the necessary algorithms, (2) skills of the development team, (3) required performance of the components, and (4) time available to develop the components. Note that item (3) is less of a concern than you might think since Visual Basic 5.0 produces native (i.e., not interpreted) code that is nearly as fast as similar C++ code. The real differentiators will be the skill set of the developer (item 2) and the language itself (item 1). C++, for example, has pointers while VB does not. Some algorithms need pointers to be implemented effectively, which would make C++ the choice in that case. Other algorithms require only simple procedural logic, in which case VB may be the best choice.

Visual J++ is also emerging as a tool to write server components. Microsoft has discussed plans to "wrap" Java applications into COM objects and run them on the server. This will be an interesting capability to watch develop over time.

Deploying Components on Transaction Server

For some data warehousing applications, it may be appropriate to deploy the ActiveX Server Components on the Microsoft Transaction Server. Transaction

Server can help those components scale and perform well under multiuser conditions. It can automatically handle the queuing of requests for objects' services and the pooling of connections to the database. Developers writing components for Transaction Server can basically ignore these issues by assuming their component is a single-user object with a monopoly on the database. Transaction Server then handles these issues behind the scenes. This approach makes it easier to develop components because developers can focus on the business problem rather than on the plumbing. As concurrent user load increases, Transaction Server can balance the load appropriately.

Note that a data warehousing application does not typically use Transaction Server's pure transaction processing features (i.e., commit and rollback of transaction performed by components) since these applications are by definition only reading the database. This accentuates Transaction Server's dual nature as both a TP monitor and an object manager.

Active Data Objects

There may be cases where a separate component is not required to perform analysis and interact with the database. For example, you may want to simply retrieve lists of unique items (regions, product lines, etc.) from the database to fill pick lists for the user interface. For situations like this, ASP provides Active Data Objects (ADO) to provide direct connectivity to the database through ODBC.

ADO is an object model very similar in nature and syntax to both Data Access Objects (DAO) and Remote Data Objects (RDO), both of which have been available to VB programmers for a long time. With ADO, we can run SQL queries and stored procedures, iterate through result sets, and display the results as dynamically created HTML pages. ADO can also be used to perform inserts, updates, and deletes.

The Data Services Layer

At the data services layer, Microsoft offers SQL Server, a full-featured relational database management system. While this chapter does not delve into the features and capabilities of SQL Server, it is fair to state that SQL Server is well suited as a platform for staging large data warehouses. Note that SQL Server requires Windows NT Server to run.

SQL Server does provide a few data warehousing-specific features. The

CUBE aggregate operator, for example, returns an n-dimensional result set rather than the typical zero or one-dimensional set. Similarly, the ROLLUP aggregate operator returns aggregates and super-aggregates for elements within a Group By clause. Finally, data pipes provide the ability to have remote stored procedures populate local tables using the Insert...Exec statement. All of these capabilities can help to simplify collecting data from disparate sources into a single warehouse.

Of course, the Microsoft architecture does not require that data be stored in SQL Server. Microsoft's ODBC service makes virtually any database accessible to the components in the business services layer.

User Interface Alternatives

Now that we've examined the typical Microsoft architecture in detail, we can examine two alternatives at the user services layer. These alternatives include using custom ActiveX Document Applications or Microsoft Excel to present data.

ActiveX Document Applications

Those of you familiar with Internet Explorer know that it makes it possible to view documents in formats other than HTML. One notable use of this feature is its capability to display Microsoft Office documents (Word, Excel, Power-Point, etc.). It does this by cooperating with the applications that create these documents through the ActiveX Document interface. Essentially, any application that is written to conform to the ActiveX Document Application specification can be activated inside the browser window. Its menus and toolbars merge with IE, so that its documents can be viewed inside IE. Users like this capability because they can jump from document to document without switching context. The technology that makes this possible is merely an extension of the OLE technology that makes in-place activation of embedded documents possible.

Why does this matter? Because it is possible to write a complete application to serve as the front end to the data warehouse and then run it in the browser. This can be particularly useful in an intranet situation when the client configuration is standardized on Windows. We could, for example, write a Windows application that communicates directly with the ActiveX Server Components via DCOM, thereby skipping the HTTP connection and ASP/HTML steps.

When we control the environment, this can be a very straightforward development approach. The result—browser-based data warehousing—is exactly the same to the user.

Building an ActiveX Document Application is no more difficult than building a standalone application. Both Visual C++ and Visual Basic provide wizards to create shells for these types of applications. VB even provides a wizard to migrate an existing standalone application to an ActiveX Document Application.

Microsoft Excel

Many data warehousing applications provide the ability to export the results of a query to a spreadsheet. This lets the user perform additional offline and free-form analysis. With the release of Excel 97, it is possible to host data warehouse front ends directly in Excel. This facility eliminates the "export" step and delivers the data right where the user needs it. Because Excel application development is a topic unto itself, this discussion focuses only on two specific features that have particular relevance to an intranet data warehouse: Web Queries and HTML Table Extensions.

Web Queries

Web Queries is a feature of Excel 97 that allows users to send a data request to a Web server and return the results directly into the worksheet. In very simplistic terms, it is a substitute for gathering user parameters on an HTML form and calling an ASP page. In Excel, the query gathers user parameters from cells on the worksheet. The parameters are then concatenated onto the URL of a server application (such as an ASP page), and the resulting HTML data is inserted into the worksheet.

Using this mechanism, we can write ASP applications specifically to process requests from Excel applications and return HTML data for insertion into the worksheet.

HTML Table Extensions

Excel 97 supports several HTML table tag extensions that permit users to insert data into Excel worksheets and retrieve pivot tables and data tables from a Web server. The idea here is that ASP applications can return data that is targeted to be viewed in Excel in HTML. Excel can activate in-place inside the IE window. The three most useful extensions are FORMULA, AUTOFILTER, and CROSSTAB, but this discussion is confined to CROSSTAB.

The CROSSTAB attribute can generate a PivotTable when the data is brought into Excel 97. There are two HTML table tag extensions associated with PivotTables: CROSSTAB and CROSSTABGRAND. In addition, there are six TH and TD extensions:

ROWFIELD, COLFIELD, DATAFIELD, PAGEFIELD, AGGREGATOR, and SUBTOTAL.

An example of the syntax is as follows:

```
<TABLE border CROSSTAB CROSSTABGRAND=ROWCOLUMN>
<TR>
    <TH ROWFIELD>Store #
    <TH>Date
    <TH PAGEFIELD>Channel
    <TH COLFIELD>Division
    <TH>Product
    <TH DATAFIELD AGGREGATOR="SUM">Units
    <TH>Price
<TR><TD>Store 2<TD>1/1/96<TD>Wholesale<TD>Brass<TD>Trumpet<TD>7<TD>325
<TR><TD>Store 6<TD>1/8/96<TD>Wholesale<TD>Electronic<TD>Keyboard<TD>8<TD>795
<TR><TD>Store 5<TD>1/15/96<TD>Wholesale<TD>Brass<TD>Trumpet<TD>4<TD>400
. . .
</Table>
```

Figure 6.6 shows how this file looks in Excel. Note that this is a fully functional PivotTable that allows the user to do extensive n-dimensional analysis on the data call from the client. Of course, only moderate amounts of data can be transferred and stored in the Excel PivotTable cache this way, but this approach can be very effective for some data analysis applications.

Related Topics

Three miscellaneous topics deserve mention in this chapter: a comparison of ActiveX controls and Java applets, a comparison of VBScript and JScript, and a brief discussion of ISAPI.

ActiveX Controls versus Java Applets

The previous discussion of controls embedded in HTML and running in the browser included both ActiveX Controls and Java applets. And while it's pos-

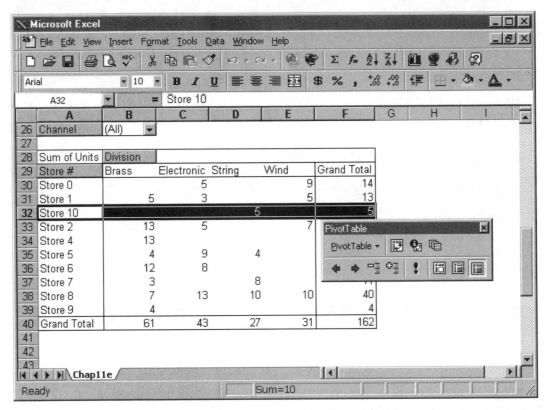

Figure 6.6 The CROSSTAB attribute.

sible to use either, it is worthwhile to note a few features of each to help determine which is most suitable for a particular environment. Although ActiveX Controls can be built with VB, VC++, or VJ++, Java applets can be built only with VJ++. Also, Java, which is certainly a well-designed language that has garnered significant industry support, is relatively new. VB and VC++, on the other hand, are mature tools with a base of knowledge and existing tools and libraries.

The two also differ in terms of execution model. ActiveX Controls are downloaded and installed (automatically) onto the client machine the first time they are encountered; thereafter, they are simply run. Applets are downloaded and executed inside a Java Virtual Machine (which is provided by the browser) each time they are encountered. Both approaches represent efficient ways of deploying functionality inside a Web page over the Internet.

In terms of support, Java applets are currently better supported on non-Microsoft platforms, most notably Netscape Navigator (although it is likely that Netscape will support ActiveX Controls in the near future). This means that for wide-audience Internet applications where you have no control over the browser, applets are probably the better choice. For intranet applications where the browser is a known quantity, ActiveX Controls are a safe choice.

VBScript versus JScript

As stated, Internet Explorer (on the client) and Internet Information Server/ASP (on the server) support both VBScript and JScript. In fact, both IE and IIS are open and provide a mechanism for third parties to plug in interpreters for other languages as well. So, how can you determine which is most appropriate?

In terms of syntax, VBScript is close to Visual Basic. It is in fact a proper subset of VB. Similarly, JScript is close in syntax to Java. It, too, is a subset. Both are easy to learn, although it can be argued that VB is less daunting to the casual or inexperienced developer. Both can implement any of the architectures discussed in this chapter.

In terms of support, JScript is currently better supported on non-Microsoft platforms, most notably Netscape Navigator (although Netscape is likely to support VBScript in the near future). Again, this means that for wide-audience Internet applications where you have no control over the browser, JScript is probably the better choice. For intranet applications where the browser is a known quantity, VBScript is a good choice.

ISAPI Applications

If you've been following the Microsoft Internet strategy for awhile, you may have heard about ISAPI (the Internet Server Application Programming Interface). ISAPI is a way to write DLLs that can be executed remotely from the browser over HTTP. To call one, you pass the URL plus the DLL name and any associated parameters as a text string. The ISAPI DLL performs its processing and returns an HTML stream to the browser. This approach has been touted as a high-performance alternative to CGI applications, which run in a separate process space from the Web server. ISAPI applications can in fact be used to implement the business services layer of the architecture we have been discussing.

Today, the existence of ASP and ActiveX Server Components obviates the need to write ISAPI applications. ISAPI is actually used as the mechanism to implement ASP and several other IIS features, but it can be considered low-level plumbing rather than the mechanism for implementing business logic. Should a need arise to write a native ISAPI application, Visual C++ provides an application template to do so.

Conclusion

Microsoft provides a robust set of tools to implement data warehousing solutions over the Internet and the corporate intranet. The key ingredients of the Microsoft architecture are:

- A browser-based client hosting HTML documents with embedded controls and client-side script.
- Business logic implemented as a COM object on the server.
- Data stored in SQL Server databases.
- ASP scripts tying everything together.

The client talks to the ASP applications via HTTP, the ASP applications talk to the business objects via COM/DCOM, and the business objects talk to the database via ODBC. The business objects themselves are likely hosted on Transaction Server to provide scalability for increasing user load. This architecture provides for a platform-neutral client (with the choice to optimize for the Windows platform) and a Windows NT Server back end.

The tools to build applications using this architecture are currently available, and provide a blend of established technology and new extensions. Developers building data warehousing solutions are likely to find that the Microsoft architecture provides a sound platform for deploying serious applications.

CHAPTER SEVEN

THE SUN INTRANET DATA WAREHOUSE: ARCHITECTURE AND TOOLS

Fast, dependable access to decision support applications and the underlying information contained in an intranet data warehouse requires a network computing architecture capable of supporting distributed databases and peer-to-peer communications among application component parts. As leading computer companies battle to dominate the desktop browser software market, a major battle is occurring in another arena: distributed network computing. Microsoft is facing off against a large number of hardware and software companies to determine who will define the development and communications standards for distributed network computing. The hardware and software companies, Sun Microsystems among them, are working together to establish open standards for distributed computing.

As discussed in Chapter 6, Microsoft advocates a distributed network computing strategy based on its ActiveX platform and Distributed Component Object Model (DCOM). This chapter presents the competing view, which supports the Common Object Request Broker Architecture (CORBA), a specification authored and published by the Object Management Group (OMG). A number of major vendors including IBM, Digital Equipment Corporation, Hewlett-Packard, and Sun Microsystems all support the CORBA specification and have released Object Request Broker (ORB) products.

Interest in CORBA accelerated with the rise of Internet and intranet computing and the growing requirement for broadly supported "open" standards for distributed network computing. Software developers have begun to rewrite application code as software components that can be downloaded to browsers to communicate with other components on servers. Sun introduced Java, a high-level programming language, in response to Web application developer's need for a language that facilitated coding components. Sun also introduced JavaBeans, a component object model for building Java components and dynamically assembling them into applications. Both Java and JavaBeans have further fueled the debate over who will define the standards for distributed computing, thereby providing the ability to deploy application components across clients and servers.

Sun's approach to meeting the challenges of the intranet data warehouse—which certainly qualifies as a distributed network-based application—is somewhat unique in that it involves both software and hardware solutions. Sun's intranet data warehousing strategy focuses on three critical aspects:

- Scalable SMP Server hardware platforms
- Superior network communications
- Java as a peer-to-peer, highly distributed, applications development tool

With this combination of hardware and software technologies, Sun is mounting a direct assault on Microsoft's network computing strategy. Although this chapter focuses on Sun, and describes its Java products and related technologies that are suitable for an intranet data warehouse, it is important to remember that many vendors are campaigning for "open" standards for distributed network computing, using CORBA as the foundation..

The need for robust software component development tools motivated Sun to develop Java and JavaBeans, as well as a number of related communication capabilities including Remote Method Invocation (RMI), Java database connectivity (JDBC), and Joe, which provides Sun's CORBA-compliant services layer for Java/JavaBean components. These tools provide the developer with ways to enhance the HTML interface and display capabilities while shifting some processing steps to the client-side, thereby providing users with the ability to, for example, rotate a 3D graph and/or modify a graphic format.

This chapter, begins the discussion of Sun's network computing model by reviewing Java and JavaBeans. It then describes some of the options available for establishing communications among distributed components developed with Java and the data warehouse and server-based components (for example, JDBC, Java RMI, and Java IDL). The goal here is to describe how developers can create decision support applications and deliver them to the browser in ways that are more visually appealing and capable than "flat" HTML pages.

Java: Component Development Tool

Java can be described as an application development tool that provides a portable, interpreted, high-performance, simple, and object-oriented programming language and run-time environment. Java completes some of computing's most important trends: the gradual linking of diverse networks, the migration of processing from the mainframe to the desktop to the network, the effort to balance the needs of system administrators against those of individual users.

Java extends the use of data warehouses to meet the needs of casual users by compartmentalizing functionality, allowing the use of certain applets (components that are downloaded to the desktop) without downloading the entire application to the desktop. Empowered with Java, the new paradigm for data warehousing is the client/universal warehouse: Java clients run the programs and display data while servers store the programs and data.

Companies are beginning to use Java-enabled browsers to provide decision-support access to the data warehouse. In addition to reducing costs by supporting the thin-client architecture of the intranet, Java can ensure that necessary features and functions are instantly available to all enterprise users, with decision support front ends accessible through a common "Web top" (i.e., a Java-enabled browser) environment.

Java is designed to be independent of both the instruction set and the operating system it runs on. Rather than calling operating system-specific calls and compiling into one instruction set, Java compilers and interpreters create a universal bytecode. This bytecode is then loaded by a Java virtual machine that translates it into the instruction set of the specific processor, and translates general operating system calls into calls specific to that operating system. Figure 7.1 illustrates the steps in the Java compilation process.

The Java virtual machine (JVM) is a "soft" computer that can be implemented in software or hardware. It is an abstract machine designed to be implemented on top of existing processors. The Java virtual machine is key to the independence of the underlying operating system and hardware; it is essentially a platform that hides the underlying operating system from Java-pow-

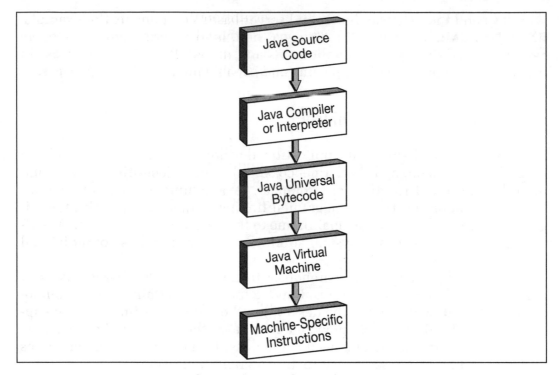

Figure 7.1 The Java compilation/execution process.

ered applets and applications. During the discussion of data warehouse implementation, we'll focus on the ways Java computing can simplify development, deployment, and management.

Java's Four-Level Security Model

Security is a critically important aspect of the Java platform. The Java API set contains four layers of security features to prevent security breaches and costly, disruptive virus distribution:

1. The language does not contain "pointers" which, in other languages (e.g., C and C++) direct memory operations and can cause memory corruption (resulting in application failures).

2. The built-in bytecode verifier checks the correctness of the Java pro-

gramming code and detects any corruption that may have taken place (e.g., by hackers) since the code was originally written.

3. The security manager checks classes of code as they're loaded and alerts users to the existence of security violations.

4. The API set contains user-implementable cryptography features that can be used to augment the security in client/server connections.

It's also important to distinguish safety from security. Security is a policy that is built on top of the safe substrate; a product cannot ensure security without first providing safety. A number of features in the Java language and the Java virtual machine ensure safety and the compiler and run-time system enforce it.

Security Manager

A Java application defines and implements its own security policy. A Java-enabled Web browser, for example, contains an applet (a component downloaded for execution on the client) security manager. The security policy imposed on downloaded applets by the applet security manager is owned, defined, and implemented by the browser. Browsers that implement the applet API also implement the standard applet security policy, all as part of the Java applet compatibility. Applets can't define their own security policies or extend or modify the security policy enforced by the browser.

The security manager prevents downloaded applets from carrying out potentially dangerous operations. For example, the security manager won't let applets

- Read or write files on the client's hard disk
- Establish network connections except to the server that the applet came from
- Dynamically load libraries
- Examine privacy-related system properties, like the name of the person using the browser
- Cause other programs to start running on the client machine

Confining an applet's execution environment in this way is referred to as the *applet sandbox.* The idea is that an applet has to play inside the sandbox, and any attempt to escape the borders of the sandbox is checked and prevented by the applet security manager.

The sandbox model distinguishes Java applets from other embedded-content models in use on the Internet. The sandbox model isn't intended to be a complete internet security solution in and of itself, but it does provide an important safety net.

Java's Key Difference: Dynamic Runtime

Java's dynamic nature offers experienced programmers a number of programming options that are unavailable in most other programming languages. In a Java program, for example, new classes can be fetched from the disk or the network at any time. The program can then start asking these objects questions such as: What is your class name? Do you respond to these methods? None of these "introspection" features (i.e., the ability to ask objects questions about themselves) is available in C++.

If an application needs to draw graphs or charts in Java, it simply asks the objects: Do you have a draw method? Can you set your own color? Do you respond to the setLabel method? Developers can add new graphs to the application months or years after it has been deployed simply by adding the new graphing objects to a directory. Because the programmer of the new graphing components simply needs to add the methods documented in the graphing class interface definition, the original creator of the graphing application does not have to know all the types of graphs that the user may need in the future when building the application.

Java on the Server

The most common use of Java is to develop application components that can be downloaded to the browser. Typically, these are the interface and display components of an intranet data warehouse application. Java also can be used to develop the application logic components that are executed on the server, based on messages sent from client-side components. Sun recommends a "pure Java" implementation in which all of the components of an application (i.e., all OLAP functions in the case of the intranet data warehouse) are written in Java.

For programming server-side components, Java offers a number of advantages over the more commonly used C and C++ languages in the areas of error-checking and recovery. When a programming fault occurs on a server, the state of the Java program is passed to error-handling objects that allow the server applications to handle the errors gracefully.

Because Java is multithreaded, it tends to scale very well in multiprocessor systems since new threads can quickly be executed on different processors. When Java is used to manage logic on central servers, many simultaneous requests are encountered with minimum latency. This is particularly relevant to the expanded user loads that result from intranet deployment of data warehouse applications.

Java application servers that implement logic are very efficient at handling requests with minimal overhead. Spawning a new thread of execution in Java typically takes about 40 kb of memory, about 25 times less than the amount of memory generally required to spawn a new process when Perl and CGI applications are running.

JavaBeans: Component Object Model

JavaBeans extends Java's "write once, run everywhere" capability to reusable component development. JavaBeans code runs on every operating system and within any application environment. Components written as JavaBeans also interoperate with Microsoft ActiveX, IBM's OpenDoc, and Netscape's Live-Connect.

The JavaBeans APIs allow independent software vendors to develop reusable software components that end users can then hook together using visual application builder tools. Several leading software development companies, including Apple, Borland, IBM, Symantec, Novell, Corel, Informix, Oracle, and Sybase have already announced their intention to support the JavaBeans component model.

JavaBeans is likely to play a key role in two aspects of intranet data warehouse application development. The first is that "palettes" of JavaBeans objects will be available to developers for use in building the presentation tier (the interface and display components that are downloaded to the browser). Instead of choosing from a relatively small number of user interface controls, the application developer will be able to select from large libraries of tools available directly from the Internet. While the early selections are likely to be limited to rather primitive components, such as simple controls for changing single data elements, as the market matures, more complex graphing and charting tools will also become available. Eventually, highly specialized JavaBeans components for viewing multidimensional data sets will become part of a toolkit available to intranet data warehouse application developers.

The second area in which JavaBeans will play a major role is in the use of JavaBeans components for server-side processing. These components will be useful for reducing large data sets into summary information, and formatting the summary information for display. Unlike the client-side processing components that will be useful to any application developer, server-side JavaBeans components are likely to evolve to meet the needs of vertical industries such as health care, finance, or retail.

Middleware and APIs

One of the challenges in data warehousing is implementing OLAP middleware components to provide the glue between the browser on the client-side and data sources on server-side. There is an increasing need for standard application programming interfaces (API) to allow heterogeneous interoperability without regard to hardware platform or operating environment. Sun has invested in the development of supporting infrastructure by helping to establish open standards for APIs and middleware.

Java Enterprise API

Java Enterprise APIs support connectivity to enterprise databases and legacy applications. By using these APIs, corporate developers can build distributed client/server applets and applications in Java to run on any operating system or on any hardware platform in the enterprise. Java Enterprise currently encompasses four areas: JDBC, Java IDL, Java RMI, and JNDI.

Java Database Connectivity (JDBC)

Java Database Connectivity (JDBC) is an ANSI SQL-2 entry-level compliant database access interface that provides Java programmers with a uniform interface to a wide range of relational databases. Sun also offers a JDBC-ODBC bridge implementation that allow many of the existing Microsoft ODBC database drivers to operate as JDBC drivers. The following is an example of JDBC code for connecting to an ODBC-compliant relational database:

```
// Connect to the database

Class.forName("jdbc.odbc.JdbcOdbcDriver");
String myURL = "jdbc:odbc:myDatabase";
Connection myConn = DriverManager.getConnection(myURL, "myName", "myPassword");

// Send SQL to the server

java.sql.Statement myStmt = myConn.createStatement();
String mySQL = "SELECT name, address, phone, FROM person";
ResultSet myResult = myStmt.executeQuery(mySQL);

// Get the results

while (myResult.next())
    { // print the values of each row
    String name        = myResult.getString("name");
    String address     = myResult.getString("address");
    String phone       = myResult.getString("phone");
    System.out.println(name + " " + address + " " + phone);
    }
```

With JDBC, it is possible to develop the presentation and logic components of an intranet data warehouse application in Java and download the application on demand to the user's browser. The resulting browser-resident code is capable of issuing an SQL query, via JDBC, with the results of the query returned to the Java code for further processing and display. The problem with this approach is the same as that encountered with any PC-centric processing of OLAP functions. The amount of raw data required, combined with the complexity of the analytic process for many types of intranet data warehouse applications, overwhelms the resources of the PC and network. The solution is to partition the logic components from the presentation components of the application and move the logic components to a server for execution. Distributing application code on both the client and server is a reliable method of communicating between client-side and server-side components.

Java Remote Method Invocation (RMI)

Java Remote Method Invocation (RMI) is a standard for communicating between components when both the client-side and the server-side components are written in Java. RMI allows developers to write Java objects that are invoked from Java code running in other virtual machines, including those running on other computer systems. With RMI, a method invocation on a remote object has the same syntax as a method invocation on a local object. References to such remote objects can be passed as parameters in RMI calls. RMI uses the Java Object Serialization protocol, which defines interfaces for writing and reading objects and classes that implement object interfaces. RMI supports a wide variety of configuration scenarios. Developers can, for example, configure servers in an open or closed fashion. Applets can use RMI to invoke methods on objects supported on servers. If an applet creates and passes a remote object to the server, the server can use RMI to make a callback to the remote object. Java applications can use RMI either in client/server mode or in peer-to-peer mode.

RMI consists of the following three layers:

- **Stub/Skeleton Layer:** The interface between the application layer and RMI, this layer does not deal with the specifics of any transport, but transmits data to the remote reference layer via the abstraction of *marshal streams.* Marshal streams use a mechanism called *object serialization* that enables Java objects to be transmitted between address spaces. Objects transmitted using the object serialization system are passed by copy to the remote address space, unless they are remote objects, in which case they are passed by reference. The appropriate stub and skeleton classes are determined at runtime and are dynamically loaded as needed. Stubs and skeletons are generated using the rmic compiler.

- **Remote Reference Layer:** This layer deals with the lower-level transport interface. It is responsible for carrying out a specific remote reference protocol, which is independent of the client stubs and server skeletons. The remote reference layer has two cooperating components: the client-side and the server-side components. The client-side component contains information specific to the remote server (or servers, if the remote reference is to a replicated object) and communicates via the transport to the server-side component. During each method invocation, the client- and server-side components perform the specific remote reference semantics. For example, if a remote object is part of a replicated object, the client-side component can forward the invocation to each replica rather than just a single remote object. In a corresponding manner, the server-side component implements the specific remote reference semantics prior to delivering a remote method invocation to the skeleton. The remote reference layer transmits data to the transport layer via the abstraction of a stream-oriented connection. The transport takes care of the implementation details of connections. Although connections present a streams-based interface, a connectionless transport can be implemented beneath the abstraction.

- **Transport Layer:** This layer is responsible for setting up connections to remote address spaces, managing and monitoring connections, listening for incoming calls, setting up a connection for an incoming call, and maintaining a table of remote objects that reside in an address space.

Figure 7.2 illustrates the relationship between RMI and the application layer. The RMI transport layer consists of four basic abstractions:

- An *endpoint,* which denotes an address space or Java virtual machine. In the implementation, an endpoint can be mapped to its

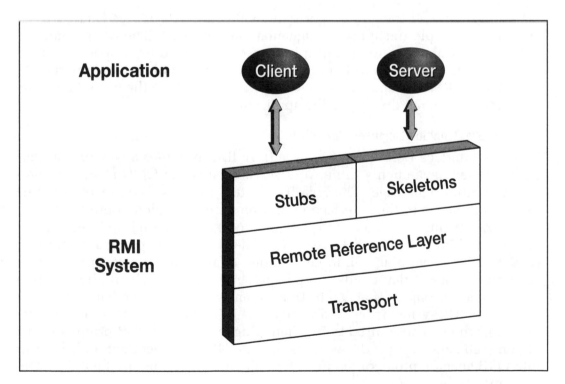

Figure 7.2   The relationship of application components and RMI.

transport; that is, given an endpoint, a specific transport instance can be obtained.

- A *channel,* which is a conduit between two address spaces. A channel is responsible for managing connections between the local address space and the remote address space for which it is a channel.

- A *connection,* which transfers data (i.e., performs input/output).

- The *transport,* which manages channels. Each channel is a virtual connection between two address spaces. Within a transport, only one channel exists per pair of address spaces (the local address space and a remote address space). Given an endpoint to a remote address space, a transport sets up a channel to that address space. The transport abstraction is also responsible for accepting calls on incoming connections to the address space, setting up a connection object for the call, and dispatching to higher layers in the system.

Because the RMI transport layer defines the concrete representation of an endpoint, multiple transport implementations can exist. The design and implementation also supports multiple transports per address space, so both TCP and UDP can be supported in the same virtual machine. It is important to note that the RMI transport interfaces are available only to the virtual machine implementation, not directly to the application.

Java Interface Definition Language (Java IDL)

The Java Interface Definition Language (Java IDL) provides a way to transparently connect Java clients to network servers using the OMG standard Interface Definition Language. The Java IDL system permits developers to define remote interfaces in the interface definition language, then compile the IDL definitions (using the idlgen stub generator tool) to generate Java interface definitions and Java client and server stubs. The Java IDL mapping specification (which defines mapping IDL to Java) allows a Java client to transparently invoke an IDL object that resides on a remote server. Similarly, it allows a Java server to define objects that can be transparently invoked from IDL clients.

The Java IDL system is based on a portable Java ORB core (illustrated in Figure 7.3), which is structured to facilitate plugging in new ORB protocols. The idlgen stub generator produces stubs that are ORB independent and that call into ORB-specific protocol modules for all data marshaling or other ORB-specific operations.

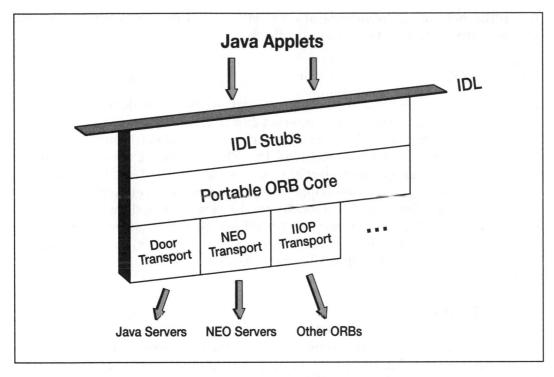

Figure 7.3   The portable ORB core.

The portable ORB core is designed to support multiple ORB protocols. The IDL stub generator idlgen generates stubs that for any given call

1. Call into the object reference to get a Representation object that is implemented by an ORB-specific transport module.
2. Use that Representation object to get an ORB-specific MarshalBuffer object.
3. Use that MarshalBuffer to marshal the arguments.
4. Call into the Representation to execute the call.
5. Use the MarshalBuffer object to unmarshal the results.

Java Naming and Directory Interface (JNDI)

The Java Naming and Directory Interface (JNDI) provides a unified, industry-standard interface to multiple naming and directory services in the enterprise, providing networkwide sharing of a variety of information about users, machines, networks, servers, and applications.

Java Server API

Java Server is an extensible framework that enables the development of a whole spectrum of Java-powered Internet and intranet servers. The framework API contains server-side class libraries for server administration, access control, and dynamic server resource handling. The framework also encompasses the Java Servlet (components executed on the server) API. Servlets are platform-independent Java-powered objects—the server-side counterpart of client-side applets. Servlets can reside locally on the server or be downloaded to the server from the Net under security restrictions. Servlet examples range from simple HTTP servlets (efficient replacements of CGI-scripts) to more complex servlets using JDBC/ODBC that offer database connectivity.

What iS CORBA?

CORBA (the Common Object Request Broker Architecture) is one of two related specifications published by the Object Management Group (OMG) in 1992. It defines a common framework for object-oriented applications, along with Object Services and Common Facilities for managing distributed applications. The related specification, the Object Request Broker (ORB), defines the key communications elements that allow applications developed as objects to transparently make requests and receive responses (i.e., send and receive messages) in a distributed heterogeneous environment.

Sun, an active member of OMG from the beginning, contributed the Interface Definition Language (IDL) to the CORBA specification. The IDL specifies the interface to objects, describing the properties and operations of objects in a language-independent way.

An updated version of CORBA, CORBA 2.0, defines the Internet Inter-ORB Protocol (IIOP). IIOP is an asynchronous protocol that enables communications between ORBs from different vendors and with "lightweight" ORBs embedded in Web browsers. (Lightweight ORBs perform a limited set of communication functions.) IIOP resolves many of the problems involved with building complex Web applications, particularly those caused by the fact that HTTP (HyperText Transfer Protocol), the default protocol for transmitting page markup information from Web servers to Web browsers, does not provide effi-cient messaging between objects running in the browser and objects in the server. Integrating IIOP into Web browsers such as Netscape Communicator adds fuel to the already burning firestorm of Web application development functionality for the enterprise.

When to Use CGI, RMI, or IIOP

Although HTML is the most common programming tool for developing user interface components for client-side service requests, it produces relatively "flat" pages that resemble the interface menus of traditional mainframe appli-cations. Using Java applets can significantly enrich the functionality of client-side application components by permitting the interface and display compo-nents to be presented in a far more graphical format than is possible with HTML pages.

In many ways, CGI is the simplest method of linking HTML user interface components with an external program (e.g., server-resident OLAP functions). CGI offers a useful means of executing relatively simple calls from an HTML interface to external application components. While the application itself can be quite complex (depending on the server-based functions that it calls), pro-cessing on the client-side is limited because there is essentially no interaction between client and server components. As the HTML interface is enhanced with the addition of Java applets, a more robust communications method is re-quired between client-side and server-side components.

RMI offers a simple way for application developers to create components that communicate between two processes running on the same or different computer systems. RMI is ideal for small departmental applications that have the source and destination "hard-coded" into each program. Because the sender and receiver of a message (i.e., the components of an application) are designed to work with each other, RMI is the ideal solution for establishing communications links between client-side and server components when both sets of components are written in Java.

The CORBA standards—IDL and IIOP—are better solutions for situations in which developers are building generic information services for the enterprise. This is particularly true if the application's source and destination compo-nents are written in different languages and the location of the services needs to be handled in a generic way that is not hard-coded into the client. IDL and IIOP are also preferable for situations in which issues like fail-over, fault tolerance, service migration, service load balancing, or naming services are important. IDL and IIOP are "open" industry standards that extend Java's interoperability in a distributed multivendor network architecture.

Sun's Support of CORBA

Sun's Solaris NEO and Java products both conform to the CORBA specification and establish the foundation for the company's network computing strategy. Java allows sophisticated applications software code to be downloaded to a Web browser and to communicate with server-based components and the data warehouse. Solaris NEO is a distributed object environment that enables organizations to deploy a corporate Web of business-critical shared services. Once deployed, these shared services are accessible from multiple, various client platforms throughout the enterprise and, if desired, the Internet. Solaris NEO objects can also interoperate with objects from other vendor's CORBA environments using IIOP.

Sun's Joe product integrates Java with NEO. Joe incorporates an ORB that connects Java applets to remote CORBA objects running on any machine across the Internet or an intranet. The Joe ORB is automatically downloaded into Web browsers along with Java applets. Joe then establishes and manages connections between local Java objects and remote CORBA objects using IIOP. Joe also includes an OMG Interface Definition Language compiler that automatically generates associated Java classes from interface definitions of CORBA objects.

NEO connectivity for Microsoft Windows provides a bidirectional bridge that enables OLE-compliant applications to access NEO objects, and vice versa, extending the benefit of NEO's network object environment to desktop users without modifying the Windows environment.

Applying Sun's Strategy to the Data Warehousing Environment

Sun Microsystems' Java platform provides a rich hardware and software development environment for building and deploying network computing solutions. As corporations look to leverage their intranets as a solution for providing decision support applications for the data warehouse, Java is proving to be a beneficial programming platform for evolving this implementation. Java offers developers and users the advantages of a write-once, run-anywhere development platform. This flexibility is particularly important as corporations begin to provide universal access to their data warehouses since they cannot generally dictate the user platform to their external customers or business partners. Java computing offers a platform-independent solution for the client-side as well as the server-side of the Internet and intranet environments. With Java, developers need to maintain only a single executable and a single source code.

Java's platform independence highlights a fundamental difference between it and Microsoft's ActiveX environment. Even if Microsoft's attempt to open up portions of ActiveX succeed, developers and users are still likely to be locked into the Win32 platform, or need to maintain multiple ActiveX controls for each different platform that they want to run on. ActiveX allows routines written in many languages (e.g., C, C++, Basic, and so on) to coexist within a single application and on a single platform (e.g., Microsoft Windows running on an Intel CPU). Java allows a single application to run on multiple platforms (e.g., Microsoft Windows, Sun Solaris, Apple Macintosh, UNIX, or the JavaOS running on a network computer). Further, the JavaBeans component API, which is written entirely in Java, allows Java components to be inserted in any other component architecture, including ActiveX, IBM's OpenDoc, and Netscape's LiveConnect, as well as any Java applet or applications.

Meeting the Dynamic Requirements of Data Warehousing

One of the key differences between the client/server (i.e., client-centric) data warehousing applications and Intranet data warehousing is the highly adaptive interface that can be delivered to users with intranet technologies. Rather than a single, feature-rich monolithic code structure installed on every user's desktop, users can download only the application components that they need, and developers can adapt the interface to the user's unique requirements. The JavaBeans component model extends this concept to include the ability to adapt applications by combining components from multiple vendors with those developed internally.

Most organizations do not need to build from scratch the necessary OLAP software to provide users with access to the data warehouse. Rather, they can integrate off-the-shelf packaged applications, and allow the IT department to act as an internal systems integrator to create value by assembling the best-of-breed technologies. This approach is usually the correct starting point to deliver a rapid return on the data warehouse investment and provide immediate benefit to the organization. This is not to say that packaged applications—no

Sun Microsystems' Development Environments

Sun provides these integrated development environments, which address the specific needs throughout an organization:

- Java Workshop for Java development
- Internet Access PlusPack for Intranet implementation
- Internet Workshop for intranet applications
- JavaPlan for enterprise Java applications

Java Workshop

Java Workshop is a complete, integrated development environment for creating Internet applications and Web pages. It includes:

- An easy-to-use Web browser user interface
- Visual Java for rapid development of your application or applet's user interface
- Integrated robust graphical development and debugging tools for Java applications
- Publication tools for Java applications on the Internet or intranets
- Multiplatform support for Solaris, Windows 95, and Windows NT systems

Internet Access PlusPack

The Internet Access PlusPack is a bundle of Internet tools designed to provide Solaris users with access to corporate intranets and the Internet. These tools also allow users to navigate the Internet and corporate intranets, create HTML-based information and Web content, and explore the capabilities of

Java through a Java desktop browser and the Java Development Kit. Components include:

- **Internet/Intranet Access:** Netscape Navigator 2.01i Web browser, including customizations for Solaris integration, FTP, and Telnet wrappers; and Solaris Common Desktop Environment (CDE) actions and OpenWindows scripts for access to Solaris FTP and Telnet capability.
- **Internet/Intranet Publishing:** SoftQuad HotMetaL Light 2.0 HTML authoring tool for Web content authoring and Web page creation; and the Java Development Kit 1.0, including the Java Virtual Machine to develop and use Java applets.
- **Internet/Intranet Viewing:** ShowMe Media Player for playing audio and WAV files, and viewing AVI, QuickTime, and MPEG files.

Internet Workshop

Internet Workshop is a development environment for building client/server applications that can operate across corporate intranets and the public Internet. It includes Java Workshop and incorporates Sun's Joe technology along with tools for developing universal client applications in Java, with tools that build scalable, manageable server applications in C/C++ languages.

JavaPlan

JavaPlan is a graphical software development tool that simplifies the process involved with developing and documenting enterprise software applications. JavaPlan provides a common framework from which both managers and developers can work, thereby integrating an organization's strategic business goals and processes with the development of information tools to help achieve these goals.

matter how cleverly assembled—can meet all the information access and analysis needs of an organization. More often, some OLAP middleware is required to act as the "glue" to integrate the off-the-shelf applications with whatever custom components are required to meet the organization's unique requirements.

OLAP Middleware as used here describes OLAP functions that are coded as components that reside between the browser and the data warehouse; these components may be executed on the client-side or server-side. By implementing interoperable applications with heterogeneous middleware, organizations position themselves to swap out applications as new products or requirements emerge. This is a relatively simple process when middleware APIs are used to insulate software layers.

As organizations move toward a network object-based component software model using JavaBeans and CORBA-compliant environments like Solaris NEO, this integration process is likely to become even more simple and require few programming changes. Today, the Java platform permits organizations to change applications on the server and instantly redeploy them as users invoke them from their browsers.

Sun provides several development environments for the Java developer, which facilitates the creation of client-side and server-side components of an intranet data warehouse. See the Sidebar "Sun Microsystems Development Environments."

Sample Data Warehousing Application Architecture

Let's now turn to sample data warehousing application architectures. Assume that the presentation layer is provided by a standard browser such as Netscape, Internet Explorer, or any other browser that supports the Java Virtual Machine. Sun also offers an alternative browser, HotJava, which is customizable to create a unique look and feel for the application and which features a thin-client interface that is appropriate for thin-clients such as network computers.

The database tier most commonly consists of a commercially available relational database management system that is organized and tuned for data warehouse queries and more advanced forms of OLAP. The focus will be on the OLAP middle tier, since that is the area with the most development options and deployment alternatives.

First I will discuss an approach that leverages a packaged Java application from Infospace (described in the next section) to illustrate how Java applications can be deployed for intranet data warehousing. Next, I will address how custom data warehousing applications can be implemented using object-based technologies and OLAP middleware offerings.

Infospace Intranet Data Warehousing Application

Infospace, Inc. is a start-up company that develops Java applications for intranet data warehouses. It is an example of the growing number of pure Java solutions for data warehousing that are highly deployable for intranet data warehouses. Combining database query capabilities with reporting and charting display options, Infospace's products enable companies to create and pub-

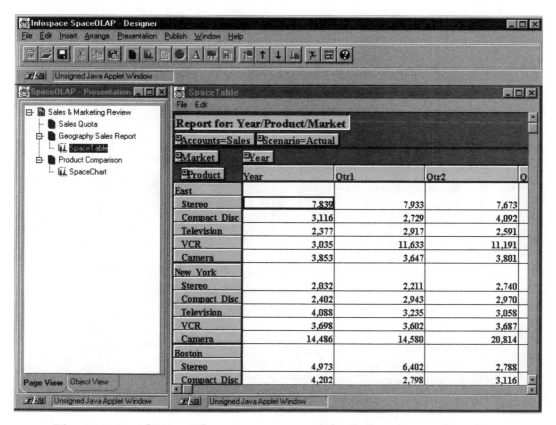

Figure 7.4   The interface component of the Infospace application.

lish information extracted from any database, data mart, or data warehouse to thousands of users, all through the single, common interface of a Web browser.

Figure 7.4 shows an example of an Infospace application. When invoked by the user, this Java application is automatically downloaded to the user's desktop, enabling the user to query the database and visualize the information with the Infospace SpaceCharts and SpaceTable technology. The same Infospace application can run on a PC, Macintosh, or UNIX desktop. The user automatically receives the most recent version of the Infospace product when the application is requested, eliminating any need to provide software change management or administration at the desktop.

The dynamically downloaded Java application applet communicates directly with the Infospace Java Server. The server that Infospace has built in Java is

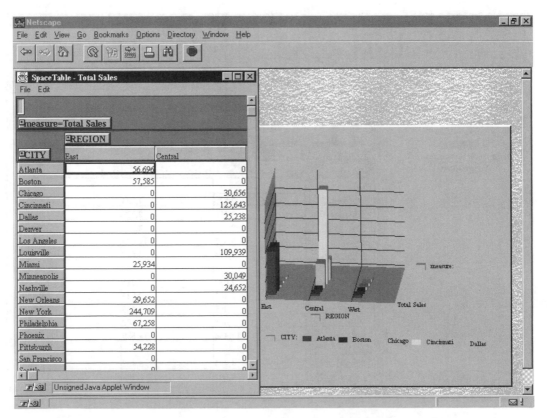

Figure 7.5   The display component of an infospace application.

scalable and multithreaded, which provides state and persistence with the client and database. By contrast, other Web applications rely on the Common Gateway Interface (CGI), which connects, starts, stops, and then disconnects from the database each and every time data is requested by the client.

Once the user receives authorization to access the Infospace Java Server, the applet is ready to run. Users can browse through the database structures for which they have been granted privileges to view. Based on the users' selections, the database query is dynamically generated and sent to the Java Server and, in turn, is executed against the database. The query results are returned to the Java Server, formatted, and sent back to the Web browser. The results can be displayed graphically with a pivot table, SpaceTable, two- and three-dimensional charts, SpaceCharts, or an HTML-based table, as Figure 7.5 illus-

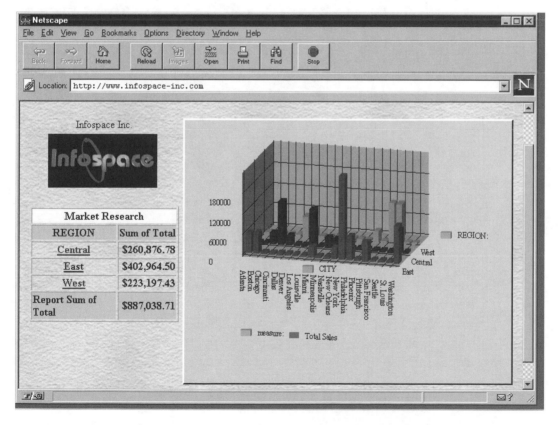

Figure 7.6   Alternate display component of an Infospace application.

trates. The results are sent to the browser in the form of Java applets, which give the users interactive capabilities such as drill-down and rotation.

The applets and data that results from the execution of the query now reside on the user's PC, which allows the user to interact with the data and application without reconnecting to the server. For example, the user is able to shift from one form of graphical display (Figure 7.5) to a new form of graphical display, as shown in Figure 7.6. The ability to interact locally with the data provides faster response for the user and frees intranet bandwidth for other users.

The Infospace application combines the point-and-click ease of the Web browser with the functionality of an ad hoc query, designer, report writer, charting, and analysis package. This level of user access is mobilized through the Java platform. With single-server installation, organizations can provide any user with access to any data through a ubiquitous browser interface.

CHAPTER EIGHT

Optimizing the Performance of the Intranet Data Warehouse

Performance is the first criterion that users will consider in evaluating the intranet data warehouse, because the data warehouse and OLAP applications place enormous processing burdens on the database management system. Fortunately, a number of vendors are beginning to enhance their relational database management systems for data warehousing and OLAP applications to address performance issues. Red Brick Systems is establishing many of the performance benchmarks for database management system software used for data warehousing. The Red Brick product is used in this chapter to illustrate the capabilities that are important in an optimized database management system, but these examples are intended to serve as guidelines for evaluating features in competing products as well.

Designing for Performance

By speeding the flow of information to many more users within a company, an intranet distribution strategy necessarily places increased performance demands on data warehouses. Consequently, intranet data warehouses and data marts will need to efficiently support increasing numbers of concurrent users, many of them casual users lacking in technical database knowledge. And as these new business users discover the value of decision support, they can be counted on to launch ever more complex queries and to seek to engage in new kinds of knowledge discovery applications—for example, predictive analysis using advanced data-mining technologies. Meanwhile, data warehouses will invariably continue to balloon in size as users require access to increasingly detailed data.

There is nothing new in this progression. The brief history of data warehousing has been defined by the mantra: "More knowledge, from more detail, to more users." But intranets promise to drastically accelerate the process, leaving data warehouses based on inadequate performance premises—premises mired in the legacy or skewed to the demands of online transaction processing (OLTP) applications—in the dust.

Throughout this book, data mart has been used to describe a single-subject data warehouse that may serve the needs of a single department or focus on a narrow set of business issues. While a data mart is often smaller than a data warehouse, this is not always true; in many cases, data marts are quite large, often exceeding several hundred gigabytes. Data warehouses, which contain the enterprise's data sources in a single integrated database, and data marts are both based on relational databases and handle the same types of queries. While the performance advantages associated with data marts are generally a function of database size, data marts may also benefit from a simpler database design that can also influence performance.

A production data warehouse or data mart application consists of many components including analysis and reporting tools, legacy and transaction data extraction subsystems, and metadata management tools. But the most important component of a data warehouse is the relational database management system (RDBMS) used to store vast quantities of information and to quickly and reliably answer a wide range of business questions.

Just as OLTP applications demand increasing performance and functionality, data warehouse applications require a similar focus, but the demands are quite different. For example, a single query on a data warehouse or data mart can require thousands or millions of times more work (and different work at that) than a typical OLTP transaction. Moreover, data warehouse applications are frequently required to support tens to hundreds of concurrent query operations—a situation that is likely to intensify as more users gain access to data warehouses via intranets.

The fact is, most of today's relational databases were originally designed for OLTP, not data warehousing. Figure 8.1 itemizes the differences in approach. Cobbling warehousing features onto these relational database engines does not necessarily result in systems that are well tuned for supporting the comparative and sequential analyses that characterize decision support applications.

Star schemas are a case in point. Most experts agree that star schemas are the preferred modeling method for data warehousing, yet as implementors have tried to host such intuitive query-centric schemas on traditional OLTP-biased databases, they have encountered a severe obstacle: poor performance. Traditional OLTP relational database engines are simply not designed for the rich set of complex queries that can be issued against a star schema. In particular, the need to retrieve related information from several tables in a single query—"join processing"—is severely limited. Traditional OLTP relational database systems can join only two tables at a time. If a complex join involves more than two tables, the relational database system must artificially break the query into a series of pair-wise joins. Although pair-wise joining is not a severe limitation for the simple requests that dominate OLTP databases, such join techniques cannot perform adequately in a data warehouse environment. They generate intermediate results on the way to a full result, and these intermediate results can be large and very costly to create. While various "patches" have been widely applied to alleviate this problem, mitigation does not equal a full solution.

This is just one example of the data warehousing inadequacies of relational database systems that have grown out of a transaction-oriented environment. The point is, given the elevated performance requirements that intranet deliv-

	OLTP	DATA WAREHOUSE
Purpose:	Automate day-to-day operation	Information retrieval and analysis
Structure:	RDBMS	RDBMS
Data Model:	Normalized	Dimensional
Access:	SQL	SQL plus business analysis extensions
Type of Data:	Data that runs the business	Information to analyze the business
Condition of Data:	Changing, incomplete	Historical, descriptive

Figure 8.1 Comparison: RDBMSs optimized for OLTP and data warehousing.

ery will engender, a data warehousing relational database system must be optimized from its very core for data warehousing. For starters, this optimization must encompass

- Load processing and high-performance updating
- Heightened query performance
- Advanced query functionality

Load Processing

Virtually all of the data stored in a data warehouse originates in external systems. Examples include retail point-of-sale data collected from store systems; telephone call detail records from switching centers; purchased data such as government census records and corporate transaction data from inventory, manufacturing, financial, and other systems. Getting this data into the data warehouse and fully preparing it for use is the key update in a data warehouse system.

Many steps are required to transform raw external source data into information ready for end-user access and business decision making:

1. Data must be read directly from a variety of feeds including disk files, network feeds, mainframe channel connections, and magnetic tapes.

2. Data must be converted to the database internal format from a variety of external representations, including fixed- and variable-length records, character and binary formats, IBM EBCDIC data, packed decimal, zoned decimal, and so on.

3. Data must be filtered to reject invalid values, duplicate keys, or otherwise erroneous records.

4. Records must be reorganized from external flat-file representations to match the relational schema of the data warehouse.

5. Records must be checked against the existing database to ensure table-level and global consistency and to maintain complete referential integrity.

6. Records must be written to physical storage, observing configuration requirements for data segmentation, physical device placement, inter-disk balancing, and so on.

7. Records must be fully and richly indexed (including building multiple indexes on new data in parallel).
8. System metadata must be updated.

A data warehouse update is not complete until all of these steps have been accomplished successfully. This requires a loading and data preparation tool that conducts all of these activities as a unified process and provides the necessary administrative controls and recovery facilities.

As with OLTP transactions, data warehouse updates require methods for recovery and restart in the event of an error or a system failure. Traditional OLTP recovery approaches fail to meet this requirement because they depend on transaction logs and rollback mechanisms, which are unable to accommodate the record counts and data volumes involved in typical data warehouse updates. Specialized recovery and restart techniques are required in the database to support data warehouse updates.

Load Performance

The ability to perform many of these load processing tasks in parallel is extremely important. As mentioned in earlier chapters, data warehouse updates are frequently very large (incorporating tens of gigabytes and hundreds of millions of rows) and generally must be accomplished within narrow batch windows. For example, point-of-sale detail records are often captured daily and must be loaded and prepared for use in the space of a few overnight hours. New applications and added levels of detail increase the size and frequency of updates, but do not add more hours to the day in which to accomplish them. The 24-hour reach of company intranets will only serve to exacerbate the load window problem.

For this reason, extremely fast update performance is critical to data warehouse success and growth. Most OLTP applications update or add data as transactions occur. As a result, OLTP vendors have never needed to focus on bulk data loading because high-performance loading never emerges as a requirement. In contrast, the "loader" subsystem of a data warehouse relational database system must be able to perform complete data loading and preparation, including format conversion, integrity enforcement, and indexing, and it must accomplish all of these steps at rates measured in hundreds of millions of rows and gigabytes per hour. To minimize elapsed time and fit short batch windows, the relational database system loader must effectively use all system resources, including being able to harness and apply the entire processing power of a large parallel processor system.

In the event of a failure, recovery and restart processes must be equally fast. Recovery and restart must be accomplished within minutes so that the full update can complete within a narrow batch window.

Data Quality Management

At this point, it is important to also consider data integrity, which begins at load time. Of course, the insights gained from a data warehouse can only be as good as the quality of the information stored in the warehouse; unfortunately, source data feeds are often "dirty" and unpredictable. The data warehouse relational database system must provide mechanisms to clean and filter input data, as well as mechanisms to continuously guarantee overall data quality.

In the context of data warehouse applications, local consistency requires that each data item be valid and meaningful; and global consistency requires that various data items across the warehouse be self-consistent. For example, it would be a local consistency error if Saskatchewan were to appear in a table containing names of U.S. states, or if a negative value were to appear in a table tracking current inventory. It might be a global consistency error if sales data from western region stores were missing for the July 25 period from the point-of-sale transaction detail table. The database server must enforce local consistency and detect discrepancies from overall global consistency.

Data warehouse schemas almost always contain multiple tables that reference each other and are brought together and matched using SQL join operations to answer queries. For example, a column containing a customer ID number in a transaction detail table might reference a matching customer ID number column in a customer information table. Accurate query results depend on all intertable references being valid at all times, a property called *referential integrity*. The database server must enforce referential integrity at all times, and must not allow dirty data or incorrect updates to breach total referential integrity. Referential integrity must be checked and enforced during load updates, SQL DELETE operations, and any other operation that changes data in the warehouse.

Load Comparisons

To illustrate the positive effects of parallel load processing (including referential integrity assurance), the load performance chart in Figure 8.2 summarizes the load process times for a loader optimized for data warehousing versus the best load performance of a test group of OLTP relational database systems. The optimized relational database system in this example (the Red Brick Warehouse) employs:

- Parallel index building, referential integrity checking, and load processing.
- Index creation as new data is loaded (OLTP databases build indexes as a separate step after all the data has been loaded).
- Optional auto row generation for incoming data that fails referential integrity checks (to reduce the time for reconciling bad data).
- Optimized sorting of data and indexes in memory prior to writing to disk (to reduce the number of disk writes and reads to populate the warehouse).
- Optimized table-locking mechanism.
- Multiple index creation as new data is loaded (build multiple index-

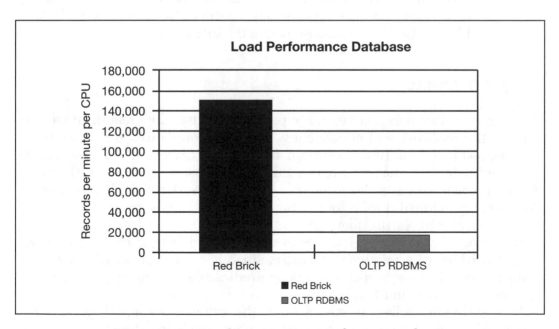

Figure 8.2 Load comparison performance chart.

es on new data in parallel; this process requires multiple passes with OLTP relational database systems).

- Code paths tuned for batch data loading (OLTP relational databases use code paths from basic Insert, Update, and Delete commands).

Overall, the parallel load process of the relational database that was optimized for data warehousing sustained a rate of more than 150,000 records per minute per CPU. Optimal load performance from the group of OLTP relational database systems used in this evaluation was 17,000 records per minute per CPU. Given the dual CPU hardware configuration, the complete load process time for a 1-gigabyte, 15-million-record database using a data warehouse-optimized relational database was less than one hour and greater than seven hours for the OLTP relational database systems.

As an aside, in an effort to improve the OLTP load performance, logging was disabled during the load process. The OLTP database performance did indeed improve, but disabling the logging feature during the load process imposed severe consequences on the integrity and quality of the data populating the warehouse. When the query results were evaluated, it was determined that the data was corrupt and yielded inaccurate result sets. Records were lost during the load process, and because logging was disabled, there was no audit trail maintained by the OLTP database to restore the lost records.

Query Performance

From an end-user perspective, query performance has the greatest impact regarding the usability and effectiveness of a data warehouse. Response times must be fast (near real time) to sustain an iterative "discovery" process. As analysts or business managers progress through the discovery process, they drill down on specific qualitative aspects of the business. A typical business question might be, How did sales for product X perform versus product Y this year versus last year in North America?

This type of complex query puts extraordinary demands on the optimization algorithms of a relational database, since it must process joins between many tables. The design goal is to ensure predictable, fast query processing for queries that require multitable joins.

As mentioned earlier in this chapter, the schema methodology that has gained widespread acceptance for data warehousing is the star schema, which provides a query-centric view of the data. The basic premise of star schemas is that information can be classified into two groups: facts and dimensions. Facts are the core data element being analyzed; dimensions are attributes about the facts. Fact: A purchase has been made. Dimensions: The item purchased and the date of the purchase. Most, if not all analysis is based on these dimensions, hence the term *dimensional analysis.*

Given this two-way classification of information, Figure 8.3 shows what a star schema for a purchase order database would look like. Asking a business question against this schema is relatively straightforward because we are looking up specific facts (PURCHASES) through a set of dimensions (SHIP_FROM, SHIP_TO, ITEM). It's also significant that, in the typical star schema, the fact table is much larger than any of its dimension tables.

Even though star schemas are the accepted method for data warehousing, a relational database system that has its roots in OLTP is likely to run into diffi-

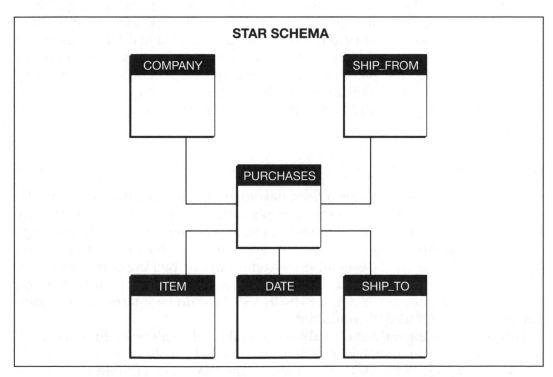

Figure 8.3   Sample star schema purchase order database.

culties with queries that involve more than two tables because traditional OLTP databases can join only two tables at a time. Thus, queries that involve more than two tables are artificially broken into a series of pair-wise joins that create intermediate results.

Not surprisingly, the order in which the joins are performed dramatically affects query performance. As an extreme example, if the join of ITEM to PURCHASES results in the selection of only a single record, subsequent joins would be joining only this one record. However, if PURCHASES is joined to COMPANY first, an intermediate result might be generated that contains every single row in PURCHASES. Because selecting the order of the pair-wise joins can have such a dramatic performance impact, traditional OLTP relational database systems waste a great deal of effort on determining the best order in which to execute those joins. After all, the number of different combinations to be evaluated grows exponentially with the number of tables being joined. While a six-table query has 720 possible combinations, a seven-table query has 5,040, and a 10-table query presents 3,628,800, and so on. In addition, the relational database system may have many different join algorithms with which the tables can be joined, and it may need to evaluate each of these algorithms for each combination. Finally, with all traditional OLTP relational database systems, it is important to remember that the task of deciding in which order to do the pair-wise joins must be completed before the query even begins to execute. In other words, all the time the database system spends evaluating pair-wise join combinations is time *not* spent running the query.

Star Schema Optimizations

A number of workarounds have been developed to alleviate this problem. Because the number of pair-wise join combinations is often too large to fully evaluate, traditional OLTP relational database systems pick an "interesting" subset for evaluation. How these subsets are selected differs from one database system to the next, but in general the system starts by picking combinations of tables that are directly related. Using the example star schema, this criterion would say that joining ITEM and PURCHASES would be interesting, but joining ITEM and COMPANY would not.

However, looking only at directly related tables doesn't work for data warehouses because, in a typical star schema, the only table directly related to most other tables is the fact table. This means that the fact table is a natural candidate for the first pair-wise join. Unfortunately, the fact table is typically the largest table in the query, so this strategy invariably leads to selecting a pair-wise join order that generates a very large intermediate result set. Generating large intermediate result sets severely affect query performance.

A common optimization that provides some relief for the star schema join problem is to try and look at more combinations of pair-wise join orderings. The basic idea is to try to get around the pair-wise join strategy of selecting only related tables. To understand how this works, it is necessary to first understand what it means to join unrelated tables. When two tables are joined and no columns "link" the tables, every combination of the two tables' rows are produced. In relational database-speak, this is called a *Cartesian product.* For example, if the ITEM table had two rows (paper, tape) and the COMPANY table had three rows (Sears, KMart, Wal-Mart) the Cartesian product would contain six rows: paper+Sears, tape+Sears, paper+Kmart, tape+Kmart, paper+Wal-Mart, and tape+Wal-Mart. Normally, the relational database logic to look only at related tables would never consider Cartesian products as reasonable pair-wise join candidates, but for star schemas, there are times when considering these Cartesian products improves query performance. Nevertheless, this is not a universal fix since it still requires pair-wise joins. It is also feasible only if the Cartesian product of dimension rows selected is much smaller than the number of rows in the fact table—otherwise the intermediate result size would be colossal.

Parallelism has also been suggested as an answer to optimizing star schema performance. While the ability to take advantage of parallel processing is an important component of a feasible data warehousing relational database management system, it alone is not sufficient to overcome the limitations of relational databases designed for OLTP. Parallelism enables users to either reduce execution time of a single query (speed-up) or handle additional work without degrading performance (scale-up). In either case, parallelism succeeds by applying more computing resources (processors and/or disks). Ideally, a multi-table query that would normally execute in 500 seconds without parallelism would execute in 50 seconds when spread out over 10 processors. But it doesn't always work that way. In an SMP (symmetric multiprocessing) system, for example, additional processors add overhead, and thus do not bring a full processor's worth of performance to the system. In some cases, you may even experience slowdown on certain queries—analogous to too many workers (processors) getting into each other's way. Similarly, a query may not be able to be broken down into an arbitrary number of pieces, leading to underutilization of processing resources, which corresponds to having too many workers for the work at hand.

The point is, parallelism is best employed when, and only when, the task at hand benefits from parallelism. For example, parallel processing can be assigned only to large queries of a certain complexity, while small queries can run without it—enabling the most efficient exploitation of system resources.

Specialized Joins and Indexes

A relational database management system that is truly optimized for data warehousing performance must employ specialized multitable join technologies and indexing. Indexes are, of course, the internal structures used to speed data location. When indexes are defined on selected columns of a table and the query constrains on those columns, the relational database system can use the index to very quickly identify the rows of interest.

A database designed for decision support should have several indexes to speed as many queries as possible. B-tree indexes are common for most relational database systems and are critical for locating information quickly. Red Brick Warehouse, for example, employs B-tree indexing as a default. However, for accelerated query performance, it is necessary to provide further choices. In the case of Red Brick Warehouse, the alternatives include a STARindex that, in conjunction with proprietary STARjoin technology, takes advantage of the full potential of star schemas without degrading performance. In a similar vein, Sybase offers the Interactive Query Accelerator (IQ Accelerator) for advanced indexing capabilities; and a number of other vendors, including Oracle and Informix, appear to be focusing on parallel processing approaches to improve the performance of SQL queries. Parallel processing architecture is covered in detail in Chapter 9.

Red Brick and Sybase also use bitmapped indexing to improve performance for queries that require very fast selection of records from a large, wide table such as a customer table containing millions of records and hundreds of attributes. Red Brick and Sybase both incorporate the proprietary bitmapped indexes as fully integrated features of the core relational database engine. In Red Brick's case, to handle the highly skewed data set frequently encountered in customer-centric applications such as database marketing, the Target index uses a continually adaptive indexing technology to automatically apply the most efficient subindexing scheme for each value in a column: uncompressed bitmapping for small domains like gender, compressed bitmap for medium domains like area codes, row-ID list for large domains like zip codes, and B-tree for unique identifiers like social security numbers.

STARindexing and STARjoin Technology

To close the discussion of star schema optimization, it is important to look at an indexing methodology like STARindexing in more detail. In Red Brick's product, STARindexes are created on one or more foreign key columns of a fact table. Unlike traditional indexes that contain information to translate a column value to a list of rows with that value, a STARindex contains highly compressed information that relates the dimensions of a fact table to the rows that contain those dimensions. This makes the STARindexes extremely space-efficient and facilitates building and maintaining them. The STARjoin algorithm can then use the STARindex to efficiently identify all the rows required for a particular join.

To fully understand the capability of Red Brick's STARjoin technology, consider again the traditional OLTP relational database approach of generating a full Cartesian product of dimension tables, which then can be joined to the fact table. This approach doesn't work well for even moderately sized dimension tables because of the size of the Cartesian product. However, STARjoin technology offers the advantage of efficiently joining the dimension tables to the fact table without the penalty of generating the full Cartesian product, because the STARindex allows the STARjoin to quickly identify which regions of the Cartesian product space contain rows of interest (in much the same way that a B-tree index can quickly identify which rows contain column values of interest). Thus, the STARjoin algorithm can generate a Cartesian product in regions where there are rows of interest, and bypass generating Cartesian products over regions where there are no rows. As a simple example, if the COMPANY dimension table contains 100 rows, a simple Cartesian product would generate rows for each of the 100 companies. If, however, the fact table contains only data for two of these companies for a particular set of other dimension values, you would be unnecessarily generating 98 combinations. The STARjoin would know, by virtue of the STARindex, that only two companies were involved, and would only generate Cartesian products for those two companies.

The net result is the ability to perform the multitable joins typical of data warehousing applications 10 to 20 times faster than traditional pair-wise join techniques. In addition, a STARjoin is inherently parallelizable. In parallelizing a STARjoin, each of the processes involved is given its own piece of the *join space* to work on, and the join space can be decomposed in an arbitrary number of pieces. Because each process works on its own piece, there is no need for coordination among the processes. The result is any number of parallel work assignments, each with no need to coordinate—a very effective answer for scale-up.

Finally, this technology is well suited for more complex schemas, such as the multifact table star schemas illustrated in Figure 8.4. In schemas with multiple fact tables, these tables typically have one or more common dimensions. Often the queries processed against schemas like this relate not only the fact tables to their associated dimensions but also the fact tables to each other. Because the tables typically have one or more dimensions in common, it is possible to join multiple fact tables by selectively accessing the STARindexes of the tables being joined. The result, as illustrated in Figure 8.5, is a complex join being processed at speeds simply not possible with traditional OLTP databases. In fact, these complex schemas are even poorer fits for the traditional OLTP relational database systems because they have effectively doubled all the problems of the single fact table schema.

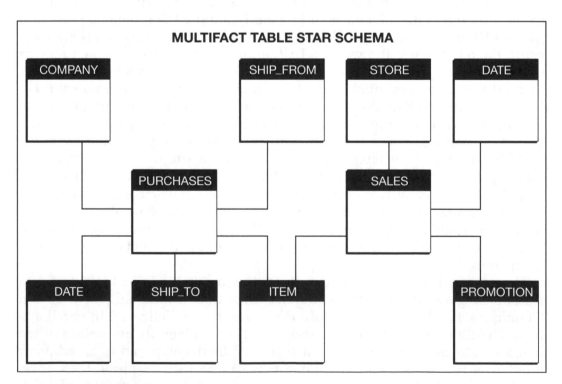

Figure 8.4 Multifact table star schema database.

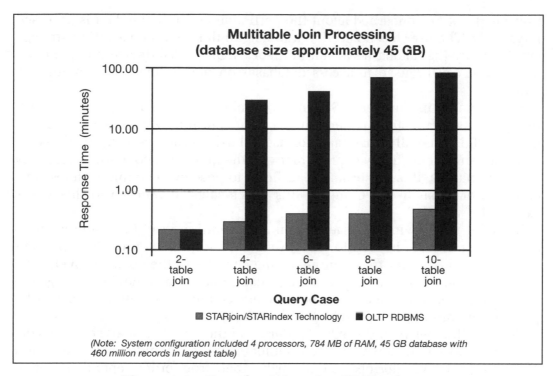

Figure 8.5 Complex join using STARindexes.

Advanced Query Functionality

Data warehouse performance is not only about faster processing of more complex queries for more users—though intranets will surely compound this issue. It is also about getting the exact information that business decision makers need, without encumbering them with details about how the data is stored. The large number of new users, many of them casual users, who are likely to use an intranet to access data warehouse information want easy ways to get answers to more powerful business-oriented questions.

SQL, which has been widely used in mainframe and minicomputer systems for many years, is now being implemented in client/server networks and increasingly over intranets, enabling PCs to access the resources of corporate data warehouses. SQL has a number of distinct advantages: It can be used with many database management packages, and it is *data independent,* meaning a user need not be concerned about the particulars of how the data is accessed physically. The user has no need to understand the internal execution strategy employed by the database system. In theory, SQL is also device independent, meaning it can be used to access databases on mainframes, minicomputers, and PCs.

But, as noted in Chapter 3, SQL has a number of disadvantages as well. Although it is an industry-standard language for computerized database management, SQL is generally unsuitable for use in business analysis applications because it cannot effectively express many of the questions commonly asked by decision makers. It is, for example, difficult to pose even simple business-oriented requests such as, "Compare this year's sales in Chicago to this year's sales in New York."

Consider the moving average, a common operation used in business analysis. Moving average is used to smooth variability in the source data, particularly when looking for trends or analyzing changes in the business over time. Unlike computation of a simple average, computation of a moving average depends on the ordering of the data being averaged and is, therefore, an order-dependent operation prohibited by standard SQL.

This conflict between the SQL standard and the business analyst's needs occurs repeatedly in data warehousing. Other examples include the computation of rankings, n-tile orderings, and so forth. Apart from order-dependent operations, standard SQL also does not include critical statistical operations such as variance and standard deviation.

These deficiencies in SQL push the problem of advanced analysis onto the client workstation, where in order to produce the desired answer, the entire database result set needs to be reprocessed using a spreadsheet, a statistical tool, or a custom program. This two-step process drastically slows effective query performance, requires the use of several dissimilar tools, and significantly increases network capacity requirements because large volumes of raw data are sent to the client workstation for reprocessing. This is not a situation that will adapt well to an intranet distribution strategy with its thin-client architecture.

Opening SQL for Business Analysis

The limitations of SQL have argued effectively for the development of a set of business analysis extensions for SQL, extensions specifically designed to simplify the creation of complex business queries and to answer them easily, quickly, and with lower application development costs. Again, it is a matter of optimizing relational database systems for data warehousing and decision support applications. For the vast majority of intranet users, such optimization will be mandatory in order to maximize the value of the data warehouse.

Red Brick's proprietary SQL extensions—RISQL (see the Sidebar "RISQL Extensions and Their Business Applications")—augments SQL with a variety of powerful operations or extensions appropriate to data analysis and decision-support applications, and offers one answer to the SQL limitations. Other vendors are likely to follow Red Brick's lead and offer SQL extensions as part of their future releases. In the meantime, however, both Oracle and Sybase offer OLAP products that perform analysis on data caches extracted from the relational database. These OLAP tools—Oracle Express Analyzer and Informix Metacube Explorer—perform the types of analysis that cannot be effectively supported by SQL. Clearly, there is a need for enhanced data analysis that is supported by the database management system and for multistep analysis that requires an external analytic data cache. The Red Brick RISQL extensions, which provide flexibility in balancing the processing load between the database and the OLAP applications, include:

- Business analysis functions that perform sequential calculations
- Numeric and string functions to manipulate character strings and numerical values
- Macro-building capabilities that simplify the use of repetitive SQL and calculations

By using RISQL to expand the SQL vocabulary used to query databases, the data warehouse system makes it easier to frame questions about vital business functions involving such attributes as rankings, moving averages, comparisons, market share, this year versus last year, and so on. And, because these actions can be performed on the server rather than the client, there is less data moving across the network, and useful business answers can be derived more quickly.

Problem-Solving Using RISQL

To repeat, it is important to remember that every data warehouse can be expected to evolve over time as user needs become more complex. Often, this evolution takes place in four distinct steps, relating to the increasingly sophis-

RISQL Extensions and Their Business Applications

Decode: Replaces or translates codes often used for internal purposes into more commonly understood values. Example: "List sales by month for each geographic region, and show the region name instead of its code number."

Cume: Computes a running or cumulative total of a column's value. Example: "Show the monthly sales for each product, along with the monthly year-to-date figures."

MovingAvg(n): Computes the moving average of a column using the current row and the preceding n − 1 rows. Example: "Produce a six-month moving average of product sales for the last two years."

MovingSum(s): Computes the moving sum of a column using the current row and the preceding n − 1 rows. Example: "List monthly sales with a rolling 12-month prior sales figure for each month."

Rank. . .When: Assigns sequential numeric value to the sorting of a column's value. Use of the WHEN clause limits the result set to the top n or bottom n rows. Example: "List the top 50 customers, based on last year's sales; sort the list by customer name."

RatioTo Report: Computes the percentage of a column's value in each row to the total of that column for all rows. Example: "Show sales by product type along with the percentage of total sales."

Tertile: Performs a three-tiered ranking by assigning the values High, Medium, and Low to each row of a result set, based on a column's value. Example: "Group products into three bands, based on revenue generated for the last year."

Create Macro: Allows commonly used queries or subqueries representing standard business calculations to be parameterized and written once to be shared by many users. Sharing these macros among users ensures greater accuracy and consistency with corporate policies. And when a rule changes, it only needs to be changed at one place. Example: "List annual sales for this year and compare this to each of the last five years."

ticated types of questions that are asked and the escalating business value of the answers that are sought:

1. What is happening?
2. Why is it happening?
3. What if I do something different?
4. How do I achieve the best possible results?

RISQL extensions to SQL allow analysts to easily gain insights into "what" is happening (e.g., How many additional lines did we sell? How does this track with last year's sales? or What were the total incremental revenues from the promotion?).

The next step in the evolutionary process is often to begin asking: Who did I sell these lines to? What kind of customers are buying this product/service? or What was the success rate of this promotion across various demographic groups? Compared to the "what" type of questions, considerably more data needs to be examined in this step, but the answers are much more valuable for it. Similarly, what-if scenarios require still more data to derive answers to such questions as: What if I tweaked the promotion by bundling call forwarding with the second line? or What if I added a $10-off certificate to my promotion?

The ultimate step—How do I achieve the best results?—requires all the preceding data, and depends on the ability to spot trends and patterns in the data. The problem is, as the amount and complexity of data in the warehouse reaches unprecedented proportions, it becomes more difficult for business analysts to identify such trends and relationships using simple query and reporting tools. At this stage, data mining holds the key.

Data-mining software attempts to discover the patterns, trends, and relationships among data—even nonobvious and unexpected patterns. This new knowledge, in turn, can be used for more effective management of the business. The beauty of data mining is that its algorithms are not predisposed to look for results in any particular spot. The more data the algorithms can "attack"—that is, the more variables they can address—the more valuable the results. Using models based on these results, users can then predict the effect of decisions on their customers, businesses, and markets. Decision makers can visualize, for example, the combined effects that sales or promotional channels, product/service mix, geography, demography, and seasonality have on sales, fraud, profit margins, or customer retention.

Data Warehousing/Data-Mining Synergy

How do data warehousing and data mining interrelate? The data warehouse, not surprisingly, is the best place to find data to mine. The data in a warehouse is complete, clean, and integrated. While it is useful to have a lot of data to mine, it is obvious that not all data is appropriate for mining. Users will want to select which data elements to mine, or decide where to look for the relationships. In seeking to identify fraudulent claims (e.g., insurance, health care, product warranty) for example, it is probably useful to have lots of information about the claimant, the situation, the policy, the award, and any relevant history, whereas it is probably not useful to consider the account number, social security number, or phone number of the claimant, the claims processor, or the sales rep who sold the product or policy. Because data that is not useful for mining is interspersed with data that is, a query engine is needed to sort through all the available data and select what is appropriate to mine. A data warehouse engine designed for fast query processing is a highly useful tool for identifying the subset of data required.

In addition, a data warehouse is required for post-mining processing. The result of a data-mining exercise ideally is a new pattern or trend that was not previously noticed by analysts using standard query and reporting tools. This new "discovery" is only the starting point for new query-based analysis. Armed with those same query tools, the data in the warehouse, and a new understanding of the relationships in the data, an analyst can investigate entirely new scenarios or follow a brand-new thought process. For example, if data-mining software revealed a relationship between customers who purchased insurance policies and their length of employment, it might spawn a whole series of queries around employment profiles of existing customers versus prospects. Another example might be the telecommunications company that finds a relationship between customers' likelihood to "churn" (switch carriers) and an increased number of service calls in the previous six months. At the very least, the analyst would want to generate a list of existing customers who have had increased service calls recently (a simple warehouse query) in order to attempt to prevent them from switching. Finally, as mentioned earlier, data mining may result in a new discovery such as a segment of the prospect population that is highly likely to purchase a specific product. In this case, the data warehouse would be required for the query to select prospects based on various attributes for a targeted mailing.

Data Mining in the Relational Engine

Today, analysts performing data-mining operations are forced to pull subsets or samples of data from the warehouse and apply data-mining algorithms at the client level. This has several negative effects on performance, both from a systems and a human standpoint. For one thing, working with subsets can be self-limiting and fly in the face of data-mining's capacity to spot patterns and trends throughout large data sets—sets that are too large for client machines to process. Second, this scenario requires much shuttling of data across the network between the data warehouse server and the client. And, perhaps most important, it breaks down the iterative querying process and stunts user creativity. As the intranet delivery model develops, all these issues will be thrown into even higher relief.

A preferable method, and one that is now emerging, is to perform data mining directly on the data already in the data warehouse. A fully integrated data-mining/data warehousing approach uses the best features of different data-mining technologies—including neural networks, decision trees, and statistics—to provide data mining against all the data in a data warehouse. These data-mining capabilities can be incorporated directly into the relational database system.

Data mining in the relational engine is accomplished by creating models that appear as tables in the database. These models can be accessed and manipulated via SQL just like ordinary tables. However, when data is inserted into the model (exactly like inserting into a table with an INSERT INTO statement), data-mining calculations are performed, which in turn create other tables containing the results of the calculations. These other tables can then be viewed to understand the results and to perform prediction on other data sets.

This integrated approach makes sense for many reasons. First, obtaining clean, integrated data to mine is a primary challenge. Traditional mining tools would typically transfer the data, possibly tens or hundreds of gigabytes, across a network in some flat-file format for loading into a data-mining tool. This proprietary tool would then be used exclusively for mining the data set that had been obtained. Obtaining more or different data would require repeating the process. Any type of data administration or security would be left to the manual processes of the handful of users performing the data mining.

In an integrated approach, illustrated in Figure 8.6, the data remains in the warehouse in relational tables and the data-mining software is brought to the data, rather than vice versa. This avoids overloading precious network band-

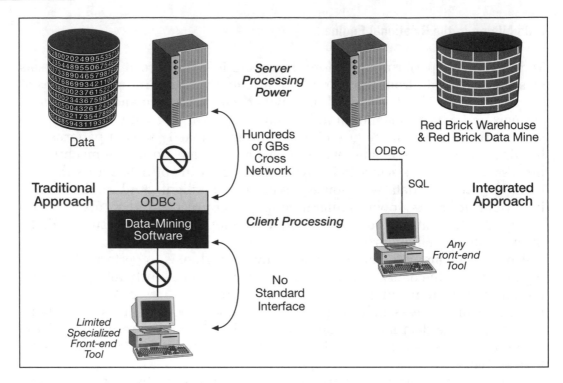

Figure 8.6   Integrated approach to data warehousing and data-mining applications.

width, eliminates the need to administer yet another large data store, and mitigates the "fat" client syndrome. Logging, locking, security, and user administration are all issues that must be dealt with separately if data mining is attempted on a separate data set. Instead, an integrated approach takes advantage of all the features of the data warehouse, including role-based security, database administration, and user statistics gathering.

Perhaps a more important benefit of integrated data mining occurs at the user interface. Typical data-mining tools require some proprietary front-end interface to manipulate the data and create models. Special expertise in using the tool is typically required for maximum benefit. In contrast, integrated functionality, as part of the database engine, is accessible via SQL. Any user familiar with database access via SQL can use the data-mining functionality. By the same token, any front-end tool that generates SQL (there are hundreds) can access data-mining functionality.

Additionally, as pointed out, the data-mining process is seldom a single operation, but is an iterative process requiring the refinement of models by adding and deleting data, grouping data differently, and so on. By integrating data mining with the data warehouse and using SQL, a fully integrated approach facilitates this iterative process without requiring any network transfers of flat files and without switching back and forth between separate desktop tools as in a nonintegrated approach. Data never needs to leave the warehouse, and both functions are performed as one, using a single desktop SQL tool. The Sidebar, "Integrating a New Business Process," provides an example of how data mining can be implemented as part of a business process.

Tailor-Made for Intranets: Data Mining for the Masses

Integrated data mining (i.e., performing data-mining functions within the database itself) is a model that is tailor-made for an intranet distribution strategy. By leaving both the data and the data-mining models in the data warehouse, this approach also facilitates sharing the data-mining models and the results of data-mining studies across all warehouse users. Any user with access to the warehouse (and appropriate security permissions) also has access to the data-mining models and results, and can use any SQL tool of choice for access.

Finally, performance and scalability are necessary for data mining. These attributes should be at the foundation of any relational database system that is optimized for data warehousing. Because only a handful of users on a dedicated system ever touch traditional nonintegrated data-mining tools, scalability (of data and users) and performance (of software processing) are not the focus of data-mining software development efforts. But data warehousing relational databases, on the other hand, absolutely must be designed to support thousands of users and massive amounts of data.

Conclusion

This brings us full circle. There are already enormous performance demands on data warehousing relational database systems. Traditional OLTP-biased database systems are already severely strained (and constrained) in a data warehousing environment. An intranet delivery strategy will bring the benefits of data warehousing-based decision support to a much wider audience.

Integrating a New Business Process

Data mining represents a new and potent business process. To illustrate the new capabilities and power that integrated data mining brings to decision-support applications it is probably easiest to use a simple example. Consider the marketing analyst tasked with generating mailing lists for various regional direct mail promotions. The goal is to maximize the response rate for each promotion. By using data collected on the customers who respond to the promotions over time, the analyst can build a model that successfully predicts response rates against various lists. This model can be built either with a graphical front-end tool designed to build and refine models using samples of data from the warehouse (such as Red Brick Data Mine Builder) or by accessing an integrated data mine option directly on the warehouse server using SQL. The latter can be accomplished with any industry-standard SQL generating tool such as Brio Query or Business Objects.

A model-building SQL statement would look like:

```
CREATE MODEL promo_list
     income character input,age integer input...
     ...respond character output)
```

Those readers familiar with SQL will note the similarity of the CREATE MODEL statement to the standard CREATE TABLE. This is intentional because the newly created model is now just like a table or a view and is available for subsequent SQL processing. The SQL statement creates a model that will relate various *input* such as income (high, mid, or low) and age to a desired *output,* such as response rate (respond = yes or no). All possible inputs are not shown in the example, but there is no practical limit on the number or type of inputs that could be considered. A real application would typically include several dozen to more than a hundred such attributes. With this many different factors influencing response rates it's clear why data-mining technology is needed.

To give the model some data to process in order to find relationships among the various inputs and possible outputs, the analyst simply inserts data into the model using a standard SQL statement:

```
INSERT INTO promo_list SELECT income,
     age, respond
FROM customer_list,
WHERE promo = "Q3_Midwest"
```

This process automatically creates additional views of the model table, which are used for understanding the relationships and predicting future outcomes (promo_list_UNDERSTAND and promo_list_PREDICT tables). Once this model is built, it represents the best information the analyst has about the profile of people who respond to his or her direct mail promotions. To view the correlation information generated by the data mining study, the analyst simply selects from the table:

```
SELECT * FROM promo_list_UNDERSTAND
WHERE input_column_name = 'income' and
      Input_column_value = 'high' and
      output_column_name = 'respond'
      and output_column_value = 'yes'
ORDER BY importance, conjunctionid
```

To generate a mailing list for a new regional promotion in Minneapolis, the analyst could again use SQL to access the PREDICT table for just the records where a positive response is predicted:

```
SELECT name FROM customer_list,
      promo_list_PREDICT
WHERE city = "Minneapolis" AND respond = "yes"
```

Notice that the model and its associated views, once created, are treated as tables in the database. They can be viewed and joined as appropriate to deliver the most benefit from the data-mining process. Also, the model tables are available to anyone with access to the warehouse and the ability to generate SQL, not just the analyst who created it. Other users may choose to use this model as a template, but modify it slightly for their custom use. This is easily accomplished:

```
CREATE MODEL new_promo LIKE
      promo_list (income integer input, ...)
```

Finally, it is worthwhile to note that as results from these new campaigns are made available and entered into the data warehouse, the data-mining model can be updated and further refined, improving accuracy for future predictions. This iterative process of continuous improvement is greatly simplified through the integrated data-mining and data warehousing approach.

This is no time for constraints! The full measure of data warehousing performance and knowledge discovery functionality is required in this environment for users to maintain confidence in their decision-support applications.

This emphasis on performance begins with continually getting data that can be trusted into the data warehouse as expeditiously as possible. It extends to finding answers as quickly as possible, even as the pool of concurrent users expands and the volume of the data balloons—and, of course, as the queries that the users launch against all this data increase in complexity (and rapidity).

Finally, it is important to continue to push the limits of available technology in order to draw more useful business intelligence from raw data assets. In other words, keep pace with the business needs of users with more advanced and increasingly fast and easy-to-employ query functionality. The intranet model assumes server-centric functionality, and tomorrow's data warehousing relational database management systems must act as robust delivery platforms. Advanced query functionality must be built into the database system where appropriate, as in the case of business extensions to SQL (RISQL) and data mining.

CHAPTER NINE

Using Parallel Processing for Scalability

As the intranet data warehouse grows, both in database size and user load, decisions regarding sever hardware become critical to meeting performance requirements. Many database vendors are relying on parallel processing hardware to improve the performance of SQL queries. This chapter provides some background on the options for parallel processing. An important part of the planning for an intranet data warehouse is ensuring that the architecture is scalable. After ease of use, users focus on the response time between requesting information and viewing a report.

Scalability, which was introduced earlier as one of the primary design goals of an intranet data warehouse, begins with the selection of servers assigned to the tasks of database management and OLAP processing. (Note that, here, scalability refers to intranet scalability—the network—and data warehouse scalability—the database and OLAP analysis requirements). When a network system architecture does not scale as the data warehouse and/or the user load grows, the usual result is poor system response to users' requests. Most users quickly become frustrated when the processing of a request takes too long or is unpredictable. While users of OLTP applications expect almost instant response to their requests, acceptable response from an OLAP application is generally more subjective. Generally, users consider a delay of 10 to 15 seconds a reasonable response for a report request, but they are not likely to be as tolerant of that delay when waiting for password authorization. Thus, the key to scalability for an intranet data warehouse is not subsecond response to any request, but rather predictable response as user loads vary. Internet users have firsthand experience with a system in which performance varies by day and time of day. In designing a network computing architecture, the goal is to provide consistent performance despite large user loads.

Scalability is not a simple concept. Each aspect of computing—the hardware, software, middleware, and applications—scale in different fashions, often in ways that are somewhat dependent on the attributes of the overall computing environment. An intranet data warehouse, for example, must address scalability on three dimensions:

- Capacity, to support the growing data warehouse.
- Concurrency, to support an ever-changing user load.
- Complexity, to support increasingly sophisticated OLAP applications.

Adding to the confusion surrounding scalability are the many and varying standards of what, exactly, qualifies as a scalable solution. Many vendors, for example, refer to their solutions as scalable if they can accommodate a range of workloads or database sizes—regardless of their efficiency in actually handling those workloads. Scalability also extends to systems administration, addressing such factors as reliability, recoverability, and consistency of response time. This chapter discusses some of the facets of scalability, exploring methods for determining what constitutes scalability and for achieving scalable solutions for particular applications.

An intranet places more emphasis on scalability than virtually any other computing environment because it is intended to provide as many users as possible with access to as many diverse applications and databases as possible. But the diversity of intranet applications and the wide range of users' technical skills compound the problem of intranet scalability significantly because it is generally easier to scale simple environments and applications than it is to scale diverse ones. This is a key difference between client/server data warehouse applications that tend to serve a relatively small homogenous user community and those designed for intranet deployment. The issue is that workloads in a diverse environment often exhibit what's called *negative affinity effects*. In other words, some workloads interfere with the performance of others; this has a very definite affect on scalability. So, while a particular application may be scalable in an isolated environment, it may not exhibit significant scalability in a more complex environment with many and varied applications. In many ways, the intranet data warehouse represents a worse-case scenario in that the workloads involve SQL queries that retrieve large data sets, which may then be subjected to a multistep analysis process. The following pages address each aspect of scalability, highlighting those that are likely to suffer most from negative affinity.

The Building Blocks of Scalability

In general, scalability means that the engines of workload processing (i.e., the microprocessors assigned to perform the database query, analytic processing, and/or data formatting) can grow in capability. Such growth can be achieved by employing more engines; employing faster or more capable engines; employing hierarchies of engines; applying groups of engines to a single problem to leverage the teamwork effect. This generalization is true whether the goal is to improve query performance or executing OLAP functions.

The easiest way to achieve scalability is to use a faster version of whatever needs to be scaled. For computers, this may mean using a 200-MHz microprocessor unit (MPU) in place of a 100-MHz unit to double the amount of work that is processed. In reality, of course, this may not be the case because computer scaling has many more relevant factors than just MPU speed, but this gross simplification illustrates the point. For pure computing capability, this is the easiest form of scalability that can take place. Unfortunately, there are relatively low limits to the scalability that can be achieved by making the MPU run faster, typically a factor of considerably less than 10 times.

Microprocessors are actually an excellent example of scalability; their performance is easily understandable. Some other components are not as scalable as they may seem. Disk drives, for example, exhibit scalable storage capacities but do not generally provide increased access performance as capacity increases. Drives of a given form factor (e.g., 3.5 inches) may have capacities that vary by a factor of four or five times, but offer similar access workload capabilities. This means that the database workload of the higher storage capacity drives may actually not perform as well as lower-capacity drives. To scale disk drive access performance, you must make the media spin faster, the recording denser, or the actuator faster.

Sooner or later, however (and usually well before reaching a scalability factor of 10), it becomes impractical to further increase the capability of an individual component. In this case, the only reasonable alternative to achieving scalability is to employ multiple components to satisfy the workload requirements. This is the step that makes scalability particularly complex.

The whole issue of scalability would be considerably simpler if all components in a computing solution exhibited scalability limits at similar levels. Unfortunately, of course, they don't. Storage devices and software are typically the first components to exhibit problems. For storage devices, the problem is usually access performance, which is why most modern servers employ multiple disk drives—even if they have only one microprocessor. In fact, the ratio between the number of disk drives required to satisfy the needs of a microprocessor is increasing because microprocessors historically double in performance every 18 months while disk drive access performance doubles only after 10 years. This maxim, which is probably familiar in one respect or another to most computer users, is known as Moore's Law after Gordon Moore of Intel, who was first to state the disparity. This particular ratio and its effects are discussed in greater depth later in the section about system upgrades.

Most application programs, and many system software and middleware programs, are essentially single-threaded. This class of software performs one function at a time and then moves on to the next. As long as computers increase in speed faster than workloads increase in size there's no problem with the approach, but the intranet data warehouse is very likely to increase its workload at a pace far beyond simple increases in hardware capabilities. The intranet user population has the potential to grow exponentially and nearly instantly since there is little (or no) need for additional software on users' PCs. The implication here is that the database management software must be able to handle multiple requests (sometimes called transactions) simultaneously; this capability, which is generally referred to as multithreading, means that each request is processed by a separate thread of execution.

Application scalability is also reflected by the amount of context necessary for each user. While separate operating system processes and address spaces may suffice for small numbers of users, for large user communities (e.g., with thousands of users), it's often necessary to borrow techniques from the transaction-processing world and share resources among the users.

When the MPU begins to exceed its capacity and experience problems, the solution is usually to turn to computers with multiple MPUs, known as *multiprocessor computers*. Multiprocessor designs are widely used in servers. Although the number of MPUs per computer varies widely, for commercial applications, the range is usually from 2 to as many as 1,000. Perhaps no other aspect of the server industry gains as much attention as the battle of multiprocessor architectures, or, in other words, the alternative schemes for banding together large collections of MPUs to form a single computer system.

Shared Memory Multiprocessor Systems

Multiprocessor architecture is somewhat complex because computers also have multiple subsystems (e.g., the main memory subsystem and the I/O subsystem) that have different scaling capabilities than the MPUs. For this reason, it is practical to build memory and I/O subsystems that provide scalable performance for multiple MPUs. It is also practical to design operating systems that can concurrently manage the allocation of application tasks (i.e., processes or threads) for multiple MPUs. Computer servers that combine multiple MPUs with common memory and I/O subsystems controlled by a single operating system instance are generally referred to as *symmetric multiprocessors*, or *SMP servers*.

SMP Servers

SMP servers are particularly attractive for many computing environments because the architectural model is actually a variation of the model for single MPU scalability. The symmetric aspect of SMP servers refers to the notion that any of the MPUs can execute instructions from any application or system process. Since most server workloads consist of many application processes, the existence of multiple MPUs can be completely transparent from an application programming standpoint, and can create an effect similar to that of a simple increase in MPU capability. The degree of actual processor allocation symmetry varies by implementation, but the overall effect is as advertised.

As you might imagine, memory and I/O subsystem and operating system scaling tapers off after a certain point. Even in true multithreaded, multiprocess application designs, there are often instances of shared information, which become bottlenecks for increasing levels of concurrent processing. SMP vendors can stretch the limits of scalability by increasing the granularity of this shared information, but the increased granularity often brings with it additional overhead for concurrency control mechanisms (programs that keep application processes from interfering with one another in shared information). Overall, the limits of SMP server scalability vary with implementation, with the sophistication of the hardware and software involved, and with the characteristics of the application workloads.

SMP servers with four processors are widely available and scale rather well, with the four MPUs often providing an effective processing power greater than three uniprocessors. SMP servers with eight processors are more rare and more expensive, and offer somewhat less effective scalability. A few vendors offer systems capable of scaling to 16, 32, or 64 processors, albeit at increasing levels of cost. The really large-scale SMP servers tend to be somewhat application-sensitive, scaling most effectively with workloads consisting of numerous compute-bound short requests (typical of OLTP applications). Stretching any technology to its limits, however, often has the effect of specializing its application.

There are a number of scalability alternatives for organizations that require processing scalability beyond the limits of SMP servers. The choice of a solution depends to some extent on the application; and, of course, each option involves some trade-offs with regard to complexity of administration, generality of application to workloads, and potential level of system availability.

The primary motivation for developing SMP servers is to simulate the scalability of MPU power beyond that practical limit of a single MPU. In addition to ease of programming and workload application, an SMP's single operating system instance enables relatively simple procedures for workload management, system administration, software upgrades, performance analysis, and configuration planning. Servers that include multiple operating systems instances (e.g., clusters) are much more complex. Given the advantages of SMPs, it is understandable that server vendors are making every attempt to increase the scalability of the single operating system environment.

Distributed Memory Multiprocessor Systems with Shared Virtual Memory

The emerging architecture that is most likely to support this increased scalability for SMP or SMP-like servers is called *NUMA*, or *Nonuniform Memory Access*. In SMP servers, the memory subsystem is often the roadblock to higher scalability at reasonable cost. NUMA architectures extend memory subsystem capabilities by using multiple, separate memory subsystems that are viewed together as a unit through a hierarchy of high-speed caches and sophisticated directory-based virtual memory addressing mechanisms. NUMA servers typically have memory subsystems that are "local" to a subset of one or more of the MPUs in the server. The architecture provides SMP-like flexibility by enabling any MPU to access any memory location, but the cost—in terms of access latency as measured in MPU clock cycles—is lower for local memories than for those associated with another MPU. This is the "nonuniform" part of NUMA.

The real potential advantage of NUMA architecture, however, is that large-scale shared memory servers can be built by tying together multiple smaller-scale classical SMP systems through a sophisticated memory management and interconnection techniques. As NUMA systems continue to gain momentum in the server architecture arena, they may be able to provide high levels of single operating system instance scalability at lower costs than the classical large-scale SMP systems.

Multicomputer Systems

While the SMP and NUMA designs both have distinct advantages, they also involve some very real disadvantages and inherent challenges. As MPU capabilities are scaled, I/O capabilities must be similarly scaled to maintain balance. Also, combining sophisticated I/O subsystems and memory management techniques leads to relatively expensive servers. Rather than attempting to improve the capability of a single subsystem, the multicomputer philosophy is to apply a team of individual computers and potentially lower-cost units, and to use a divide and conquer approach to resolve large problems. Building large servers from *loosely coupled* collections of smaller servers is one example of this approach. Computers are considered loosely coupled if each participating computer has separate memory and I/O subsystems and runs a separate copy of the operating system. These collections are usually called *clusters*.

Clusters can consist of collections of SMP or NUMA servers tied together by one or more communications networks. The key difference between clusters and the SMP or NUMA architectures, however, is that a cluster involves multiple operating system instances. In other words, a cluster uses distributed computing concepts to achieve scalability. Clusters have two key characteristics, one positive one somewhat negative. The negative is that multiple operating systems instances magnify the problems of administration, performance tuning, and software upgrades and installations. The positive aspect, which generally outweighs the negative, is that the potential availability of a cluster is greater than that of a single server. This is because the servers that make up a cluster are almost completely independent and autonomous; if one of the servers in a cluster fails, the others are likely to survive and continue to function.

It is probably worthwhile to point out that in general, as any device gets bigger and more complex, it is more difficult to ensure its reliability and availability. Clustering technology enables designers to provide much of the throughput of a single monolithic server with the fault resilience of redundant hardware and software. In fact, clusters are often used simply for high availability, ignoring their potential for scalability. Assuming the proper software and workload, however, clusters do have the potential to be both highly scalable and highly available—attributes that can make clusters pivotal to the success of Internet applications.

Clusters come in several variations. Some share disk storage among the servers in a cluster, some share portions of memory, and some—usually those targeted simply for increasing availability—share nothing but the interserver communications network and alternate paths to disk storage. Others incorporate several of these attributes. Appropriate software and applications are the keys to making clusters successful.

Appropriate clustering applications are characterized by their use of client/server architecture and a user base with many concurrent users. The typical workload management strategy is to distribute requests across the participating servers; this can be accomplished either by network partitioning (i.e., each server in the cluster has a different IP address) or through middleware, such as NCR's TOP END, which automatically distributes and load-levels incoming requests to the participating servers. Various strategies may be used for file or database access, from distributed file systems to reserving one or more of the servers in a cluster for intracluster, client/server database process to cluster-enabled databases such as Oracle's Parallel Server.

In theory, because the servers in a cluster can be autonomous, the scalability of clusters is unlimited. In the real world of practical computing, however, a number of constraints generally limit clusters to between 8 and 16 servers. This is largely because most application workloads are not perfectly partitionable and distributable among an arbitrary number of servers; and because applications that are very distributable often require shared resources, such as a common database; and shared resources tend to limit scalability. Also, the administrative challenges of making more than eight autonomous servers act as an ostensibly single system can be daunting. Regardless, a cluster of eight servers, each with eight microprocessors and upwards of a gigabyte of memory, can generally accommodate thousands of concurrent users.

As mentioned earlier, clustering is based on loosely coupled multiprocessing (LCMP), a model that can provide nearly unlimited scalability. It is only the lack of a technique to distribute work among participating servers without requiring shared resources to be present that keeps clustering from reaching its scalability potential.

Parallel Processing

In a client/server data warehouse environment, scalability tends to focus on meeting performance objectives as the data warehouse capacity increases. Unfortunately, scalability is somewhat more complex in an intranet data warehouse environment because query performance (how fast results can be returned from the database) must be considered in the context of what happens when many users are executing data warehouse queries concurrently. While scalability issues are certainly not unique to the intranet data warehouse, they are generally more apparent and appear earlier in the system life cycle.

Parallel processing represents a divide and conquer approach to speeding up application processing or to maintaining response times as user loads increase. At the core of parallel processing is the notion of collective operations. While the act of processing many independent requests simultaneously is actually a form of parallel processing (in effect, the entire workload is being parallelized), generally, parallel computing is thought of as the act of breaking a single request into many smaller component requests, running each concurrently as specified by a parallel execution plan, and then assembling the results for transmission to the client. Parallelism can be initiated manually or automatically, but the complexity of the process really makes only automatic parallelism practical for most commercial applications. Figure 9.1 illustrates the spectrum of parallel processing approaches.

Modern computers actually employ parallelism at every level of their operation. Today's microprocessors often execute several instructions in parallel to speed up processing. A classic parallel processing technique, also used extensively in microprocessors, is called *pipelining*. Pipelining is the act of breaking down a computing task into stages, executing them from several requests concurrently (the number of stages and, therefore, the degree of parallelism, is called the pipeline depth), and delivering the effect of a task being executed in a time duration only as long as one stage in the pipeline. Microprocessors use pipelining by breaking the execution of an instruction down to multiple stages and filling the pipeline with stages from several instructions.

Parallelism can also occur for subfunctions of a problem, intrafunction processing, and between multiple problems. These higher levels of parallel processing are the focus of interest for data warehousing.

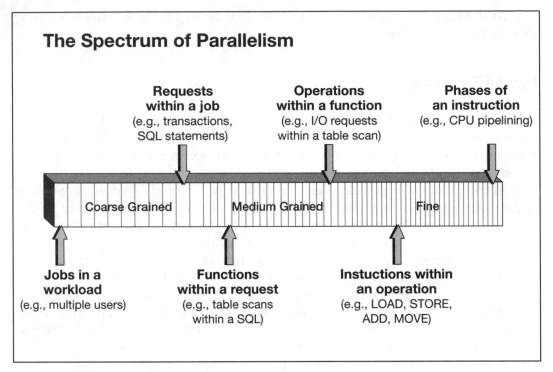

Figure 9.1   The spectrum of parallelism.

Massively Parallel Computers

Commercial parallel processing computers, sometimes called MPP or massively parallel processing computers, typically use an architecture similar to server clusters. MPP systems usually consist of a collection of independent *server nodes* that are interconnected by a special network for message passing between the nodes. Each node runs an independent copy of the operating system, which is usually some variation of UNIX.

MPP computers typically use a distributed processing technique called *function shipping*. Since MPP computers partition data among the processing nodes in a system, occasionally one node will need information available only on another. Rather than simply requesting an I/O operation (this would be *data shipping*), the requesting nodes send a high-level function request to the other node that may return complex or calculated results. Function shipping allows a so-called shared nothing architecture, based solely on message passing. Another, more familiar, example of function shipping is a remote procedure call (RPC).

The Difference between Clusters and MPPs

It is reasonable to ask, just what is the difference is between an MPP computer and a server cluster, beyond the sheer number of servers or nodes in the network. Since both are loosely coupled multiprocessors, the two models are similar architecturally, nevertheless, they have some critical differences:

- MPP computers have scalable interconnection networks between the nodes. This means that the bandwidth of the network increases as the number of nodes connected increases (though the scaling factor differs for various network topologies). Clusters generally use non-scalable networks such as buses, rings, or loops for best price performance.

- MPP computers provide support for parallel processing functions such as broadcast or multicast messages, group membership functions, collective operations, parallel process controls (e.g., barriers), and information distribution. Clusters generally do not provide these capabilities; or if they do, they don't provide special hardware or system software performance assists.

- MPP computers provide development and execution environments for parallel processing programs. Nearly every MPP vendor has developed a proprietary environment, but standards such as Message Passing Interface (MPI) and Parallel Virtual Machine (PVM) are becoming commonplace.

- MPP computers generally use sophisticated server management software to make the multiple computing nodes in a system appear more like a single configuration. Clusters usually allow the participating servers to be much more autonomous, and are often only loosely associated through administration tools.

MPP Systems with Hierarchically Differentiated Architectures

Early MPP computers, such as the Teradata DBC1012 incorporated hundreds of computing nodes, with each node employing only a single processor. This is often referred to as the *skinny node* approach. Modern MPP computers, however, use more sophisticated architectures that leverage SMP and clustering approaches (and may eventually leverage NUMA concepts) before using MPP techniques to scale further. This strategy is based on the notion of maximizing the leverage of the most inexpensive scaling technique, for example SMP, before employing a more ambitious scaling technique like loosely coupled multiprocessing. The NCR 5100M, for example, is essentially a cluster of clusters of SMP nodes. This means that each computing node in the 5100M is an SMP server, with up to 16 MPUs; the nodes are grouped into clusters, called *cliques*, for high-availability considerations; and the system scales by adding cliques, hence a cluster of SMP clusters.

MPP Availability

High availability is a critical consideration for MPP computers. Systems that use hundreds of MPUs, many gigabytes of memory, and potentially thousands of disk drives are vulnerable to failures simply by the mathematics of large populations. For example, a 5 terabyte MPP data warehousing system may incorporate well over 2,000 disk drives. Assuming a mean time between failure (MTBF) of 500,000 hours for each disk drive assembly (not an unusual claim), a disk failure can be expected every 250 hours, or about one every 10 days. The issue of availability has driven information services management to demand disk arrays or mirrored disks, hot spare hardware, redundant I/O paths, sophisticated diagnostics, and the implementation of various strategies for fault containment.

Relational Database Queries: The Killer App of Commercial Parallel Processing

It is important to understand that not all OLAP applications can take full advantage of parallel processing computer systems, particularly those classified as MPPs. Many OLAP applications require a specific sequence of processing steps where the output of one calculation or decision serves as the input to the next. While the query functions can be parallelized, the results set needs to be cached for subsequent analytic steps. However, the performance advantage achieved by speeding the query process can be substantial with large data warehouse applications.

There are several reasons why relational database queries are inherently parallel applications. For one, as discussed in Chapter 3, relational databases are composed of two-dimensional tables consisting of rows and columns. The rows in a table are not supposed to have any special physical ordering; there are no hierarchies or linkages allowed. Queries involving multiple tables are resolved by joining the information in one table to the information in another, forming a result table.

Because the relational model is based on set mathematics, tables have a number of properties that are very significant to parallel processing. As illustrated in Figure 9.2, this attribute allows us to divide large database tables into many subtables, and to assign each subtable to a different processor in an MPP computer. This subdivision of tables is responsible for the superior row selection capabilities of parallel databases on MPPs. The following example illustrates the power of parallel searching and selection. Assume a database of 100 million rows. If searching each row requires one unit time, on a nonparallel computer, a complete table search takes 100 million units of time. For a parallel processing implementation, assume an MPP computer with 200 processors. Making a subtable for each processor produces 200 subtables, each with

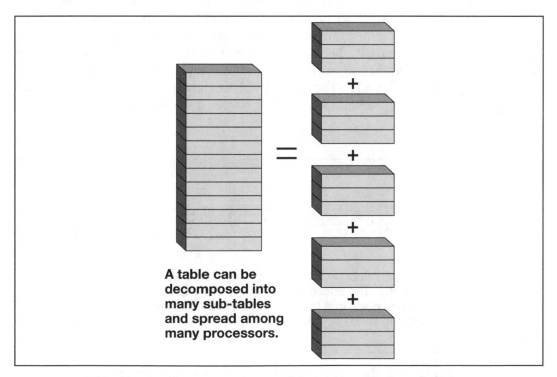

A table can be decomposed into many sub-tables and spread among many processors.

Figure 9.2   Decomposing a table into multiple subtables.

500,000 rows. Since each subtable can be scanned and searched simultaneously, the query can be satisfied in about 500,000 units of time, or a 99.5 percent reduction in wall-clock time.

Another important attribute of the relational model is that the order independence of the rows in a table allows us to assign any row of the overall table to any subtable we choose (see Figure 9.3). While the importance of this characteristic may not be immediately apparent, keeping all of the participating processors in a parallel system equally busy is one of the most critical problems in parallel processing. This can be particularly challenging for database processing with real-world information. For example, consider a table with a primary key of peoples' last names. There are far more people that have last names that begin with J than there are that begin with X. Dividing the last name table into subtables based on alphabetical order is not a good idea because the processors assigned names beginning with J will have far more work to do than the processors assigned names beginning with X. It is a rule of parallel processing that any parallel operation will execute in a time period determined by the length of the slowest participating processor. This means that if the processors searching the J portion of the table took five times as long to complete their function as the processors searching the X portion, the X processors will theoretically be idle 80 percent of the time while waiting for the J processors to finish. Not indicative of a very efficient MPP computer.

Database scientists leverage the order independence attribute of rows in tables by defining clever schemes to assign particular rows to particular data-

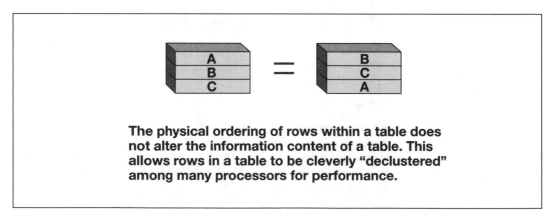

The physical ordering of rows within a table does not alter the information content of a table. This allows rows in a table to be cleverly "declustered" among many processors for performance.

Figure 9.3 Physical ordering of rows in a table.

base subtables (often called partitions). There are many types of partition assignment strategies (technically called declustering strategies). Some popular examples include key hash, key range, and round-robin (see Figure 9.4). A key hash strategy subjects a specific table column or group of columns to a mathematical hash function, with the output of the hash function providing the designator for the database partition. Key range declustering strategies assign a range of key values (e.g., A to F) to a particular database partition, and round-robin strategies simply deal out rows to be added to partitions, much like dealing cards.

A related technique to declustering strategies is called partial declustering. Full declustering means that every processor owns a partition of the database. While this is appropriate for very large tables, it can be inefficient for small ones. Partial declustering, which is generally more efficient for small tables, is the technique of assigning only a subset of the processors to own partitions of

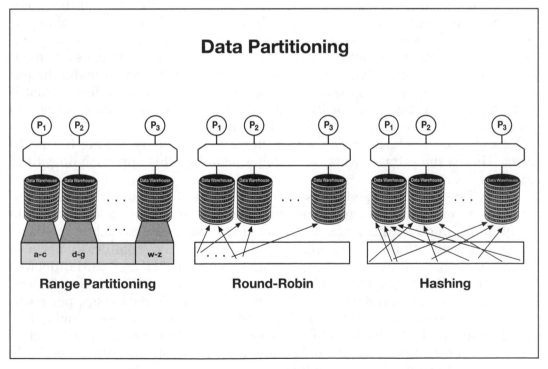

Figure 9.4 Database partitioning (declustering) strategies.

a given table. In fact, for very small tables, it may be best to assign the whole table to only one processor.

All of the various partitioning strategies aim for an even distribution of the workload to the MPUs, disks, and I/O subsystems in order to achieve maximum utilization of the computer. Experience shows that clever selection of partitioning strategies can improve performance and system utilization, but often at the price of complex database administration. Key range declustering, for example, is often useful for OLTP activities because it can reduce the number of processors participating in short transactions, but contributing little useful work. If the database tables are volatile, however, with an increasing number of rows or dramatic differences in key distributions, the effectiveness of the partitioning strategy may be compromised and require frequent readjustment. The adjustment may involve changing the number and key ranges for each partition, a situation that may involve table unloads and reloads. Unfortunately, the inefficiency of the table structure typically becomes apparent only when users begin to experience performance degradation.

Although partial declustering is often efficient for small tables, if the tables are not static, frequent adjustments may be necessary to ensure acceptable performance as the tables grow in size. A table that works well with three partitions this month may need five partitions in six months. This constant readjustment can be expensive. Also, using partial declustering to maintain numerous small tables raises inevitable questions about the most effective distribution algorithm for table partitions to available processors. Guessing wrong can result in idle resources or poor performance.

Round-robin declustering only distributes rows equally among the partitions. Unless the primary workload is table scanning, this approach does little to avoid hot spots.

NCR's Teradata DBMS, which is widely viewed as the leader in parallel processing, supports only hash declustering and full declustering. The Teradata solution is aimed at practical application of very large-scale database management and parallel processing, minimizing administrative complexity because the tuning capabilities of multiple declustering strategies and partial declustering are difficult to sustain in most dynamic commercial databases. In fact, Teradata manages each database partition using a single data space per partition, storing every table (including logs and work tables) using a single clustered index with the hash code value as the key. This allows the Teradata DBMS to automatically adjust to dynamic table populations without periodic reorganizations, while also providing consistent response times.

Parallel Query Optimization

Another attribute of relational databases that makes them friendly to parallelization is the capability to decompose complex functions into many simpler functions that can be executed in parallel. For example, complex queries often result in multiway joins that can be decomposed into parallel searches, simpler two-way joins, sorts, merges, or aggregations, all of which may execute in complex hierarchies, themselves parallel through pipelining. The key enabler of this parallel processing is a program called a query optimizer. The optimizer is the part of the database that accepts parsed SQL commands and produces a result called a query plan.

A query optimizer is actually a type of expert system. Formulating an efficient query plan is a very complex task, and one that is generally not suitable for the writer of an SQL statement. Query plans are also dependent on the structure of the physical database: How many rows are in the tables to be accessed for the queries, which indices should be used, which join strategy to choose, how and when to materialize the results. The most sophisticated optimizers are called cost-based, because they make query plan formulation decisions based on statistics about the physical database. These statistics enable the optimizer to select an efficient plan by comparing the processing costs (processor time and the number of I/O operations) of alternative plans. The optimal query plan for a given database function is determined by applying rules, formulating alternatives, estimating the costs for each alternative, and, finally, selecting the lowest-cost alternative.

Parallel query optimizers are particularly complex since they are responsible for all of the decisions required from nonparallel optimizers in addition to the decisions required to use parallel processing efficiently. Two overall goals drive the decisions in parallel optimization:

1. Maximize the amount of independent concurrent processing that can be performed by each processor.
2. Minimize the amount of data movement and message passing that must occur to satisfy the query.

The primary task of a parallel optimizer is to reduce query execution time, which may mean that some costs can be higher overall than in nonparallel environments. A good example of this is higher processor time costs, but lower actual runtime because the processor resources are being used in parallel.

Parallel processing databases executing on MPP computers require optimization choices beyond those of conventional systems. The database partitioning common to parallel databases and the availability of numerous processors requires decisions about the number and type of processors that should participate in a given function. For smaller joins, for example, it may be best to send all of the relevant rows to a single processor, but all processors should probably participate in larger joins.

Data movement is also particularly important for very large databases. To support joins based on columns that are not partitioning keys, for example, rows must be redistributed to dynamically create tables that are partitioned on the join key. This process, which is sometimes called row redistribution, can generate many gigabytes of data movement traffic for each query involving such an operation. This is one of the reasons why MPP computers should have scalable interconnection networks between the processor nodes.

Issues for Very Large Systems with Terabyte Databases

Beyond simple storage and physical table-mapping considerations, a data warehouse capable of holding a terabyte or more of data, introduces several other factors that determine the practicality of such large configurations. One such factor is data loading, the ability to import information into the data warehouse. Loading 100 million rows one row at time is impractical, even with a load rate of 100 rows per second. At 100 rows per second it would take more than 11.5 days to load 100 million rows. For terabyte databases, parallel processing offers the only practical loading technique because it can simultaneously insert multiple rows.

After the data is loaded into a terabyte data warehouse, it becomes even more valuable because of the significant time and effort necessary to re-create the database in the event of a failure. If a database is used simply for noncritical business functions, a long recovery period may be acceptable; but most enterprises do not create terabyte databases for noncritical functions. In these situations, a data loss can dramatically affect the viability of the business. For this reason, it's often necessary to take extraordinary measures to ensure high availability.

Although it is somewhat more costly to store the physical database in mirrored devices or disk arrays, this approach offers a number of distinct advantages. For example, a terabyte database typically occupies at least 500 2-gigabyte disk drives. If we assume an MTBF of 500,000 hours, we can expect a disk drive failure to occur every 1,000 hours, or every 41 days. Without mirroring or disk arrays, the failure can result in a data loss that requires re-creating the database or recovering it from a backup copy.

In addition to problems with data loading and database availability, large-scale systems and terabyte databases involve numerous administrative challenges that far surpass those of conventional computer and database systems. The sheer magnitude of managing computer systems with hundreds or thousands of disk drives, hundreds of processors, and huge amounts of memory presents a host of configuration, performance management, and operational problems. It may, for example, be necessary to schedule a regular monthly purchase of replacement disk drives since some are likely to fail during the course of a month. Complex data placement strategies, such as determining which tables and indices reside on which disk drives, may be practical for systems with 50 or 60 disks, but is unmanageable for systems with hundreds of disks. In fact, most of the fine tuning minutiae so common in smaller systems often proves impractical or ineffective in very large ones.

Parallel processing itself raises some complex performance issues for IS managers accustomed to addressing performance questions in nonparallel environments. In a parallel processing environment, correctly allocating the workload among processors and I/O systems is essential for achieving good performance. Imbalances that are tolerable with 10 processors are far less tolerable in systems with 256 processors. Unfortunately, the database partitioning schemes offered by some database vendors offer little more than a hit-or-miss approach to large-scale workload balancing. In general, there are two key points to remember about workload balancing in a parallel environment:

- Changing the partitioning strategy requires an unload and reload operation.
- In a parallel system, the operations may process in 1/NbrThreads duration compared to a single-threaded system, but the apparent speed of each parallel operation is determined by that of the slowest processor participating.

Workload management is another factor that is far more important in very large databases than in smaller ones. Poorly formulated queries that result in so-called product joins, unnecessary complete table scans, or huge quantities of intermediate or final results can produce much more devastating effects when there is a terabyte of information with which to make errors.

Issues surrounding system upgrade and expansion are often overlooked with terabyte data warehouses. Commercial databases tend to increase at a rate of 30 percent per year, and this rate is likely to increase as a result of the wide use of the Internet. The associated hardware systems typically grow in two dimensions: computing power and storage. For smaller systems, upgrades are generally handled as "box swaps," with the older, smaller system often reemployed in a less demanding application. Terabyte databases, however, typically run on MPP computers, which have very significant maintenance costs, and are suitable for only a relatively small number of applications (e.g., relational databases, transaction processing, and data mining). Unfortunately, adding processors to MPP computers is not as simple as it may sound.

First of all, the "new" processor is likely to be more powerful than the older, existing processors. This creates some problems since parallel computers operate most efficiently with compute nodes of equal power. A parallel system that incorporates processors with unequal capabilities requires redistributing data ownership to ensure that the more powerful processors have more work to do, while the less powerful ones have less work. Depending on the particular database product in use, this redistribution may be relatively simple or quite complex. And, if you use multiple partial partitioning strategies to spread the data among the processors, the task may be very difficult.

Expanding or upgrading storage systems can be especially challenging. While disk drive technology does change more slowly than other component technologies from a performance perspective (average disk access times are improving at only about 10 percent per year), modern disk array-based storage systems with caching and other performance enhancements are evolving at a much faster rate. For terabyte databases to function consistently, the entire database should reside in devices of equal performance. Thus, the unit of upgrade for a terabyte database can be very expensive, and is likely to require unloading and reloading the database.

Conclusion

Parallel processing offers performance and scalability benefits that are essential for intranet data warehousing applications directed at large databases. Recognizing this, a number of the relational database vendors are adding capabilities to their latest software releases that take advantage of parallel processing to improve query response. As the data warehouse grows, the logical migration path is to move the applications onto SMP or MPP platforms.

The ongoing challenge for developers of OLAP analytic functions, such as multidimensional analysis, statistical analysis, and data mining, is to balance the processing load between functions performed in the database and those performed against an extracted analytic cache. Essentially, using a parallel approach to process a database query speeds the creation of the analytic cache (i.e., the query result set) that is used by multistep OLAP functions. Assigning as many of the processing steps as practical to the database management system improves the efficiency of creating the analytic cache. The vendors of database management system products and OLAP tools are likely to continue enhancing their products to take greater advantage of parallel processing architectures. The performance requirements of the intranet data warehouse will demand continuous improvements in this area.

CHAPTER TEN

Securing the Intranet Data Warehouse

As many organizations are discovering, an intranet—especially one with links to the Internet—can change the way business is conducted. Many are taking advantage of the same technologies that they use to extend their core business applications within the enterprise to trade information and resources with their business partners, suppliers, distributors, and affiliates. (This is sometimes referred to as an *extranet*. But despite all the positive aspects of intranet technology, some organizations are discovering—the hard way—that not all of the changes are positive. Security is the one of the biggest obstacles to implementing an intranet data warehouse solution, particularly if it is linked to the Internet. Providing large numbers of users, internal and external to the enterprise, with access to some of the enterprise's most valuable data assets immediately raises serious concerns about data security. An intranet makes it possible to provide access to information and resources that, until very recently, were locked securely inside the enterprise. An extranet is created by providing strongly authenticated user password access to the private intranet network. In addition to supporting business-to-business applications, an extranet permits corporate users to operate from remote offices or home, or to access the intranet from the Internet when traveling.

Companies must begin to address the issues associated with security in the initial planning stages for the intranet data warehouse. Establishing the data warehouse and/or associated data marts actually provides the most basic form of security, granting users access to valuable information resources without compromising the underlying operational databases. Historically, data warehouses provided users with read-only access to information resources, but as data warehouses become the foundation for applications such as sales forecasting and budgeting, many data warehouses grant limited insert and update privileges to some users. Providing even limited database write privileges to users, however, significantly increases security concerns because users can corrupt the data warehouse contents—accidentally or intentionally.

The operative concept in securing the intranet data warehouse is to allow only certain individuals access to selective company information to ensure that the security of the enterprise is not compromised. And, while the benefits of providing extranet access are compelling, exposing a company's private network to the hazards of the public Internet presents serious security challenges. Approximately 75 percent of the corporate, university, and government sites that responded to an FBI-sponsored survey conducted by the Computer Security Institute in early 1996 said they feared attacks from independent hackers and information brokers. Half the survey respondents said their computer systems were attacked by people inside the company, while one-third said break-ins had been attempted from the Internet.

It follows, then, that security is also a major concern in selecting which data sources and data elements to place in the data warehouse. For example, many data warehouses that contain sensitive information about individuals do not include the individuals' names, addresses, or telephone numbers. After all, analyzing purchasing patterns or customer retention data does not require the business analyst to know any confidential information about the customers. Once the analysis is complete, the customer number contained in the data warehouse can be rejoined with name and address files retained in a separate database, for example, to create a mailing list for a direct mail campaign. Similarly, the data warehouse may contain concisely summarized financial data that is adequate for departmental financial analysis but does not include the underlying details of income, employee expense, and so forth, all of which remains securely stored in the operational database.

Planning for Security

Chapter 5 introduced a model for planning an intranet data warehouse, which comprised three tightly integrated strategies: the database strategy, the applications strategy, and the deployment strategy—all of which must incorporate elements of security planning. Again, it is crucial to address security issues at the initial stages of planning for an intranet data warehouse, and then to continually review security measures throughout the implementation and maintenance phases. Furthermore, executive management and intranet users alike need to fully understand the threats posed by security breaches and to support the measures taken to reduce or eliminate such threats.

Security issues that should be addressed in the database strategy include questions of content, data mart partitioning, and data summarization. In general, organizations should avoid placing extremely sensitive data in the data warehouse, particularly an intranet data warehouse that is accessible to a large number of users. In many cases, one or more separate data marts may provide users with the necessary data access while maintaining tighter security. Finally, by summarizing data stored in the warehouse and deleting highly sensitive information like customer names and addresses, the organization can "desensitize" the data warehouse or data mart.

Security issues that need to be addressed by the application strategy include the implementation of user names and passwords, including the means by which these safeguards travel between the layers of a distributed, multitier application. The application strategy should incorporate a policy that clearly states how user names and passwords are to be issued and administered. In general, organizations should enforce a minimum length for passwords, avoiding the use of two- or three-character passwords since short passwords are significantly easier to break down than long passwords. Also, the policy should encourage users to change passwords frequently.

Security issues related to the deployment strategy include means for safeguarding the integrity of the network and for developing proper procedures to ensure the authentication of users, authorization for access to intranet resources, and confidentiality of information communicated over the network. At a minimum, the strategy should define requirements for encrypting user names and passwords, but may extend to guidelines for encrypting the entire transaction between the client and server. In addition, the strategy should clearly define methods for detecting security breaches and implementing corrective actions to minimize damage in the event of an incursion.

When planning security for an intranet data warehouse, the primary concern is to prevent motivated "hackers" and "crackers" from using the intranet to access information resources in the data warehouse. Unfortunately, threats from hackers are not unique to the data warehouse environment, and not all hackers are outside the organization; studies indicate that disgruntled employees initiate a significant share of hacker attacks. In fact, the security threats in an intranet data warehouse environment are much the same as those in any network application, but the data warehouse—with its vast stores of information—and the intranet—with its gateway to the Internet—make the intranet data warehouse a particularly inviting target.

Of course, the underlying database must be secured. The majority of intranet users are authorized to access only a limited portion of the data contained in the intranet data warehouse—the information they need to perform their jobs effectively. Too often, poorly designed applications facilitate breaches in security. For example, in a multidimensional OLAP analysis application that permits users to "drill up and down" in the database dimensions, the software must be designed to prevent users from drilling into any portions of the data warehouse for which they are not specifically authorized. Similarly, in the highly collaborative world of an intranet data warehouse, the software should restrict users' ability to breach security by sharing sensitive information with unauthorized users. Although it is not possible (or even practical) to completely control such information sharing, users should not be able to easily exchange passwords or applications that provide access to the data warehouse.

When database security breaches do occur, they are often inadvertent, caused by "bugs" or gaps in the application tier that enable users to access portions of the data warehouse database for which they have no legitimate authority—or need. But in truth, businesses don't generally use sophisticated "hacker" techniques to breach security. The primary concern in such cases is to locate the easily exploited bugs and gaps in the system and plug them before they begin to threaten the integrity of the database. It is important to remember that, as more users gain access to the data warehouse via intranet deployment, the security risks increase dramatically. The challenge is to plan a secure system initially, then continually monitor that system to discover the bugs and gaps and resolve them while the intranet data warehouse system is still relatively small. It is infinitely more difficult to monitor security and resolve problems after the system is fully deployed throughout the enterprise.

This chapter presents three views of intranet data warehouse security. The first portion addresses the network security issues, focusing on the ways to protect the intranet data warehouse from intentional and unintentional breaches of information "over the wire." The second part of the chapter describes the security issues specifically associated with database security in an intranet data warehouse environment. The third and last section describes one vendor's (Hewlett-Packard's) means of dealing with data warehouse security issues in an intranet and Internet environment.

The Basics of Network Security

Security breaches that result in unauthorized intrusions into the enterprise's private network not only expose sensitive corporate information to unauthorized users, they also give hackers the opportunity to corrupt the contents of the database. Data integrity is crucial in an intranet data warehouse environment, for it loses much of its utility if users cannot be assured that the data is complete and accurate at all times, that it has not been destroyed or altered by a virus or a Trojan horse. Unfortunately, network security is more complex than a simple product or marketing proposition can address. In looking for a clear idea of what "network security" means, there are as many descriptions as there are contexts, but, in general, organizations need to consider security from three perspectives:

- **Prevention:** The most frequently discussed aspect of security, prevention deals with eliminating the possibility of an unwanted incursion.
- **Detection:** Detection is the ability to determine when and where incursions are attempted and whether they are successful.
- **Correction:** Correction deals with resolving gaps in security after an incursion occurs, determining the extent (if any) of damage, and, if necessary, repairing that damage (i.e., restoring the data to an uncorrupted state).

In many cases, detection and correction, coupled with effective prevention measures, can serve as powerful deterrents to potential security violations. Many security breaches actually occur by "accident." By combining careful planning with an effective system of continuous monitoring, it is possible to greatly reduce, or even eliminate, the risks of inadvertent security breaches. And, by building systems that appear to be secure—or at least very difficult to breach—we can often discourage hackers, even motivated hackers, from attempting security incursions. Continuous monitoring, which enables us to quickly detect and respond to attempted security breaches, is also essential for determining where security weaknesses exist in order to initiate preventative measures.

Prevention

All of the following network security measures focus on preventing breaches of security, and are well suited to protecting information resources in an intranet data warehousing environment. Certainly, network security issues are not unique to the intranet data warehouse but, as mentioned earlier, the importance of these issues is amplified by the decision to deploy applications over the intranet and Internet. A basic understanding of network security issues is essential in planning a secure intranet data warehouse.

The following paragraphs list some common security measures (and the threat that they're designed to protect against) that should be considered during the planning stages of an intranet data warehouse.

- **Authentication (Spoofing, Masquerade):** Authentication substantiates that the user is, indeed, communicating with the correct enterprise. Similarly, the enterprise must be certain that it is dealing with a legitimate and correctly authenticated user. For example, when a sales manager accesses the intranet data warehouse to check sales figures, he or she must be certain that the Web server with which he or she is communicating is his or her company's—not someone masquerading as that company to catch authorized passwords. And the company needs similar assurance that it is truly communicating with the legitimate sales manager.

- **Authorization (Inside Job, Unauthorized Access Permissions):** Authorization deals with granting selective access to corporate resources. Since a majority of successful computer intrusions originate within an enterprise, companies must limit internal user access to the intranet data warehouse and maintain effective read/write controls. It is also important to remember that Internet connectivity increases the threat that someone outside the organization can collaborate with someone inside to gain unauthorized access to valuable data resources.

- **Data Protection (Unlawful Disclosure, Industrial Espionage):** Data protection measures ensure that users can choose when and with whom to share data. This kind of security is often called *multilevel* because it defines a need-to-know or safe-to-know strata that specifies who has access to what. All multilevel security measures are designed to keep sensitive data from ending up in the wrong hands. In many segments of the financial services and telecom markets, regulatory requirements and disclosure laws provide stiff civil or criminal penalties for failure to maintain the privacy of data. Examples of the types of data that might require data protection measures in an intranet data warehouse include an individual's credit history, medical records, or financial account.

- **Nonrepudiation (Spoofing, Denial of Receipt):** Nonrepudiation provides irrefutable proof that a user and enterprise have completed a transaction. Each user and each enterprise must be certain that answers and acknowledgments to messages are not forged by a third party, and that the person who submits a requests cannot later deny making it.

- **Access (Denial of Service):** Access involves ensuring that users are able to access corporate resources when needed. Of all threats, denial of service is the most insidious and the most difficult to prevent. A simple example is flooding a Web site with fake information requests, preventing legitimate customers from being serviced.

Detection

If a security breach does occur, an organization must be able to quickly and accurately determine the cause of the breach and assess the damage. Detection involves monitoring such things as log files, CPU loads, altered system binaries, password files, and so forth. But monitoring is only the first step in detecting security breaches. Companies also need to establish real-time alarms to notify IS administrators of security incursions and attempted incursions. Alarms can be very effective in initiating damage control mechanisms, pinpointing security gaps, and preventing future breaches. In effect, they help companies to avoid "locking the barn door after the horse has been stolen." Alarms are usually configured to notify administrators about such specifics as:

- User login from a particular terminal.
- Events that happen at an odd time of day (e.g., login at 3:00 A.M.).
- Events that happen too often (e.g., five consecutive failed logins).
- Events that happen in too short a time interval (e.g., two system backups in one night).

In addition to detecting security breaches and alerting IS administrators, a good security system must be capable of implementing protective measures.

For example, it may be configured to immediately shut down all user access to the data warehouse or to allow very limited access to specific portions only.

Correction

Correction plays a major role in ensuring the integrity of a data warehouse. It involves assessing the damages after a security breach and implementing actions to ensure the integrity of the data. The first step in correction is determining whether damage has occurred; for example, has the information in the data warehouse been corrupted or a virus introduced? The second step is to initiate recovery actions, to repair any damage, and search and destroy any viruses. The third and final step is to determine the cause of the breach and take corrective actions, implementing detection or prevention measures to patch any gaps in the existing security system. Corrective actions may involve something as simple as changing all user passwords after a breach to something as complex as implementing new security software capable of protecting against new viruses or masquerade techniques.

Three Network Security Zones to Protect

Although internal access via the corporate TCP/IP network is the most common method of accessing an intranet data warehouse, most organizations inevitably face the need to link the intranet and the data warehouse with the Internet to meet the needs of users in remote offices and those who travel frequently. And, once the intranet evolves into an extranet, the circle of authorized users widens to include nonemployees such as suppliers, customers, and investors. As soon as an enterprise decides to permit external access to internal data warehouses, its challenge becomes one of allowing such access without opening security holes in the corporate intranet. Typically, externally focused (i.e., public access) Web servers are placed outside a company's firewall precisely to prevent creating a security hole. Because these external servers are prone to many known security risks, however, organizations typically post only information that is static in nature and has relatively low strategic value to the enterprise (e.g., product advertising or job postings). In contrast, a Web-enabled data warehouse contains sensitive corporate information that must reside behind the corporate intranet firewall.

Essentially, once an organization makes the decision to permit Internet access to its Web-based data warehouse, it must address three basic security zones. Figure 10.1 illustrates the three zones of network security in an intranet

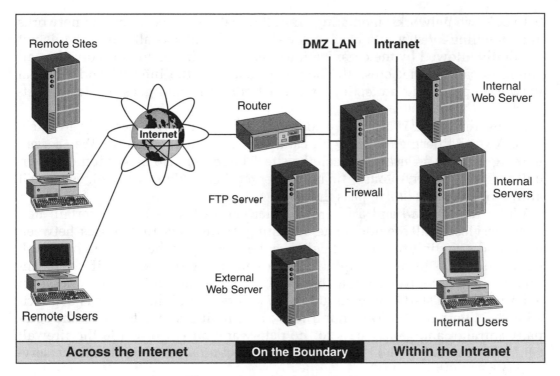

Figure 10.1   Security zones.

data warehouse application that is linked to the Internet and shows the flow of information through the three zones:

- Security on the boundary between the Internet and an intranet
- Security across the Internet
- Security within an intranet

Network Security on the Boundary

Security on the boundary is probably the most overlooked aspect of end-to-end security. The boundary can be likened to the front door to the enterprise, and, like the actual front door, it provides the first line of defense for valuable information resources inside.

Firewalls are the accepted technology for protecting a company's internal network from the Internet. Essentially, they enforce an access control policy between two networks, mediating all traffic that passes between the networks and watching for suspect data. A firewall typically blocks all traffic that is not explicitly allowed by the organization's security policy, and is involved in all communications that cross the boundary between the internal and external networks, providing protection over what comes in and goes out to the network.

A filtering router is also a key component in any network security architecture. A good filtering router significantly reduces the load on the Web server, making it easier for users to reach the site. The router also makes it more difficult for people to frivolously tie up the server (i.e., to deny service), because it allows only Web traffic to pass through.

While the firewall and a filtering router can restrict access to certain network services and provide some screening of the data that passes between users and a service, they do not enhance the security of the platform on which the service runs or of the application implementing the service. If, for example, we inadvertently install a "buggy" Web server that mistakenly allows an external user to start a program on the Web server (and that server is connected to the internal network), an intruder can exploit that bug to attack the company intranet and gain access to the data warehouse. So, while the firewall can restrict access to the Web server, it does not enhance security on the server itself.

Network Security over the Internet and within an Intranet

Network security over the internet and within an intranet are very similar. Both deal with securing data "over the wire," as well as authenticating users and servers. Participants communicating on a network have three basic security requirements:

- **Confidentiality:** The exchange of information should be private.
- **Integrity:** Messages should not be altered in transit.
- **Authentication:** The sender and receiver should be certain of each other's identity.

When communicating with someone in person it is fairly easy to be certain of these things, but once that communication moves onto a network, it introduces an element of doubt into all three requirements. The elegant solution to this problem is encryption. Encryption transforms data, called plain text, into an unintelligible form, called *ciphertext*. All encryption methods involve mathematical algorithms that scramble (i.e., encrypt) the message beyond recognition. The reverse process, decryption, unscrambles and reconstitutes the original message in readable form. Network security typically begins with password encryption, and supports user authentication as well as user access authorization. Both are described in more detail in the next section.

Since an encryption program performs the same steps for every user, we need different keys to get different results for each user. A key is simply a long number that the program incorporates into the scrambling process. Both the sender and the receiver need the key to communicate, because without it, the messages can neither be encrypted nor decrypted. Since key numbers are very long, it is useless for eavesdroppers to try to guess them, even if they know which encryption algorithm is being used.

While there are many of encryption programs, there are basically only two types of encryption systems: secret-key cryptography and public-key cryptography. In secret-key cryptography, which is also known as symmetric-key cryptography, the sender and receiver share the same key. If a third party gets the key, there can be no more secrets. In public-key cryptography, one key is used to encrypt a message and a different key is used to decrypt it. In this method, keys come in pairs: one is the public key and the other is the private key. Messages encrypted with the public key can be decoded only with the private key, and vice versa. Users share their public keys with one another, but keep their private keys to themselves. Most Web browsers incorporate Secure Sockets Layer (SSL) encryption technology, which uses public/private key pairs to encrypt messages.

SSL is a protocol for communicating between the client and server that uses public key cryptography. SSL also requires a certificate of authenticity to ensure that unauthorized users do not put their name on an authorized user's public key. A certificate is an electronic document that verifies the identity of a server or individual. Certificates have the public key mathematically embedded in a special digital signature that cannot be forged. Authorized users must obtain their certificates from a certificate authority (commonly called a CA), which is a program specifically designed to generate and issue certificates.

A public key certificate is the digital equivalent of a passport. The public key certificate and corresponding private key identify the user to someone or something that needs proof of identity. In an intranet data warehousing system, the certificate identifies the user to a server on the network. The public key certificate and private key authenticate the user, but that authentication must still be translated into database access authorization, which is granted by the database administrator and checked by the relational database management system software each time a user establishes a connection into the data warehouse.

Often, information resources, including the intranet data warehouse, are secured separately. In this situation, the user must have both a public key and a password for each secured site. A number of vendors are beginning to move toward centralizing authentication and authorization on a single server in order to provide users with single sign-on access to intranet resources.

The Basics of Database Security

Where network security is largely concerned with preventing "strangers" from accessing a secure environment "over the wire," database security is primarily concerned with protecting the integrity of the data in the data warehouse. Database security restricts access to the underlying databases, preventing users from accessing portions of the database for which they have no authorization. Network security generally stops with user authentication and authorization to access the content on a secured server. In the case of most Web servers managing unstructured content (i.e., text, image, and audio information), once access is authorized, users have complete access to the entire content; there are no further security restrictions. This arrangement is clearly not sufficient for an intranet data warehouse environment where additional security is required to control access to the data that is stored on the server.

When an organization establishes a data warehouse, it separates OLTP operational systems from broadly available data warehouse decision support data, thereby establishing an important line of defense against unauthorized incursion into the operational databases. Even if a hacker does manage to break through all levels of network security to gain access to the data warehouse, the operational databases themselves remain inaccessible. The hacker may be able to change (or corrupt) data in the warehouse, but he or she cannot alter the underlying account balances or billing statements in the operational database. Of course, this assumes that network security systems are in place to prevent intruders from gaining network access via the data warehouse server.

Intranet data warehouse planners have the opportunity to create a second layer of database security when they specify the data warehouse content. The data warehouse contents can be largely desensitized through data summarization or by omitting certain data elements. In many cases, data marts are useful for creating desensitized versions of the enterprise data warehouse, providing access only to "slices" of the data that are of interest to specific departments or that are required to make decisions about specific business issues.

User authorization privileges provided by the data warehouse's underlying relational database management system (RDBMS) actually provide the primary level of database security. Database authorization privileges, which are based on the SQL standard, include Select, Delete, Insert, Update, Reference, and Usage. System administrators can grant some or all of these privileges to individual users or groups of users and/or specify privileges for specific portions of the data warehouse. For example, the eastern region sales manager may be granted read-only (Select) access to eastern region data only. All relational database management systems provide this level of security, and most OLAP functions inherit that level of security and may add one or more additional levels.

In practice, the majority of today's data warehouse users have only Select privileges; they can retrieve and read data from the data warehouse, but cannot alter that data. As applications such as sales forecasting and budgeting are deployed on the intranet, however, more users are likely to be granted Insert and Update privileges, meaning that they will be able to change the values of the data in the data warehouse (but not the operational databases themselves). The ability to write data to the warehouse changes the read-only characteristics of the data warehouse and significantly increases the risks to database integrity.

Accessing the intranet data warehouse and associated server-based OLAP functions via a Web browser requires passing an encrypted user password through an intranet firewall for authentication and authorization. An authentication server (which ensures that users are who they say they are) and an authorization server (which determines what users can access on the intranet) can be used to centralize security to provide users single sign-on capabilities. If these steps are not performed at a single point on the intranet, they must be performed separately by each secure information resource on the intranet. Even when authentication and authorization steps are completed at an application server (containing OLAP functions), the server issues a request for services from another secured server. In the case of an intranet data warehouse, the OLAP functions generate SQL database queries and must attach a password to gain database access authorization. Vendors are presently addressing these administrative issues, all of which arise from the distributed nature of the intranet, with the goal of centralizing authentication and authorization and providing users with single sign-on access to the intranet resources.

The fact that the Web server is stateless (it drops the connection to the browser after it passes each page of HTML content) further compounds the problem of single sign-on access. User authentication and authorization are lost when the connection to the server is dropped. The security steps must be repeated each time a user accesses the Web server. In a worse-case scenario, this means that the user would have to enter a password to gain access to the intranet data warehouse and reenter the password each time he or she requests additional information. To eliminate the need for the user to reenter a password for each data warehouse access attempt in a single session, all Web browsers now support Netscape's *cookies*. As discussed in Chapter 2, cookies provide a mechanism for storing and retrieving the server-side connections on the client, thereby creating a persistent client-side state. Once the server verifies user authorization at the application level, the authorization is stored as a cookie on the client. The cookie, containing the authorization code, is passed to the server each time the user reaccesses the data warehouse.

As part of the query generation process, the server-based OLAP functions are tasked with associating a user's database access password with the encrypted network password. Because the user name and password implemented for database security authorization generally differs from the user name and password assigned to secure network access, users cannot automatically access the data warehouse even if they do gain access to the network. In essence, a user's information request must first successfully clear multiple network security layers, then must be granted database access security in order to successfully process an information request.

Hewlett-Packard's VirtualVault

Hewlett-Packard's VirtualVault Web technology is an example of how one vendor deals with the issues of providing network security for the intranet and Internet data warehouse environment. Although VirtualVault is used in this chapter to illustrate how a single product can provide many of the features necessary to safeguard security in such an environment, a number of other companies offer comparable products that are also well suited for this environment. In fact, every major vendor, including IBM, Sun, and Microsoft, are actively addressing the challenges of Internet and intranet security.

VirtualVault is a secure Web server platform that sits on the boundary between the Internet and an intranet. Although it was originally designed for the UNIX operating environment, Hewlett-Packard is currently porting Virtual-Vault to Microsoft's NT environment. In VirtualVault, a secure CGI gateway that passes database calls (i.e., SQL queries) or parameters (i.e., messages or remote procedure calls) for executing server-based OLAP functions is the only communication between the public Internet and enterprise itself. All other access to the intranet world is prohibited.

VirtualVault is based on an operating system that has no single point of control, no superuser, no root, and no rlogin capabilities for accessing remote platforms. This substantially reduces the possibility that an intruder can exploit a security breach by gaining access to all of the server's functions and, by doing so, gain general access to applications on the server.

VirtualVault uses a combination of high-level security features to ensure that only properly authenticated users have access to the data warehouse for which they have legitimate authorization. In essence, VirtualVault assures that only appropriate transactions occur between the Internet and the intranet, and severely inhibits the ability of a nonauthorized user to gain access to internal programs and data. Figure 10.2 identifies the security threats that VirtualVault is designed to protect against on the boundary.

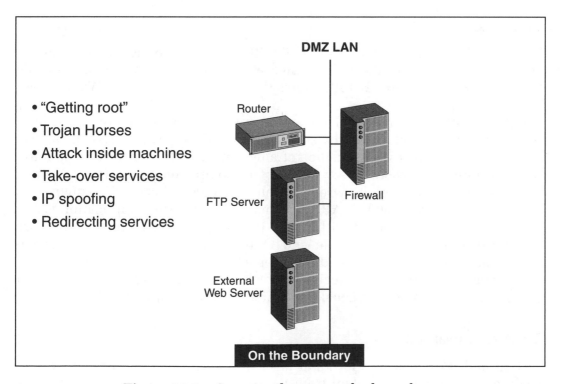

Figure 10.2 Security threats on the boundary.

Data Partitioning

VirtualVault partitions enterprise data into three compartments: Inside (intranet), Outside (Internet), and System (configuration files and other system-specific files needed by system programs and applications). In general, VirtualVault prevents programs running on the Outside from accessing files on the Inside, and vice versa. Hackers coming in from the Internet cannot reach into the Inside compartment to access data files, run programs, or download/upload files. Only the minimum necessary information is stored in the Outside environment, such as descriptive Web pages, and simple forms. All mission-critical data and applications are stored in the Inside compartment or on intranet systems. Two copies of a Netscape Web server run on the Virtual-Vault. The Inside Web server, also referred to as the internal Web server, is used by enterprise employees to administer VirtualVault, applications, and the outside Web server via the Web-based administration interface. The Outside Web server interfaces with users on the Internet.

The Trusted Gateway

VirtualVault acts much like a firewall, sitting on the boundary between the corporate intranet and the public Internet to bridge the enterprise with the "outside" world. Figure 10.3 illustrates the location of the VirtualVault server on the boundary.

But VirtualVault's Trusted Gateway feature does not replace the need for a firewall; instead, it adds security access for specific applications such as server-based OLAP processing for the intranet data warehouse. In a data warehouse application, where a browser interface component requests data from a data warehouse, the Web browser program executes either an SQL query or a set of calls to server-based OLAP functions. If the requested application is registered with the Gateway, it will invoke the program and then handle secure communications between Inside and Outside compartments, but only between that specific program and the user who invoked it. The Gateway program ignores requests for unregistered or nonexistent programs. Figure 10.4 provides a diagram of the VirtualVault internal architecture.

Directory Concealment

VirtualVault provides an additional layer of security for the intranet by concealing most of the file system from the Netscape Web server running in the

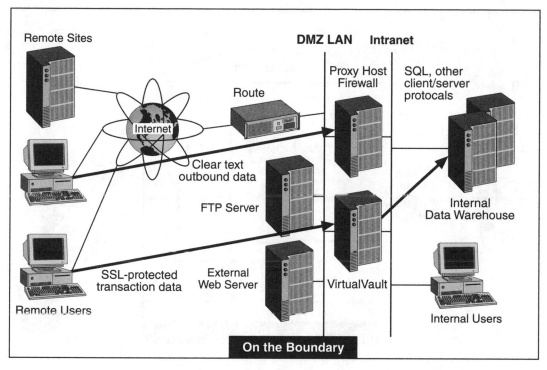

Figure 10.3   VirtualVault security solution on the boundary.

Outside environment. Not knowing something exists is an effective way of deterring break-in attempts. Although users can modify the restrictions to suit their particular needs, Hewlett-Packard presets this feature to permit only a specified directory and its subdirectories to be visible to the Outside Web server. This prevents a potential perpetrator from examining and modifying files in the Outside compartment, and perhaps gaining a clue to an unknown security hole.

Authorizations

Because VirtualVault was originally designed for the UNIX operating system, it incorporates a number of specialized features to provide security in that environment. For example, because one of the most common means of penetrating a UNIX system is to obtain the superuser (root) account password,

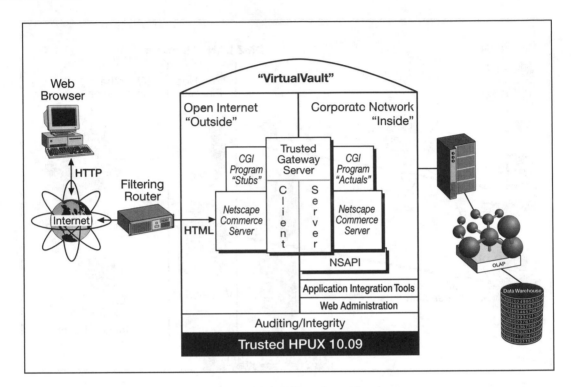

Figure 10.4   VirtualVault architecture.

VirtualVault does not support a root account. Instead, it breaks the capabilities normally assigned to the root account into authorizations, each of which permits access to a limited set of capabilities. Even system administrators must have proper authorizations; in fact, VirtualVault provides individual authorization levels for five types of system administrators.

Privileges

Because programs can inherit privileges on an operating system, one known security breach in the UNIX environment is to have a malicious program inherit superuser or root privileges. VirtualVault eliminates this threat by restricting what programs can actually execute and ensuring that no program can inherit a root or superuser authority.

VirtualVault also uses privileges to limit user access to the secured application (i.e., server-based OLAP functions) through the Trusted Gateway to protect against one of the very real threats that all computer users face, that of the Trojan horse, which is a kissing cousin to a computer virus that lurks within the computer until a prespecified time or event, then attacks the integrity of the system, altering files, directories, or applications. Unfortunately, these "time bombs" are a common occurrence, often introduced into an enterprise by files that are downloaded from the Internet.

Conclusion

Security is a matter of probabilities. An organization contemplating putting its enterprise data on the Internet must recognize that there is no such thing as impenetrable security; there are no perfect locks. Therefore, the security goals for any enterprise must center around reducing risk to a level that makes the required investment attractive and the business return worthwhile. Clearly, establishing and maintaining both network security and database security is a complex process that requires continual review and modification.

In many cases, establishing a sound security policy is the most important aspect of security planning. Although it is important to take advantage of advancements in hardware and software technology to secure the network and database resources, it is equally important to determine which users or user groups should be allowed to access which resources. Establishing a good security policy begins with determining data warehouse and data mart content, and continues with sound administration of that content.

It is equally important to communicate the security policy to users. Ultimately, they are responsible for following the policies and monitoring system usage to ensure that information resources remain secure. By encouraging users to exchange and share information, the intranet data warehouse environment substantially increases the possibility of unintentional security breaches. Users must have a firm grasp of both the threats to and their role in protecting the information resources of the enterprise.

CHAPTER ELEVEN

AUTOMATING INTRANET INFORMATION SEARCHES

One of the challenges of deploying data warehousing applications over the intranet is reaching passive users. Most decision makers do not have the time nor the inclination to embark on information searches. They are accustomed to having information delivered to the them. This chapter discusses how intranets can support "push" as well as "pull" strategies for information delivery. (The Information Advantage product is used here as an example of how these capabilities can be provided, but note that all vendors of OLAP tools are rapidly evolving to integrate more effectively with the intranet data warehouse environment.)

Prior to the advent of the intranet, corporations used a "push" method of delivering information to users. Reports and memos were delivered to users based on a distribution list that delineated who needed the information. Decision makers were trained to react to the information that arrived on their desks. In contrast, the Internet requires that users proactively initiate, or "pull," information from the vast store of available resources. The pull model works for the Internet, but simply making information available fails to meet critical decision support requirements of Intranet users. Too often, decision makers are unaware that information exists unless they are notified in some manner.

Search engines provide data about the information resources available on the Web and thereby provide needed assistance in pulling information from the intranet and Internet. In many respects, they perform a service similar to that of the Yellow Pages or *TV Guide*, enabling users to determine whether information exists about a certain topic, and directing them to the information location. But, though extremely valuable, search engines rely on active user participation. A means of pushing information to passive users on a "need to know" basis is essential for business applications. Agent technologies, which enable background processes to be automated on behalf of the users, provide an efficient means of pushing information to individual users. This chapter discusses the importance of using search engines and agent technologies to fully integrate intranet deployment of data warehouse applications. In the lexicon of the Internet, pushing information out to users is referred to as *Webcasting*.

This chapter also explains the importance of search engines and agent technologies to fully integrate intranet deployment with data warehousing applications. Without integrated search engines and agent processing technologies, many users would be unaware of much of the valuable information available to them to support decision making. And, in many respects, the intranet data warehouse would fail to achieve its intended goal of improving information-rich communications and collaboration.

Large and Diverse User Community

As discussed in Chapter 5, the user community of an intranet data warehouse is both very large and very diverse. The power users of the system typically spend several hours a day building analysis models and scouring the data warehouse to uncover trends, problems, and opportunities. Often these power users are the authors of applications used by others, and although they represent the smallest segment of users, their analytic requirements are the most complex.

In contrast, active users rely heavily on the intranet data warehouse to analyze business issues; they generally don't have the time or the inclination to aimlessly search for information. Active users want solutions to business issues.

Casual users, who span the organizational structure from executives to first-line managers, represent the largest segment of users but are typically rather infrequent users. They generally are seeking answers to specific business questions.

One challenge that developers face in building an intranet data warehouse involves creating a user interface to instruct OLAP functions in analyzing the data warehouse content. While ease of use is important to everyone, it is viewed differently by each type of user. The problem is compounded by a rapidly changing set of business management requirements. Certainly, attempting to build a separate desktop application for each user is not realistic, nevertheless, a system tailored to the needs of the individual is necessary to maximize productivity. Meeting this challenge is accomplished by deploying OLAP capabilities in the form of decoupled user-interface (UI) objects rather than monolithic application programs. This object-oriented view of constructing OLAP applications from parts is consistent with the distributed network computing model of the intranet. In fact, the architecture of the intranet is accelerating the development of applications in the form of distributed objects.

OLAP Interface and Display Objects

Interface and display objects provide intranet users with a powerful set of reusable software components, written as downloadable applets that allow users to interface with OLAP functions from a Web browser. Interface objects communicate instructions (i.e., messages or remote procedure calls) to invoke OLAP functions. These instructions provide the variables to generate a database query, the messages, or calls that identify which analytic process to perform and how to format the data file. Display objects provide the user with options for viewing the information in report or graphic form in the Web browser. Interface and display objects represent the application presentation tier that separates the complexities of the underlying database design, OLAP application logic, and network architecture.

By using a library of UI objects, developers can quickly assemble the presentation tier from components, to provide the wide range of business applications that the authors and active and casual users require. There are a number of OLAP products, including Information Advantage's DecisionSuite, that partition the application logic from the interface and display components of an application's presentation tier. Each vendor relies on a proprietary API to communicate messages or remote procedure calls generated in the presentation tier to the server-resident OLAP logic. DecisionSuite, for example, provides server-based multidimensional data analysis capabilities that include Report Template, Filter, Calculation, Display, and Drill. These constitute the basic set of multidimensional analysis capabilities provided by most vendors, even though each vendor uses different terminology to describe them.

The Report Template is an instruction script containing the filters and calculations necessary to generate a user-requested report (typically displayed in tabular or graphic output format). A "virtual" document, the Report Template dynamically executes OLAP functions to produce an HTML page when it is requested to do so by a browser. A closer look at some of DecisionSuite's capabilities may illustrate how various server-resident OLAP functions and interface objects interact.

Filters package groupings of dimensions, attributes and calculations together as a single item for measurement. Simple filters represent groupings of elements that exist in the warehouse and that are typically dynamic in nature, such as "diet soft drinks with unit sales in Chicago greater than 1 million." Complex filters represent groupings of elements not represented in the warehouse, such as a realigned organizational chart or sales territory; they enable users to perform powerful, tactical what-if analysis without modifying the data warehouse. Calculations, which are used to measure dimensions, attributes, or filters, can be facts taken directly out of the warehouse or represented by arithmetic formulas (a ratio such as X/Y), nonarithmetic functions (COS, moving averages), or programs that derive values from the data warehouse.

Display objects are the mechanisms used to view the results produced by the OLAP functions; these may be spreadsheet grids, graphs, spatial dimensional models, or geographical information systems.

A well-designed OLAP system provides power users with the ability to author complex filters and advanced calculations without requiring programming skills or knowledge of SQL and database design. These filters and calculations become the enterprise's business rules, and themselves take the form of reusable objects. Once the filters and calculations are developed by authors, they should be readily available for use by active and casual users in their own applications.

The drill object gives all users advanced navigation functionality to drill up, down, and across dimensions, attributes, and calculations in pursuit of answers to rapid-fire business questions. The complexity of drilling is dependent on the need to navigate user-defined filters and calculations. Drilling should not be limited to navigating the content of database. As a user drills up or down dimensions, OLAP functions must be called to maintain the integrity of the filters and calculation at the new reporting levels.

OLAP Metadata

Interface and display objects are linked to OLAP functions and the data warehouse by metadata, which (as discussed in Chapter 4) provides information about the data warehouse content as well as the data used to execute OLAP functions. Because all OLAP tool vendors create proprietary metadata layers, these layers vary significantly among OLAP products. DecisionSuite is used here to illustrate the critical role that metadata plays, but the role is much the same in all OLAP tools.

Metadata serves several purposes in DecisionSuite. It provides a repository for business rules and inserts a semantic layer that isolates the user from the complexities of the data warehouse and OLAP application logic. It also describes the contents of the data warehouse to the OLAP application logic, and provides the additional information needed for the general OLAP functions to generate a database-specific query strategy. This strategy is responsible for efficient, pinpoint access to the warehouse content and optimal distribution of join, aggregation, and calculation processing between the RDBMS and OLAP application logic layer.

DecisionSuite's OLAP metadata model includes a very diverse description of the data warehouse, phrased in terms that are used by the OLAP functions:

- **Physical Location:** The database and server name that contain the data warehouse and data marts. Proper implementation should enable simultaneous access to multiple, heterogeneous relational database management systems (RDBMS) in a manner that is transparent to the user.

- **OLAP Processing Rules:** Complex forms of data analysis often require a multistep process. OLAP processing rules define the most efficient means of processing joins, aggregations, and calculations. These rules determine how processing is distributed between the database management system and OLAP functions. For example, it may be most efficient to perform simple aggregations in the database and to transfer the results into an analytic cache for more comprehensive multidimensional analysis. The effect translates into an optimized query strategy that can take advantage of SQL extensions like Red Brick Systems' RISQL, which was discussed in Chapter 8.

- **Aliasing:** Provide alternative, more descriptive names for dimensions, attributes, tables names, column names, calculations, and filters so that users can browse and select information in terms they understand.

- **Navigation Map:** A navigation map for the data warehouse includes the physical definition of dimensions, attributes, base facts, and the relationships among them. An important structure of the map includes the parent/child-level descriptions that drive the drilling process.

- **Summary-Level Information:** Information that identifies data redundancies, such as those created by storing frequently requested aggregations necessary to drive an aggregate-aware query strategy. The OLAP query logic must be aware of aggregates that are put in the data warehouse to improve response time for frequently requested summary data.

- **RDBMS Key Information:** Information to drive query strategy to leverage prejoined data and eliminate table scans.

- **Filters:** Rules that describe both simple and complex filters.

- **Calculations:** Formulas or programs that describe calculated facts.

- **Objects:** Instructions that describe all other interface objects including agents, formatting, exception rules, formatting, and reports.

- **Descriptions:** A repository for commentary concerning anything contained or derived from the data warehouse, including original author and date of the information, and perhaps a paragraph describing for what the information is intended.

This metadata model provides information that is used at runtime to formulate an efficient SQL query and the enterprise-specific business rules that are necessary to perform the analysis. Because the business rules are stored in the metadata, they are accessible to all users, just as if they were facts or dimensions of the data warehouse itself. Users need not know what data are stored as facts in the data warehouse or created as calculations by the multidimensional OLAP functions.

Barriers to Timely Access of OLAP Information

For power users, applications that allow *direct pulling* of information from the metadata directory provide the greatest flexibility in directing OLAP functions. Authors typically create new calculations, filters, and report templates for their own use and publish the results so that other users can take advantage of their work. But selecting calculations, filters, and report templates from a series works well only as long as users are familiar with specific operations of the OLAP system.

The major challenge to individual productivity among active and casual users is determining where to find the information that already exists. These two classes of users are likely to have only superficial knowledge of OLAP and data warehousing. Consequently, somehow the system must connect people with the information they need, quickly and easily. Users require a mechanism that provides *indirect pulling* of information from the metadata directory, enabling them to intelligently ask for known *and unknown* information. For example, many active and casual users would be baffled when faced with the task of trying to find last week's eastern regional sales report for a specific product in the corporation's traditional client/server system. Many would not know that the eastern regional report contains the necessary information, and some proportion probably would not know that such a report exists. Most of the nontechnical users would have a difficult time determining the file type and traversing the network directory structure to look for a report name that sounded like a match. Intranet-based search engines provide the solution for this indirect pulling of information by allowing the user to focus on content rather than the application.

Search Engine Operation

The World Wide Web serves as a useful model for capabilities that users expect to find on intranets. Search engines, which represent one such capability, are crucial to the success of an intranet data warehouse. They provide the mechanism by which relatively nontechnical users can locate information that already exists within the warehouse. The World Wide Web has created a single information-access and processing interface that makes all underlying tools and disparate data types work like a single integrated application. Finding information on the Web is surprisingly easy. The user does not need to know the information exists, does not need to know where it is located, and does not require knowledge of its data type, or the tools used to access it. In fact, to find information on the Web, the user requires only an inkling of what he or she is looking for and access to one of the many search engines.

For example, let's say we're planning a business trip to New Orleans and we're hoping to spend one evening dining on Cajun cuisine. A logical thing to do is get on the Web and see if we can find the name of a good restaurant. Using Excite, Yahoo, or a similar search engine, we would probably just type something in like "New Orleans" and "Cajun food" to derive the type of results illustrated in Figures 11.1, 11.2, and 11.3.

The result is a list of relevant content that may include links to restaurant

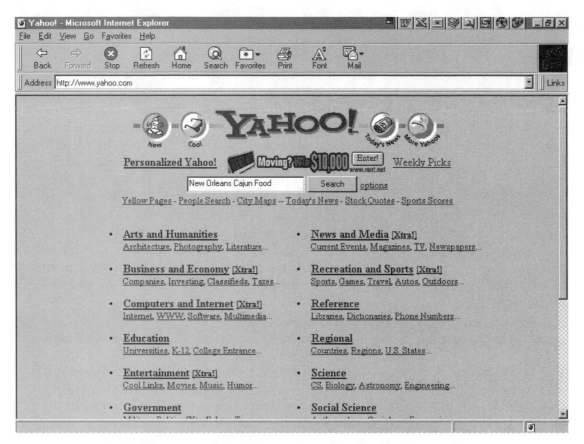

Figure 11.1 Search engine results and sample content.

home pages, critics recommendations, and/or newspaper and magazine articles. To pull this information from the Web, we focused entirely on content, without concern for whether the web pages actually existed, where they were located, what they were called, or what type of information they contained.

Publishing information on the Web so it can be "found" by search engines is quite easy. If, for example, you're the owner of one of the restaurants in New Orleans, once you've finished defining the content of your Web site, you need only request that the providers of the Internet search engines (Yahoo, Excite, etc.) index your site in their search engine. This is usually done by e-mail and should include a list of keywords that would indicate a likely interest in your

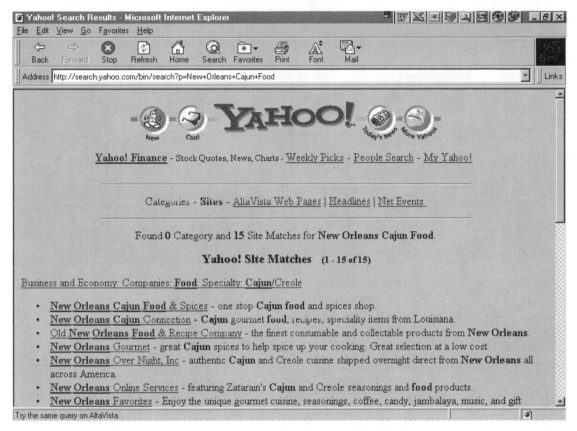

Figure 11.2 Search engine results and sample content.

Web site's content, such as Cajun, New Orleans, blackened, catfish, crawfish, and so on. Once the information is compiled into the search engines, anyone requesting a search using one of the keywords would find their way to your site. Figure 11.4 illustrates indexing Web content to a search engine.

Users do not need to know the network address and name of your Web page or even of its existence to retrieve information about the restaurant. Similarly, knowledge of how to use and operate your Web site is not required. Anyone with a browser can find and use the information.

There are a number of search engines in use on the Internet, but two companies in particular offer products that focus on corporate intranet applications

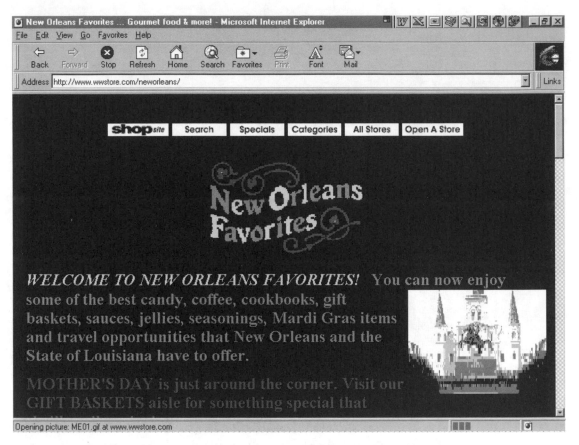

Figure 11.3   Search engine results and sample content.

and are especially well suited for intranet data warehousing. Both companies are focusing their products to respond to the unique requirements of intranets by adding database links and agent-processing capabilities.

- Fulcrum Technologies' SearchServer is a multiplatform indexing and retrieval search engine that organizes and references information through a table structure in which every row corresponds to a document or object (i.e., the link to OLAP functions). Columns contain profile information like author, title, or other keywords associated

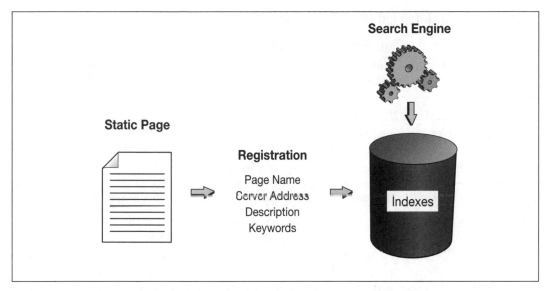

Figure 11.4   Indexing existing content into a search engine.

with the document/object. SearchServer supports Boolean operators like AND, OR, and NOT, which allow users to construct highly targeted queries, and relies on comprehensive indexing of terms to support high-performance searches. SearchServer is accessed by an API that uses Microsoft's ODBC. Tables are accessible through Fulcrum's SearchSQL language.

- Verity Inc. offers SEARCH '97 Information Server, an integrated search engine and Agent Server that allows users to establish queries as agents. Agents continuously monitor the database to detect when information that matches the query is detected or changed. The agents then notify users that the information exists or that updated information is available.

Agent technologies bridge the gap between more effective pulling and efficient pushing of information to users. When the technology is extended to the intranet data warehouse, agents must be capable of monitoring what is occurring within the database and of notifying users that a change in business conditions has been detected.

Extending the URL to Find OLAP Resources

Using a search engine to access information on the Internet or an intranet merely involves finding the server and locating the requested Web page on that server. This is because most of the information resources available on the Internet and intranets is unstructured content, which is stored as static documents. Accessing information that involves instructing OLAP functions to dynamically *create* documents based on the data contained in the warehouse adds a new twist. Because the document must be created, the traditional method of finding the server address and document page name is not a valid option.

The solution lies in a well-designed object environment integrated with a search engine like Fulcrum's SearchServer or Verity's SEARCH '97. Decision-Suite's Report Template, for example, contains the filters and calculations that define report content and their resulting analysis. Because it is a "virtual" report, created online when requested by a user, it can be represented to a search engine and indexed as if it actually existed. In fact, it is a program script that defines the SQL generation, data processing and formatting, and the location for the content after it is created.

The program's parameters are the necessary filters and calculations. By indexing a URL to a search engine that launches a program script to generate the resulting report content at runtime rather than displaying a precreated content page, the user is able to access OLAP services in the same seamless manner as finding any other content on the web. For example, you could access the report template shown in Figure 11.5 by typing a URL, which in turn links the

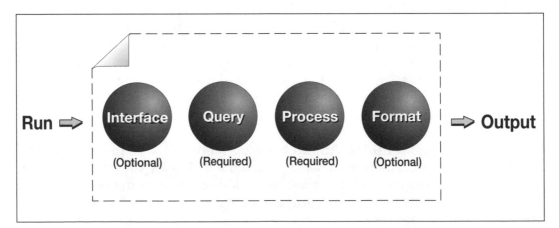

Figure 11.5 Report template script with parameters.

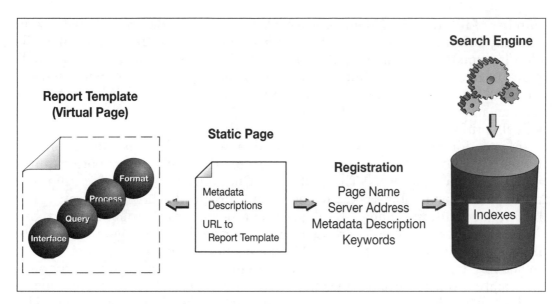

Figure 11.6 Indexing a report template script to a search engine using an indexed URL.

address of a program and launches that program with parameters. This is illustrated in Figure 11.6.

From a search engine's perspective, an index containing a URL redirects the link from the URL to the OLAP program script. Indexing this type of URL is the same process as any other search. Properly designed Web-enabled OLAP tools provide administrators with a means for creating these specialized URLs by automating the use of the existing name and description from the OLAP metadata model, as well as providing a wizard for building the syntax of the URL. Integrating intranet technologies with OLAP and data warehousing resources places significant demands on the application architecture. Products that can best support this level of integration are those with a server-centric view for executing OLAP functions.

Information Resource Overload

One barrier to individual productivity on the Internet that is likely to become evident on intranets is the effort and time it takes to wade through the growing number of information resources available to users. The data warehouse is one of many information resources that share an intranet. As the number of available information resources multiplies, it is understandable that only a small percentage of the information will have relevance to a user's immediate decision-support requirements. Not only does wading through the information take an unacceptable amount of time, it can also cloud users' ability to see valuable information when it crosses their path.

Information services must have a way to automatically push important information into the user community based on the decision-support requirements of individual users. The challenge is not only to detect when information becomes available or has changed, but also to detect when operational business conditions change. By delegating a portion of the data analysis and filtering processing to software agents, the intranet becomes a more complete information delivery mechanism. Without agent technology, users are limited to actively pulling information. Agents provide a means of pushing important information out to decision makers, monitoring changes within the database, and ensuring that users are promptly notified of critical business issues. The result is an OLAP system that is not only "online" for active searches, but one that is also continuously processing information on behalf of users.

OLAP Agent Technology

By definition, agents are self-contained software processes that run in the background and perform a useful action on behalf of a user or group of users. Agents come in a variety of models. Simple agents perform small, repetitive tasks, while intelligent agents can decide which tasks are to be included in processing by choosing from a library of simple agents to perform several tasks in proper sequence. Learning agents observe how users perform tasks and then automate those tasks based on that behavior.

Most production systems have literally thousands or tens of thousands of agents deployed across the system to help users monitor business issues. Maintaining such an environment is almost impossible if agents are not designed as self-contained processes. Unless the agents can stand on their own, be called by other processes, and be nested together as intelligent agents, it is impossible for them to be self-maintaining as the data around them changes. For OLAP, this means the query and processing steps must be linked at runtime.

For example, a simple OLAP agent may automatically run the weekly sales report at 1:00 A.M. every Monday morning for the entire calendar year. In order for this agent to be completely independent of changes in the database, it must execute the entire OLAP process at the strike of 1:00 A.M. Figure 11.7 illustrates an encapsulated OLAP process being executed at 1:00 A.M. with the results delivered to the sales directory.

A system design that executes the query step and only schedules the SQL to be processed at 1:00 A.M. every Monday will, of course, eventually start yielding inaccurate results since the database and/or metadata changes over time. This design is useless and impractical in production systems that run thousands of reports with agents in a given week because of the maintenance overhead incurred. The SQL must be generated by the agent at runtime *and* be based upon a run-time consultation of the metadata to ensure a maintenance free agent environment.

By definition, an agent must also be a background process. A true background process, like the one illustrated in Figure 11.8, is invoked or awakened

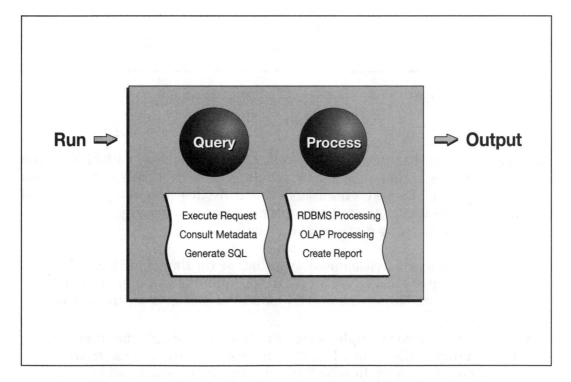

Figure 11.7 Example of an agent-directed OLAP process.

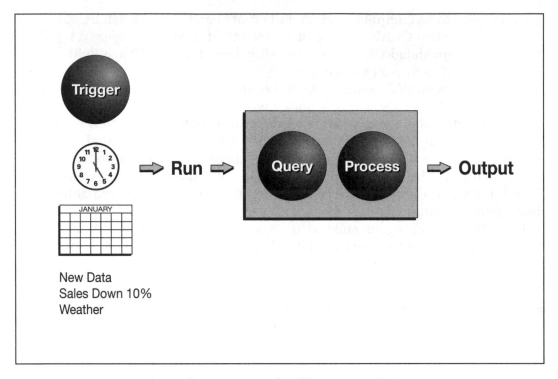

Figure 11.8 Example of a background process.

by a trigger rather than the user, and does not depend on the availability of the user's PC. In this manner, the agents are able to automatically perform tasks without *any* dependence on the users. This truly delegates the processing of the task from the user to the agent to optimize user productivity.

Triggers come in many makes and models:

- A trigger may be a scheduled event based on time and date. This type of trigger is used extensively to schedule the running of agents on a recurring basis (e.g., every Monday morning or on the 5th of every month).

- A trigger can also be implemented as a Boolean variable that invokes the running of the agent when its value becomes true. These triggers are used extensively to schedule the running of agents when new data in the warehouse is available, or when a value in the data warehouse exceeds a threshold. For example, if fewer than 1,000,000 units of diet cola sold in Memphis last week, the trigger would become true and would invoke an agent to run one or more reports that would allow a decision maker to correct the problem.

- A trigger can also be based on a value that is in the OLTP system database rather than the data warehouse. For example, if the number of inventoried units of diet cola in Memphis falls below 10,000,000, the trigger would become true.

- Triggers can also be based on a nondata event like a worker strike, or when a certain weather condition occurs. Triggers that extend beyond the warehouse environment offer a powerful tool for tying the OLAP environment to the rest of an organization's IT investments, and provides the user with a powerful workflow application.

By definition, once an agent passes the self-contained process and background process requirement, it must also perform a useful task on behalf of the user.

Standard Reporting

Even an agent that meets only the bare minimum requirements of the agent definition can delegate an enormous amount of work from the user to the OLAP system. The age-old mainframelike delivery of standard reports on Monday morning is still the most widely utilized task for agents today. Figure 11.9 illustrates this common use of agent technology.

Although simple in nature, these agents provide enormous benefits to the user and IT organization. The user automatically receives reports without hav-

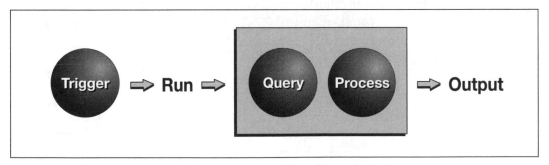

Figure 11.9   Example of standard reporting.

ing to manually build and run them, thereby saving valuable time. The IT organization is able to drastically reduce processing resources by running each report only once and delivering it to hundreds or thousands of users.

User Notification

A powerful concept in agent technology is the ability notify the user that an agent has completed its task and inform the user(s) where to get the results or output. Standard reporting works well as long as the user knows or expects the results of an agent at a certain time. However, for those agents that are triggered by a value in the data warehouse, OLTP database, or some other nonpredictable event, the user must be notified in order to take action on those results in a reasonable time (see Figure 11.10).

In this model, the agent automatically carries out the action and notifies the users of the new information via e-mail, pager, or a customizable user interface. The agent's results can also be attached with the message—for example, as an e-mail attachment—further benefiting the user by delivering the results with the notification.

Exception Reporting

The sheer size of most data warehouses (containing gigabytes and terabytes of data) makes it virtually impossible for users to "surf" through the data to find nuggets of vital information that require immediate attention. The prolifera-

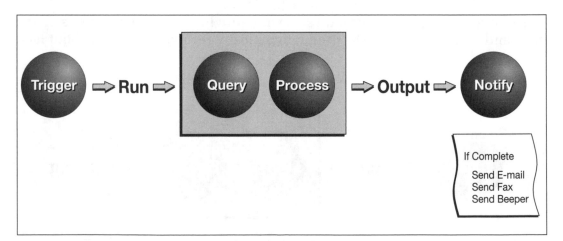

Figure 11.10   Example of user notification.

tion of nondata warehouse information in the form of documents, coupled with the infinite amount of information available on the World Wide Web also drives business users to view the data warehouse as just one of many sources of available information. In reality, the data warehouse, though large in size, is a small fish in the big pond of information. Looking for relevant information is much like looking for a needle in a haystack, and most business users just can't afford the hours it takes to perform this process.

With all this information readily available, the challenge is no longer empowering users to access and surf for information, but rather to provide them with a means of automating the surfing process. This process is called *exception reporting*, and when delegated to an agent provides a necessary tool for any enterprise decision support system. In the case of OLAP, exception reporting extends the agent capability with additional background processes that work off the *derived* data in the report, as shown in Figure 11.11.

The exception-reporting process runs through the derived values in a report and compares them to thresholds or limits defined by the user. For example, a user can request an agent to automatically run the national sales report whenever the warehouse is updated with new data. Once the report is created, the exception-seeking process can check to see, for example, whether any of the "% Change Year Ago" values have dropped by more than 5 percent. If they have, the agent notifies the user that the acceptable threshold for "Sales versus Year Ago" has been exceeded. If none of the values in the report exceeds the

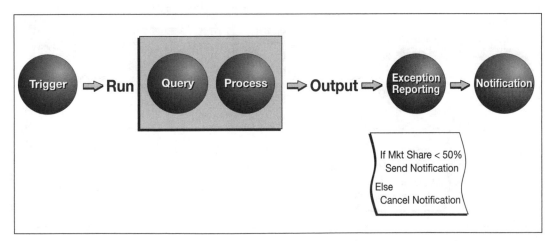

Figure 11.11 Example of exception reporting.

exception threshold, the notification is canceled and the user is not bothered with the unimportant information.

In practice, this technology enables a user not only to invoke the services of a dozen or so agents to analyze the entire business model, but also to have those agents look specifically for the conditions that matter most, thereby filtering only the most urgent information back to the user. The result is a system that delegates costly "surf" time to the decision-support system, and directs the user to the tasks involved with resolving the most critical business issues.

Intelligent Agents

Intelligent agents have the unique ability to make decisions at runtime based on the current status of the data, system, or environment. For example, a retail organization may develop an agent that analyzes the inventory for a given product, but the product to be analyzed depends on a trigger. When the designated trigger becomes true (for example, because the weather report forecasts a blizzard), the interface process may feed the report template "snow shovels" as the product filter and "Minneapolis" as the market filter (see Figure 11.12). If another trigger becomes true when the Green Bay Packers win the Super Bowl, the interface process may feed the report template "football jerseys" and "Wisconsin" as the market filter.

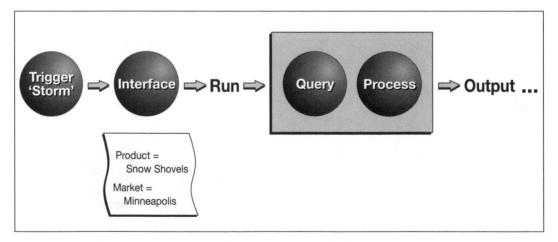

Figure 11.12 Intelligent agent with dynamic content.

By adding an interface process to the agent, the ability to dynamically pass the agent filters and/or calculations can be based on a given event. Such agents can drastically reduce the development effort of agents by allowing a single agent to be utilized for multiple purposes. This is another reason to link the query and process steps at runtime. Architectures that separate these processes cannot support intelligent agents.

Intelligent agents can also comprise the background execution of two or more agents where the agents are dynamically linked at runtime based on conditional logic. For example, one agent executes an exception report and a second initiates a detailed analysis for each exception (see Figure 11.13).

Intelligent agents provide the unique ability to automate decision makers' workflow. An intelligent agent can, for example, take the results from an agent that discovered an out-of-stock situation for a product in a retail store and use it to call another agent that automatically orders the out-of-stock product from a warehouse for next-day delivery.

All types of agents can be scheduled to work on behalf of individual users, all members of a workgroup, or all users within an enterprise. It is important when managing a large number of agents working for a large user community that system administrators have the authority to cancel agents, alter priorities, and restore agents and triggers in order to ensure that processing is administered without requiring user intervention.

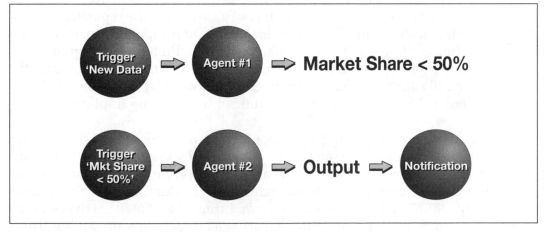

Figure 11.13   Intelligent agent driving workflow.

Team Productivity

The most valuable corporate information is not stored in the data warehouse or any computer system; rather, it is the opinions, experience, and personal knowledge of the individuals in the organization that is most important. Maximizing an organization's productivity can happen only if those individuals work together as a team, sharing their knowledge with colleagues during the decision-making process. The data warehouse and OLAP functions provide only the resources to help decision makers become more informed.

That said, an intranet data warehouse can facilitate collaboration among individuals to correctly interpret information and implement decisions. Successfully integrating the data warehouse and OLAP functions into groupware systems, which are the evolutionary path of intranets, is crucial to ensuring information sharing and collaboration within an organization.

The intranet data warehouse addresses many of the issues involved in optimizing teamwork and user productivity by providing:

- Consistent data and information
- Effective communication of the information
- A means for users to share work in progress

Shared Metadata

Using a shared metadata repository on the network is one way to help ensure consistent OLAP information. Because metadata serves as the repository for the business rules in the form of filters, calculations, and report templates, a network location centralizes its maintenance and facilitates synchronizing the rules for each user's application, ensuring accuracy and consistency across the system. Not only is the collaboration process improved by ensuring consistency across users, but productivity is maximized by reducing duplication of effort.

The disadvantage to placing metadata on the network rather than on the desktop, thereby making it immediately accessible by every user, is that it raises some security concerns. Any environment that promotes the sharing of information must also provide a secure framework in which that sharing occurs. An elegant solution is achieved by combining distributed network-based metadata with powerful workgroup security. The metadata model described earlier in this chapter can be easily advanced to support secure enterprise-sharing of its elements by applying individual network-based user or group profile user IDs and privileges to each object in the metadata structure. All read/write privileges are thus automatically built in to the distribution mechanism, achieving complete enterprise management and control over authoring and publishing of each business rule.

The flexibility of such an implementation is easily recognized when multiple workgroups use different business terms for the same business purpose. For example, the marketing organization may view the number of products sold as volume while the finance department may view the same fact as units. Under such a scenario, the number of products sold is actually represented by two instances of that rule in the metadata. Members of marketing are aware and have corresponding authoring and publishing privileges associated with only the volume instance. Meanwhile, members of finance are aware and have corresponding authoring and publishing privileges associated with only the units instance.

Effective OLAP Communication

Problems resulting from ineffective communications are responsible for consuming a great deal of decision-makers' time—often needlessly. Duplication of effort frequently occurs because users are simply uninformed—and therefore unaware—of work that has already been done. Effective communication requires more than just reporting the news. The *assumptions* behind the news must be communicated as well. Only when a group of people understand what must be done and why it must be done can a coordinated, collaborative team effort be put forth toward a common goal.

Shared Notification

Notification is the first step in effective communication in an intranet data warehousing user community. Direct notification through electronic messaging is a common means of getting the news out. Users broadcast the availability of new business rules, reports, and ideas through an organization's e-mail system. In some cases, the reports may even be attached to the messages, giving the recipient immediate access to the new information. Agents can also broadcast their findings across the organization's e-mail system—often targeting a group of users based on subject area and exception criteria.

Shared Assumptions

Getting the information out there is only part of the battle. Ensuring proper interpretation of the information is another matter entirely. In trying to make sense of any information or analyses, understanding how the idea was derived is key to creating an environment for effective discussion of the topic. In other words, the first part of any conversation usually starts with understanding the assumptions behind the analysis.

Thus, effective OLAP groupware must also provide recipients of analyses with the assumptions used to derive the result. For example, the assumptions behind any sales analysis include the definition of each territory, product, and time period measured, as well as the actual formulas used to calculate those measures. In addition, there may also be a need to inform the recipients about when the report was last generated, any data warehouse inconsistencies that may have existed when the report was run, the names of the users who authored the business rules, and any commentary other users or authors may have about the report. Figure 11.14 shows how a report might look if a user chose the option of displaying information about the report. Information of

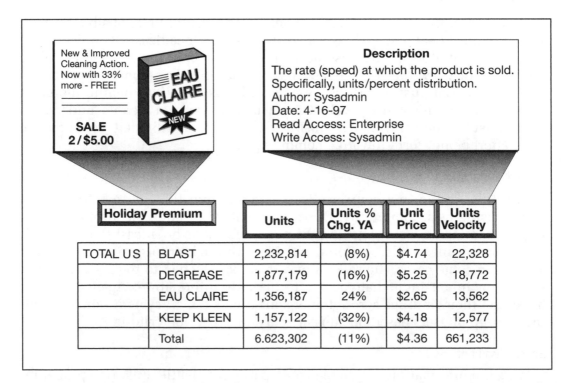

Holiday Premium		Units	Units % Chg. YA	Unit Price	Units Velocity
TOTAL US	BLAST	2,232,814	(8%)	$4.74	22,328
	DEGREASE	1,877,179	(16%)	$5.25	18,772
	EAU CLAIRE	1,356,187	24%	$2.65	13,562
	KEEP KLEEN	1,157,122	(32%)	$4.18	12,577
	Total	6.623,302	(11%)	$4.36	661,233

Figure 11.14   A report is based on assumptions that must be communicated.

this nature is vital to the recipient's ability to assimilate the information and to quickly and accurately interpret the report.

The metadata model described earlier can be advanced to support the secure enterprise sharing of its elements, as well as their corresponding assumptions. Adding another attribute to the metadata structure for storing each element's detailed description, annotation and commentary, and name and time stamp of authoring is the optimal way to deliver such a solution. When information is delivered in this manner, along with its assumptions, the magic of collaboration can begin.

Sharing OLAP Work in Progress

Collaboration is the cornerstone for a successful decision-making process. Interaction between appropriate analysts and decision makers is the best way to guarantee proper interpretation of opportunities and problems, to identify the best solutions, and to pave the way for consistently making informed decisions. Expedience in decision making correlates directly to the degree of real-time interaction. Live information makes collaboration possible, allowing users to explore and offer suggestions regarding the information and analyses throughout the enterprise.

Referring to information as live implies it has intelligence about how to interact with its surroundings. For example, assumptions provide users with information on how to interpret a situation: For example, to determine what level they are currently at within the Territory dimension; or by whom, when, and for what purpose the market share calculation was originally authored; or even the newspaper ad that was tied to the product promotion. Live information also provides users with the capability to *challenge each of those assumptions* by drilling in or out to different levels of detail and to build upon the initial thought by extending the analysis from where the last person left off.

Figure 11.15 provides an example of how members of a team might carry out the analysis process. In this example, an agent that was originally authored by an analyst organization notifies a marketing manager that units sold in the western region dropped by 15 percent in the past week, and delivers substantiating reports along with the message. The manager immediately verifies the source of the information (e.g., determining where the agent came from and when it was run). In this way, the manager can assess the validity of the information, for example, to be sure that the data in the warehouse was complete at the time that the report was run and that the decrease is not mere-

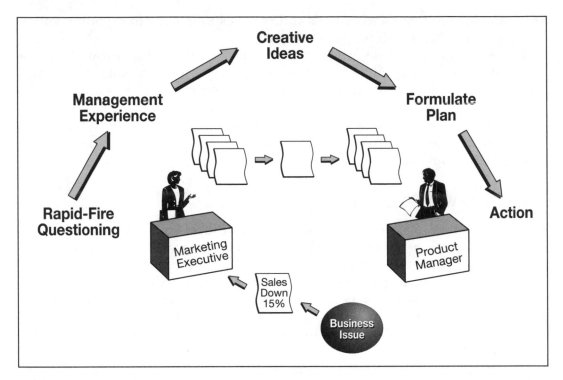

Figure 11.15 Multiple decision makers must work collaboratively to solve business problems.

ly the result of incomplete sales information. After the information is verified, the manager can drill deeper into the report to determine the specific products contributing to the decline. When the manager has isolated the decline, which in this case we'll assume was due to a decrease in the sale of frozen breakfast products, he or she can route the analysis to the manger of frozen breakfast products. At this point, the product manager extends the analysis by comparing performance across the region with several competitors and adding measures to determine whether the decrease in volume was due to lower prices or increased advertising. The organization can then use the resulting analysis to make an informed decision on how to best correct the problem.

In this manner, users engage in real-time, interactive discussions of problems, directly leveraging the accurate and consistent data found in the warehouse. In effect, users are *sharing work in progress*. The recipients of such information are able pick up the analysis where another left off. Obviously, the value of such an activity is incalculable for making informed business decisions quickly.

Sharing live OLAP information requires exchanging the OLAP analytic logic in midstream. Sharing at this level requires an information-rich report model that must contain not only the resulting report data set, but also its assumptions and instructions used to build the report and manipulate it. In this way, the report recipient is able to use the network-based, shared metadata repository to reestablish a live link to both the data warehouse and the OLAP analytic logic so the analysis process can pick up at the point where the previous user left off. Live information technology lets users instantly explore and offer suggestions on all shared information, analyses, and assumptions, regardless of their location. Live information is fundamental for teams of analysts and decision makers to interactively work together on a single problem.

Conclusion

The Internet, today, relies on users to initiate an information search, essentially "pulling" information from Web servers to the browser. Search engine technologies simplify the process of seeking meaningful content. Within a business management context however, users are accustomed to being alerted to business issues. It is essential that intranets provide information push technologies to alert users of any business issues that require a user's attention. The enormous power of an intranet data warehouse begins to be apparent when the user, once alerted to a business action issue, is able to employ additional mechanisms to initiate further information searches and to collaborate with other users to resolve the issue.

CHAPTER TWELVE

INTEGRATING THE PIECES

Throughout, this book has stressed the concept that the convergence of three technologies—data warehousing, OLAP, and the Internet and intranet—are establishing a new enterprise information infrastructure. This new infrastructure provides the raw data, comprehensive data analysis functions, and expanded communications capabilities for information-rich collaboration among decision makers.

Today, the concepts surrounding these three technologies are often discussed as separate, loosely related topics. Each is evolving at its own rapid pace, largely driven by software vendors focused on solving one piece of the information management challenge. Amidst this seeming chaos, there is one simple shared vision: Corporations must find ways to accelerate effective decision making and successful decision implementation. Each of the three technologies plays a crucial role in achieving those goals. When combined, they provide the tools for establishing the overwhelming superiority needed to outsmart the competition.

Lessons from the Past

Internet technologies are in many ways causing us to relearn many of the lessons from the mainframe computing era. As discussed in the earlier chapters, we are once again facing issues of scalability, security, and information sharing that were largely overlooked in the era of power PCs and the rise of client/server computing. Data warehousing, particularly intranet data warehousing, requires discipline in managing information resources, a necessity often ignored by PC users accustomed to charting their own course.

At the same time, the Internet is a source of new lessons. If traditional project planning methods were used in the design of the World Wide Web, we would probably still be at the user requirements definition phase. Instead, many of the tenets of systems planning were abandoned in the process of developing the world's largest information store. The Internet is based on rapid evolution in response to users' needs, and involves multiple, parallel development activities. But the process works because the initial development effort was guided by a set of simple standards.

As corporations adapt Internet technologies for corporate intranets, they must provide access to structured content (i.e., the data warehouse) as well as the unstructured content that is typical of the Internet. The fundamental challenge in establishing an intranet data warehouse is to meet the need to dynamically transform raw data into meaningful information. Similarly, the role of OLAP functions is also evolving, moving beyond simply providing users with an easy means of executing SQL queries and formatting the result set for display to bridging the "static" Web content with "dynamic" document creation using data retrieved from the warehouse. In many respects, the data warehouse is becoming one piece in an integrated set of enterprise information resources all accessible from a single universal interface. The Web browser, in conjunction with one or more search engines, serves as the universal interface to all of the corporation's information resources.

By now, it should be clear that planning and implementing an intranet data warehouse is a complex and challenging task, particularly in an era of rapidly evolving technologies and shifting business requirements. Many of the crucial issues were addressed in previous chapters, and much like the three technologies themselves, the issues are closely related and must be integrated in the planning and implementation process. To illustrate this integration, this chapter uses a hypothetical company—the Raleigh Candy Company—to track the development of an intranet data warehouse from the initial planning stages through implementation.

Raleigh Candy Company: Planning the Intranet Data Warehouse

The Raleigh Candy Company is a leading manufacturer of candy products, which sells its products through small retail stores located in shopping centers throughout North America. Product sales are highly seasonal, with peak sales occurring at Halloween, Christmas, and Easter. Raleigh devotes the majority of its marketing budget to promotions during these three holiday periods. In addition to offering competitive promotions, Raleigh's store managers work closely with regional sales managers to ensure that inventories are at the proper level during key promotional periods. Too little inventory results in out-of-stock situations and lost revenue opportunities. Because products are specially packaged to correspond with promotions, it is often necessary to discount excess inventory remaining after the promotions in order to liquidate the stock. Although promotions are important for increasing sales, if they are poorly executed, they are costly in terms of income and lost opportunities.

Raleigh's sales and marketing managers have expressed increasing frustration with the quality of sales and marketing data available from outdated information systems. More important, the management team believed that it was no longer responsive to rapidly changing competitive conditions at the local retail level. Until recently, the sales and marketing managers were apprised of sales results through hard-copy, batch reports. Several months ago, the company installed a network and upgraded the users' PCs to Window 95. At that time, the managers began to receive sales reports via company e-mail, which improved information distribution but did not alleviate the managers' frustrations over the quality of the available sales data. In a further attempt to upgrade its corporate information network, the company installed a Web server that enabled customers to access information about the company over the Internet.

When information services (IS) managers proposed replacing the outdated mainframe-based management reporting system with a data warehouse, they received quick approval to begin the planning and implementation process. IS management recognized that the success of the data warehouse hinged on a quick response to high-priority business issues.

Corporate Mission and Goals

Raleigh's first step in the planning effort was to define the corporate mission and goals to ensure that the database, applications, and deployment strategies for the data warehouse system were aligned with the business goals of the enterprise. IS management, along with senior company management and managers in the marketing, sales operations, and finance departments joined to develop a corporate mission statement and define specific goals for the organization. The management team agreed that Raleigh wanted to become the leading supplier of premium brand confection products in North America by the year 2000; they identified four goals that the company would need to achieve in the next three years to meet the objective:

- Increase its market share leadership position by 10 basis points.
- Increase profitability by 10 percent over the same time period.
- Produce the highest-quality confection products, based on consumer satisfaction measures.
- Reduce supply chain costs by 15 percent within three years.

Management Decisions

Raleigh Candy's ability to achieve its corporate mission and goals is largely driven by its ability to make and implement effective and timely decisions at all levels of management. Decisions in the areas of sales and margin analysis, inventory management, pricing, promotion effectiveness, and category management span all functional areas of the company.

Representatives of the management team turned their attention to the task of defining the specific goals of the data warehouse application. The first priority was to limit the scope of the initial development to meet users' needs based on corporate priorities. The seasonal nature of the candy business placed a high priority on the informational requirements of the marketing department, with particular emphasis on the operational and tactical decisions associated with product promotions. Figure 12.1 illustrates the focus of the initial phase of Raleigh's intranet data warehouse plan.

Focusing on the operational and tactical decision-support needs of marketing department managers revealed the need to respond to the following types of questions:

- Did we supply the right amount of product to our retailers in support of the holiday promotion?
- Did the promotion actually drive incremental profitability or did it simply cause consumers to purchase our products earlier and at a lower margin?
- Can we raise the product price or will the increased margin be offset by lower sales velocity?

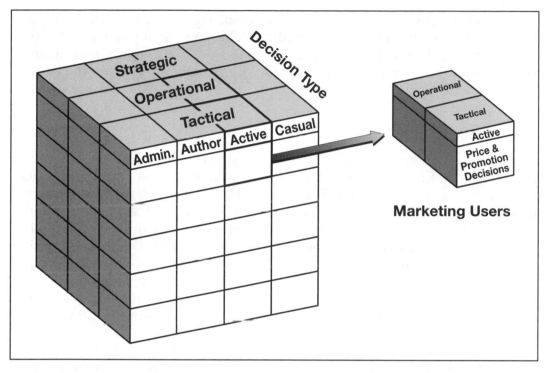

Figure 12.1   Raleigh's initial intranet data warehouse development phase.

- Is our new product driving new customers to the category or is it simply cannibalizing existing product sales?
- How can we help the retailer better market at the individual store level?

Identifying the Users

The next step in the Raleigh planning process was identifying the users, assessing their technical skills, and defining their decision-support requirements. Investigation revealed that the potential users included nearly 2,000 marketing managers, sales managers, and store managers, all with relatively minimal technical skills. In addition, the users were dispersed over a wide geographic area, ranging from the corporate office to regional sales offices and individual retail stores; even the marketing managers at corporate headquarters were frequently away from the office. The need to support a large, geographically dispersed user community convinced the Raleigh management team that an intranet data warehouse could most effectively meet the organization's decision-support requirements.

Defining Requirements

The data and analytic requirements of the system began to emerge when the team reviewed the decisions that users were tasked with making and the information they needed to make those decisions. Representatives of the various user departments were added to the original management team to bring hands-on expertise to the planning process. The team proceeded to identify operational systems that would serve as the source for sales data, as well as pricing and promotion allowance data. The team also identified the need for information about the promotions, including promotion calendars, packaging changes, and coupons associated with each scheduled promotion. It soon became apparent that much of the information that users would find useful in answering their questions existed in text and image form.

The necessity of incorporating multidimensional OLAP capabilities was indicated by the users' need to perform extensive ad hoc data analysis. In addition, users required standard and exception reports, with automatic delivery to specific users to update them with the latest available information or notify them of exception conditions. Users also expressed the desire to be able to share knowledge, experience, and analyses in a proactive, real-time environment with both their peers at headquarters and with retail store managers. They felt that such sharing would improve communications between headquarters and store managers and ultimately lead to faster response to local opportunities.

Users also wanted the ability to seamlessly initiate a decision without having to exit one system and enter another one. If, for example, a report indicated a need to mark down a product to reduce inventory, users wanted to be able to initiate the change from a single system interface.

At this point, the planning team felt that it had sufficiently narrowed the scope of the initial phase and had defined user requirements to a level that permitted implementation planning. The team itself served as the core development group that would eventually become an information resource management department. The department would gradually assume responsibility for all intranet applications development including the intranet data warehouse. The team's charter was to solve the immediate business problem while establishing the technology foundation for the ongoing evolution of the intranet and intranet data warehouse.

Database Strategy

The first decision that the planning team made concerned the database strategy. Because there were compelling business reasons to improve the decision-support and implementation process within the marketing department, the team decided to focus the initial development efforts on building a data mart based on a dimensional model. At the same time, they decided to begin developing a strategy for implementing a more comprehensive data warehouse, a central data warehouse that could more efficiently feed multiple distributed data marts.

The team chose a simple star schema, as illustrated in Figure 12.2, for the

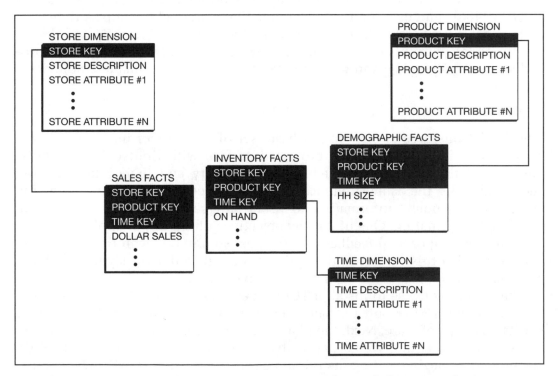

Figure 12.2   Raleigh Candy Company's logical data mart design.

design of the data mart. Once the design was chosen, the team was able to define methods for data extraction, preparation, and validation to create and update the data warehouse. Then members of the team evaluated extract software tools, hardware platforms, and relational database management systems based on the requirements for the initial data mart, as well as their capacity to scale upward to meet the requirements for the larger enterprisewide data warehouse.

Application Strategy

In reviewing users' information needs, the planning team determined that multidimensional OLAP capabilities were required to support ad hoc analysis and reporting. Because corporate management elected to develop the actual application interface in-house to meet the specific requirements of the large user community, the planning team had to select a multidimensional analysis tool that incorporated an API that developers could use to design browser interface and display objects. Team members conducted a thorough evaluation of OLAP tools and eventually selected one that provided the appropriate analytic capabilities (for multidimensional analysis), was sufficiently scalable to accommodate current and future needs (for a server-centric architecture), provided agent processing, and was capable of supporting intranet technologies.

Deployment Strategy

The initial business application, a basic set of sales reporting applications, was designed as a simple Web browser interface with limited functionality. Because of the widely dispersed user community and their relatively low technical skills, the data warehouse application incorporated agent processing functions to "push" information to users and search engines to facilitate "pulling" information. One of the key objectives of the initial application was to gain user support and feedback for the next step in the evolutionary design. To accomplish this objective, the application had to deliver significant business value while providing a simple, intuitive interface.

The company chose to install a TCP/IP network and adopted Microsoft Office, along with Microsoft Exchange and Microsoft Explorer, as the standard for its desktop software. Next, the planning team supervised the installation of an NT Web server and Web server software for the intranet, and worked with developers to begin creating the initial pages of text using HTML. The company's stated objective in providing information over the intranet was to ensure that the widely dispersed user base would have consistent online access to the most current product information. In keeping with that goal, the initial text pages for the intranet provided users with product information and marketing program schedules. But the planning team still had to deal with the task of converting existing documents into electronic form, which required tagging the documents in HTML in order to link them to one another to provide pre-defined paths for information searches. As the intranet application began to evolve, the team added images so that store managers could visualize promotional material (e.g., coupons, banners, and displays) and product packaging that would be used to merchandise upcoming promotions.

In formulating the deployment strategy for the data warehouse, the team elected to integrate the intranet data warehouse content with the unstructured content being organized on the intranet. By integrating the two types of information, users were provided with access to accurate text descriptions (planning documents) and images of the upcoming promotions, as well as to sales data for performing a complete analysis of performance.

IS managers determined that they would need to upgrade the Web server to a UNIX platform to accommodate the additional processing required to support the increased traffic for intranet data warehouse access. The planning team elected to begin "pushing" information over the intranet by providing users with a basic set of sales reports derived from data in the warehouse. Knowing that the users' appetite for information was very high, the team used these initial applications to refine system requirements. The planning team also recognized that users would eventually expect to have ad hoc data analysis capabilities, that is, to be able to initiate their own analysis without starting from a predefined report. To provide these additional capabilities, the interface (method of defining a new report) and data display (definition of format and graphical output) components of the browser would have to be more functionally rich. By adding Java applets to the basic HTML interface, the development team planned to roll out additional features in phases. Remember, the first goal in deploying a simple application is to minimize the training and support burden.

Raleigh's Intranet Data Warehouse: Implementing the Applications

This section describes the implementation of Raleigh's intranet data warehouse application from two perspectives: the interface and display screens that appear within the context of the users' decision-support requirements, and a technical overview that summarizes the activity that occurs "under the covers" on the intranet and at the server. Figure 12.3 illustrates the initial Raleigh screen or home page for the company's intranet data warehouse application.

User Perspective

At the hypothetical Raleigh Candy Company, user Sam Sweet arrives at work and, from his desktop, accesses a personalized version of the intranet home page using Microsoft's Internet Explorer browser (Figure 12.3). The home page contains a wealth of information, including the corporate newsletter and links

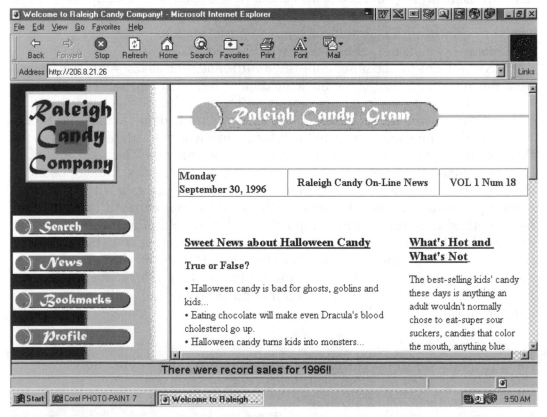

Figure 12.3 Raleigh's intranet home page.

to a broad range of intranet information resources. Sam clicks on the News link to see if anything requires immediate attention, then begins to review the latest news (Figure 12.4).

Technical Overview

Sam can employ any of the usual Web browser methods (e.g., typing in URLs or using hotlinks or bookmarks) to navigate through the corporate intranet to retrieve specific information. While some pages are stored on one or more of the several Web servers as static, preexisting HTML documents, others are created on the fly based upon the user's request for information. The intranet

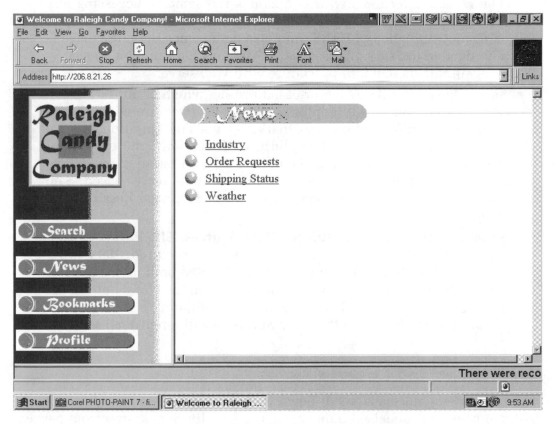

Figure 12.4 Raleigh's intranet news link.

home page, for example, represents a static Web page, while an OLAP report that is obtained by drilling in an existing report is an example of a dynamically created Web page. The corporate intranet contains Web pages with unstructured data (e.g., an image of a promotional coupon) and Web pages with structured data (e.g., an OLAP report that analyzes a specific holiday promotion). Security and a user profile determine which pages, or information sources, the user can access. The user can control standard browser settings and configuration options to customize the browser environment based upon personal preferences:

- **Universal Resource Locator:** When Sam types the intranet home page URL into the Microsoft Web browser, the browser downloads the associated Web page, an HTML document, from the Web server (Figure 12.3). Technically, this operates the same as accessing any standard Web page from a browser. The home page was developed using a combination of HTML and Java code. Once the home page is downloaded to Sam's browser, he is disconnected from the Web server; again, this is standard procedure with Web servers.

- **Server-based Profile:** A server-based profile, which is initially created by the system administrator based on user requirements, determines the specific content, bookmarks, agents, configuration, and security of the user's intranet application. Essentially, the user interface "adapts" to the needs of the individual user based on specifications provided by the user. Because the profile is server based, Sam has the same desktop and security access rights, regardless of what PC he is using.

- **Seamless Integration of Multiple Data Sources:** The intranet seamlessly integrates data from a wide range of structured (data warehouse) and unstructured content that are located both internally and externally to the company. When Sam clicks on the News button, the browser issues another URL (Figure 12.4) initiating a request for a second HTML document that may reside on a different Web server.

User Perspective

When reviewing the most recent news, Sam notices that an alert was received by the northeast regional sales manager, Jane Goodly. Sam knows from past experience that an alert contains both a message and attached report. He clicks on the Alert to explore the information in more detail, but because the requested information resides in the intranet data warehouse and is protected by access controls, the system prompts for a user name and password (Figure 12.5). This security feature ensures that only authorized users have access to company sales and financial information.

Technical Overview

Several areas in the corporate intranet require security authorization. In this case, Sam is attempting to access a report based upon information stored in the data warehouse, a secure area of the corporate intranet, thus he is required to provide authorization information before gaining access.

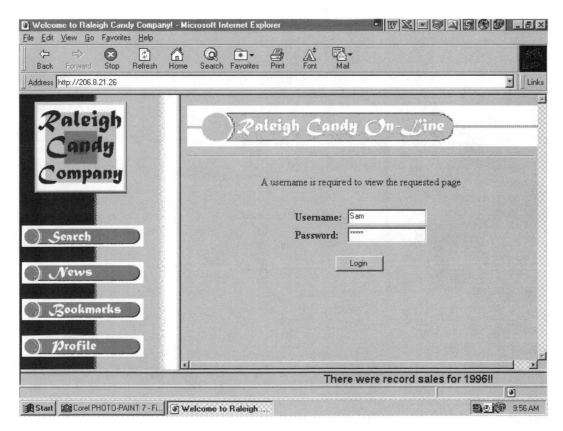

Figure 12.5   Login screen.

When Sam supplies the necessary user name and password to access the data warehouse, the security services of the OLAP server validate security and generate a cookie for Sam (refer back to Chapter 2 for more details on cookies and their application). The system will use the cookie to process subsequent warehouse requests made by Sam, thereby eliminating the need for Sam to repeatedly log in.

User Perspective

After the system verifies Sam's authorization to access the data warehouse, it displays the report illustrated in Figure 12.6. This is a promotion analysis re-

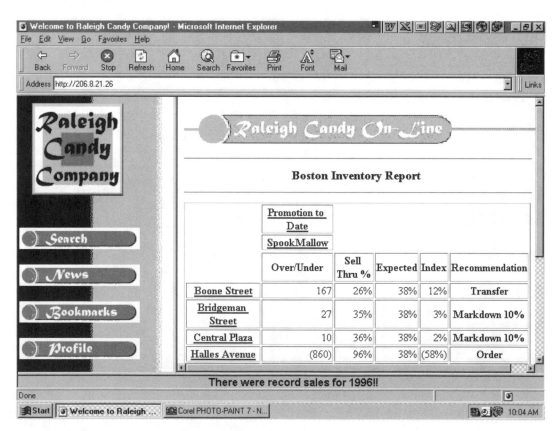

Figure 12.6 Promotion analysis report.

port that tracks the results of the promotion on behalf of the regional sales manager. The report, which is scheduled to run every time the warehouse is updated with the latest information, provides the regional sales manager with an up-to-date status of the promotion. In this case, when the regional manager, Jane, received the most recent report, she noticed some potential issues, and sent an Alert to the corporate user with a request for assistance. Both a message and report are attached to the alert. Specifically, this report indicates the current status of the SpookMallow Candy Bar Halloween promotion run in the Boston stores. It shows the projected inventory position at the end of the promotion, indicated by the Over/Under measure, and proactively recommends what to do to avoid an out-of-stock or overstock problem. Sam quickly notes that several stores are likely to run out of stock before the end of the promotion while other stores are overstocked. A message attached to the report from Jane provides Sam with specific action items:

> "The attached report shows substantial sales variation across our stores. Send additional stock to the stores indicated on the report. Also, help us better understand why there is so much variation from store to store so that we can more effectively plan for these promotions in the future."

The ability to immediately share information in a secure environment fosters a highly collaborative environment for accelerated decision making.

Technical Overview

Both Sam (the corporate user) and Jane (the regional sales manager) need to closely monitor performance of this promotion to take midcourse corrective actions, if necessary. Agent technology automates this delivery process. A proactive agent runs and delivers the promotion analysis report to the regional sales manager each time the data warehouse is updated with new information. A robust server-resident multidimensional analysis program generates this seemingly simple report. The program obtains the data from the data warehouse, performs aggregations (i.e., it calculates summary data from low-level data) and calculations, and formats and prepares the report for display.

The report shown in Figure 12.6 was run by a server-resident agent based on a trigger that detected that the data warehouse had been updated with new information. The agent requested a server-resident multidimensional analysis program (written in C++) that produced the report. The multdimensional analysis program performed the request and generated the report in the following manner:

1. It consulted the metadata to determine what SQL should be generated to obtain the information required for the report and to optimize performance. (For example, some data joins and aggregations are performed in the database engine depending on the type of SQL strategies required to optimize application performance.
2. It generated the SQL and submitted it using native database drivers.
3. It performed additional aggregations and calculations such as Over/Under on the result set, using C/C++ server-resident aggregation and calculation engines, required for the report.
4. It applied formatting to the final report.

The agent then saved the final report on the server, in this case a UNIX server. All of the processing required to initiate and generate this report occurred on the server, an absolute requirement for a thin-client intranet implementation.

Since the data warehouse contains weekly data, every number displayed in this report was aggregated by the multidimensional analysis program from lower-level detail. Specifically, the multidimensional analysis program dynamically consolidated the weekly data, physically stored in the warehouse, to represent the Promotion to Date time frame required for the report. In addition, all of the "facts," or measures, on the report had to be calculated from base elements stored in the data warehouse. For example, the Over/Under measure was calculated as follows:

Average Weekly Sales × Promotion Length) – Beginning Inventory

The Recommendation measure is even more complex. It was calculated by using if-then-else logic that assigns the value of the recommendation based upon threshold differences between the Expected Sell Thru and Actual Sell Thru. These calculations were performed using a server-resident calculation engine, separate from the database because they cannot be calculated efficiently (if they can be calculated at all) using multipass SQL and temporary tables.

Universal Resource Locator

The report attached to the alert was assigned a URL address by the OLAP server when it created the page. The URL contains the report path and name, the

OLAP engine command (i.e., the get report), and any formatting requirements of the generated HTML page. The following is an example of the assigned URL:

```
URL=http://raleigh_server/cgi-
bin/olap/bin/olap.exe?method=ReportDisplay&path=/home/olap/shared&fname=Inventory+Report
```

In this example, CGI scripts are appended to the URL following cgi-bin to run a C++ program (olap.exe) that resides on the Web server (raleigh_server) with specific parameters (display the Inventory Report located in shared OLAP directory). The C++ program uses the parameters found in the URL along with Sam's state information (including his encrypted user ID and password) to create a variable file (which is stored on the OLAP server) with the OLAP multidimensional engine call. The OLAP multidimensional engine then executes the retrieval of the alert and formats the report as an HTML document. It is important to note that, although only the key items are included in this example, the actual URL would include additional parameters.

When Sam clicked on the report attached to the alert, the report was translated into HTML format by the OLAP engine and downloaded to the PC for display in the browser. The report was not actually run again since it had already been run by the agent. The OLAP engine formatted the HTML document to include the links for drillable report elements such as the SpookMallow product. It accomplished this task by using the report metadata to identify the drillable items and then assigning URLs to these drillable items. Following is an example of the URL associated with the drillable item SpookMallow:

```
URL=http://raleigh_server/cgi-
bin/olap/bin/olap.exe?method=Drill&path=/home/olap/shared&fname=Inventory+Report
&target=SpookMallow
```

In this example, CGI is again used to run the C++ program (olap.exe) that resides on the Web server (raleigh_server) with specific parameters (drill on SpookMallow, found in the Inventory Report that is located in the shared OLAP directory). The C++ program uses the parameters found in the URL along with Sam's state information (including his encrypted user ID and password) to create a variable file (which is stored on the OLAP server) with the multidimensional OLAP engine call. The multidimensional OLAP engine then executes an SQL query, process, and formatting logic (HTML markup) to produce the requested report at the next level down a defined drill path. Again, only the key items are included in the sample URL; the actual URL would include additional parameters.

This assigned URL contains the OLAP engine command (e.g., drill) and parameters (e.g., the report name and location), and any formatting requirements of the generated HTML page. Sam can now drill on the SpookMallow item, causing the OLAP engine to dynamically generate the drill-down report (i.e., consult metadata, generate and submit SQL, perform calculations and aggregations, and format the final report).

User Perspective

Sam requests a product reorder to meet retail store requirements, but then begins to investigate the cause of sales variation among the stores. First, he reviews the specific promotions that each store is running. Not knowing where to look for this information, he elects to use a search engine. (It is important to note that most search engines operate in essentially the same manner and produce the same types of results. Most intranet users, including Sam, have access to multiple search engines, but often develop a preference for one.) In this case, Sam chooses to use Excite, and types in the keyword Promotion (Figure 12.7). This initiates a search of the corporate intranet, and leads to the required information about the various store promotions. Sam often resorts to a search engine to retrieve information "on demand."

Technical Overview

The Excite search engine allows Sam to locate valuable information on the corporate intranet. The search engine index is updated nightly to reflect the latest information available on the intranet.

When Sam enters the keyword Promotion, the search engine finds and obtains the URL for any HTML document that has been registered with the engine and tagged with the keyword Promotion. The search engine then dynamically generates an HTML page that contains the titles and associated links to the documents that were found (Figure 12.8).

User Perspective

The search engine delivers several "hits" on the search for Promotion and prioritizes the results according to its confidence in the "closeness" of the match to the original search request. In reviewing the list, Sam notices the link Spook-Mallow Promotions—Boston. This link looks promising, so he clicks on it.

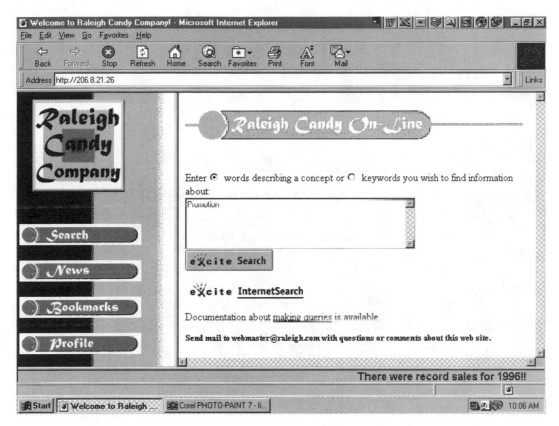

Figure 12.7 Search engine with "Promotion" keyword.

Technical Overview

The search engine delivers the list of hits matching Sam's request, along with the associated URL for the information. Sam can click on any of the hits to retrieve a specific document from the Web server.

User Perspective

The system displays an image of the actual coupon, as illustrated in Figure 12.9. The image provides a wealth of useful information including the coupon value and expiration date, and specifics on the promotional product, as well as valuable information about the appearance of the coupon. This type of in-

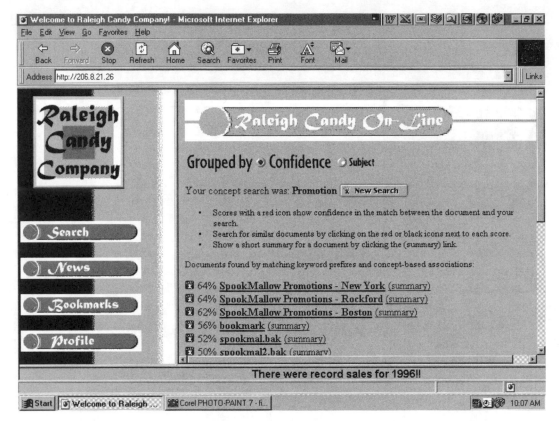

Figure 12.8 Search engine results for "Promotion" search.

tangible information cannot be quantified or expressed as a number, yet may provide the key to differentiating successful and unsuccessful promotions. Concluding that the sales variation was not related to the promotion, Sam hypothesizes that the variation may be based upon the demographic differences in the neighborhoods surrounding the stores.

Technical Overview

When Sam clicks on SpookMallow Promotion—Boston, the browser uses the URL to find and then load the HTML document that contains an image of the coupon used in the Boston market.

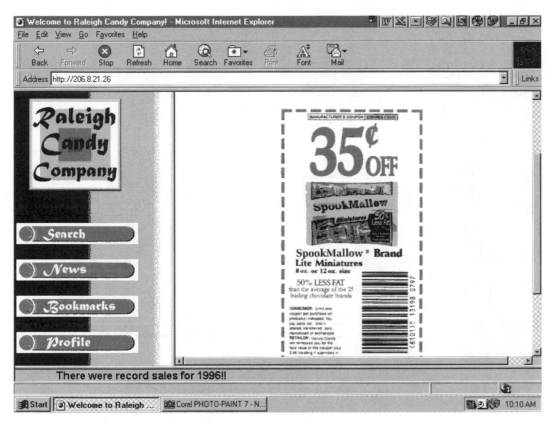

Figure 12.9 Promotion coupon.

User Perspective

Sam wants to compare the household demographics of the various store locations in the Boston area. Not knowing where to find this information or even if the information exists, he once again turns to a search engine. Sam initiates an information search by typing the word Demographics into the Excite search engine, as illustrated in Figure 12.10.

Technical Overview

When Sam enters the keyword Demographics, the search engine finds and obtains the URL for all HTML documents that have been registered with the en-

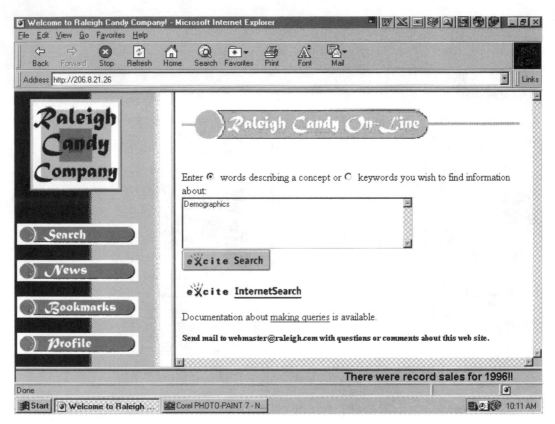

Figure 12.10 Search engine with "Demographics" keyword.

gine and tagged with the keyword Demographics. The search engine then dynamically generates an HTML page that contains the titles and associated links to the documents that were found (Figure 12.11).

User Perspective

Again, the search engine returns several hits. Sam clicks on a link titled "Market Demographics Report," hoping to find useful information about retail stores in the Boston area. The system then prompts him to specify the markets and products to be included in the report (Figure 12.12). Essentially, the system prompts Sam to select criteria for the market demographics.

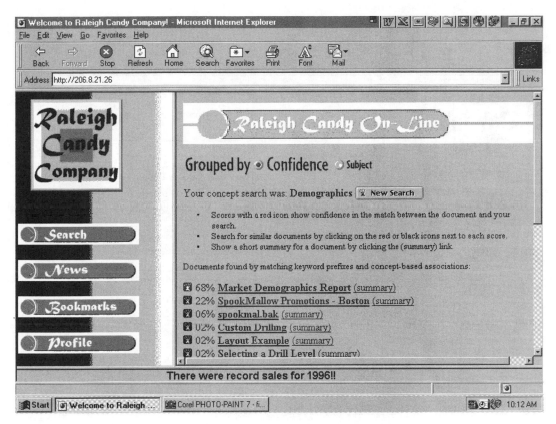

Figure 12.11   Search engine results for "Demographics" search.

Technical Summary

The Market Demographics Report link that Sam selected is, in fact, a reference to an OLAP report that must be generated on the fly based upon desired selection criteria. Unlike the SpookMallow Promotion—Boston URL, it does not represent a preexisting HTML document that is simply loaded into the browser. Instead, the OLAP server must present a browse list to the user and dynamically run the report after the user selects the demographics.

When Sam clicks on the Market Demographics Report link, the browser loads the HTML document associated with the URL assigned by the OLAP server. However, this page is in fact a "redirection" page that was indexed into

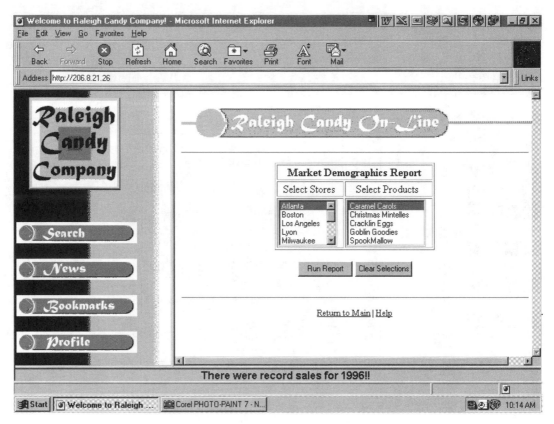

Figure 12.12 Demographics report prompt.

the search engine. It contains the report path and name, the OLAP engine call (i.e., run report), and any formatting requirements that are required to dynamically run the report. This call looks something like the following:

```
URL=http://raleigh_server/cgi
bin/olap/bin/olap.exe?method=RunReport&path=/home/olap/shared&fname=Market+
Demographics+Report
```

Here again, CGI is used to run the C++ program (olap.exe) that resides on the Web server (raleigh_server) with specific parameters (run the Market Demographics Report located in the shared OLAP directory). The C++ program uses the parameters found in the URL along with Sam's state information (including his encrypted user ID and password) to create a variable file (which is stored on the OLAP server) with the OLAP engine call. The multidimensional OLAP engine then executes the SQL query, process, and formatting functions (HTML markup) necessary to display the report in the Web browser. Here, too, only the key items have been included in this sample URL; the actual URL would include additional parameters.

This call causes the OLAP engine to run the report specified in the call. Since the report is in fact a "prompt" report, the OLAP engine generates a browse screen, requesting that Sam select desired store and product selections. Once Sam makes his selections and clicks the Run button, the OLAP engine generates the report in the same manner described earlier in this chapter.

The browse list presented to the user is constrained based upon the user's security level. Specifically, as a corporate user, Sam has access only to a subset of the company's products. The OLAP engine constrains this browse list by reviewing both the metadata and database security. The system does not prompt Sam for security because he already provided a user name and password at an earlier time.

User Perspective

After Sam selects the specific markets and products for the report, the system gathers the necessary data from the warehouse and runs an analytic report with the requested information (Figure 12.13). The report indicates household size and income for the selected market and stores and compares this information to averages for the chain. Because Sam is actually interested in variation at the store level, he clicks on the Boston market to drill down to more detail.

Technical Summary

The displayed report provides Sam with full interactive capabilities (e.g., drilling, pivoting). Clicking on the Boston market signals the server-based OLAP engine to drill down, initiating dynamic generation of a new report at the store level. As discussed earlier in this example, each drillable item on a report is associated with a URL that contains an OLAP engine command (e.g., drill) and parameters, as well as any formatting requirements that should be applied to the HTML page. Once again, all OLAP processing, including query, processing (aggregation and calculation), and formatting, occurs on the server. The report resulting from this processing is translated into an HTML document, including all hotlinks, and is sent to Sam's PC for display.

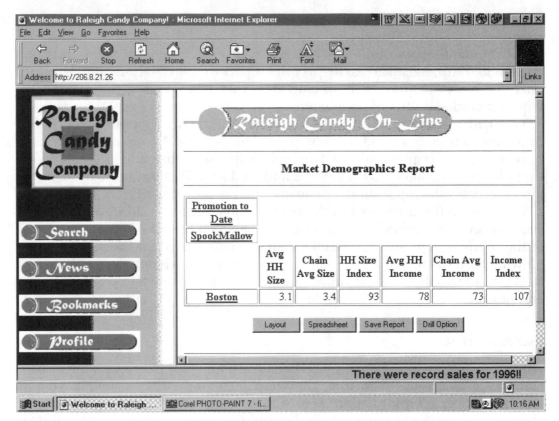

Figure 12.13 Report results.

User Perspective

As shown in Figure 12.14, the store-level detail indicates a substantial correlation between the characteristics of the shoppers and the stores that were out of stock. According to the report, stores that experienced out-of-stock situations generally have smaller household sizes and higher income levels than the retail chain average. The store managers can use this information to better plan promotions and manage inventories in the future. Sam sends the results of this analysis to Jane, the regional sales manager, along with a note describing the situation. He then bookmarks the market demographics report for future use. When the Jane receives the report, she can use the OLAP functions to

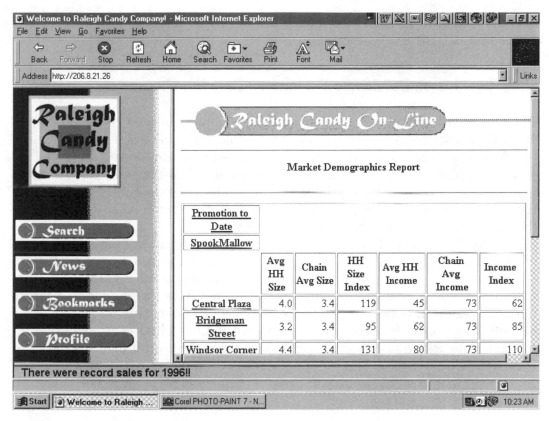

Figure 12.14   Demographic report drill-down.

elicit additional information, perform further analysis, and continue the collaboration with marketing managers at Raleigh headquarters.

Technical Summary

Jane bookmarks the original prompt report for future use. This stores the URL for the market demographics report URL with the related bookmarks that Sam already saved.

While this example of the hypothetical candy company is admittedly very simplistic, it does illustrate the value of an integrated structure in which the planning and implementation process interweaves the three technologies. It also indicates the value of integrating structured and unstructured content in a single system with analytic capabilities.

Final Thoughts on Developing the Intranet Data Warehouse

Despite its simplicity, the Raleigh Candy Company intranet data warehouse example illustrates a key concept of this book: Data warehousing and OLAP technologies, when integrated with intranet technologies, result in decision-support applications that far surpass comparable client/server applications. In many ways, intranet data warehouse applications are more robust, easily linking text and image information with data from the warehouse. Furthermore, the application interface is far more intuitive, especially to anyone who has ever used the Internet. Search engines eliminate the need to know what information exists on a particular topic, and agent technology ensures that users automatically receive updated information about important issues.

In determining how best to employ an intranet data warehouse to address business issues, it is essential to break free of the "conventional" client/server model. That model focuses on the needs of the individual users, whereas an intranet data warehouse is intended to link many users and data resources to resolve business issues. The best applications for an intranet data warehouse are those that benefit from improved communications and collaboration among decision makers.

Focus on the Business Issues First

In planning the intranet data warehouse, the appropriate database design, tools, and deployment strategy are those that provide the analytic functions required to answer users' questions. Before we can make logical choices in these areas, however, we need to fully understand the users' information needs—what questions are they asking and what decisions are they tasked with making. The true value of an intranet data warehouse lies in its ability to provide increasingly detailed answers to users' rapid-series questions that drill into the information for valuable insights that help them to make sound decisions about key business issues.

Architecture Is Important

As this book has stressed repeatedly, the intranet data warehouse must be sufficiently scalable to accommodate a large number of users who are accessing large or distributed data warehouses in the search for answers to business questions. Scalability is an issue on three fronts: capacity, concurrency, and complexity. While hardware vendors are promoting parallel processing solutions to address the issue of scalability, relational database management software vendors are enhancing their products to support extended SQL and OLAP functions. At the same time, many OLAP tools vendors are shifting from a PC-centric applications architecture to a server-centric architecture. Ultimately, performance gains will be achieved by combining the hardware and software technologies that provide optimal performance at the data tier and logic processing tier and that minimize network traffic. A server-centric distributed application provides flexibility in achieving and maintaining acceptable performance as the data warehouse and user base grows and the analytic complexity increases.

The Application Interface IS Becoming Irrelevant

Although the following statement may seem like heresy in view of the emphasis on ease of use, the application interface is actually becoming irrelevant in the selection of OLAP tools. Because technical skills and functional responsibilities differ widely in a large user community, it is far more beneficial to be able to tailor the interface and display objects to the various classes of users than it is to force all users to accept the same tool, no matter how usable that tool may be.

As discussed in Chapter 2, in order to support an adaptable interface, the presentation tier (the interface and display components) must be partitioned from the logic tier (the query, process, and format components). Partitioning makes it possible for the application interface to adapt to the needs of individual users. Employing intranet technologies, the adaptable application interface is presented to the user in the form of applets that are downloaded as necessary to meet each user's specific requirements. No two user's desktop applications must look the same, even though the users may be accessing the same information resources and/or performing the same functions. In an intranet data warehouse, adaptability is the real criterion for evaluating ease of use.

In many respects, the debate over database design centers on entity modeling versus dimensional modeling. The entity modeling approach typically yields a database design that is complete and easy to manage. This approach is popular with the database administrators responsible for maintaining it. Conversely, the dimensional modeling approach yields a design that facilitates

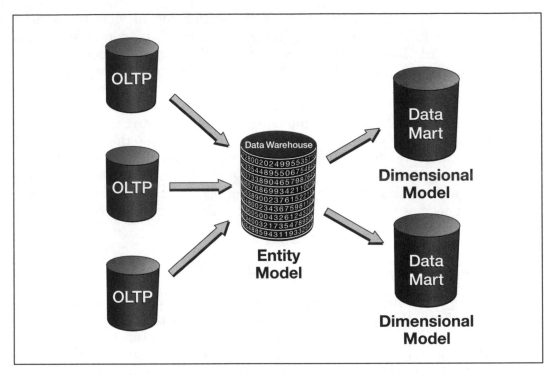

Figure 12.15 Ideal data warehouse and data mart integration.

data retrieval and analysis. This approach is popular with users who need to access and manipulate the data. Entity modeling is appropriate for creating a data warehouse that serves as a central data archive, while dimensional modeling is well suited for creating a data warehouse or data marts that are used for OLAP applications that extend beyond simple data retrieval.

The Bottom Line

The single greatest benefit of an intranet data warehouse is its ability to facilitate communications and collaboration throughout an organization (Figure 12.15). It is important to remember that decisions are generally not made by technology; decisions are made by people. And people—their ideas and experiences—are some of the most valuable information resources that an organization has.

An intranet data warehouse offers these people the opportunity to efficiently gather, analyze, and communicate information throughout an enterprise and to accelerate decision implementation. In this way, it combines the users' ideas and experience with the vast stores of structured and unstructured data available to organizations so that they can outsmart competitors! The enterprise that is capable of consistently outsmarting its competitors has gained true superiority.

INDEX

A.C. Nielsen, case study, 87–89
access to data warehouse, 121
  unauthorized, 258
Active Data Objects. *See* ADO
Active Server Pages (ASP), 157, 166–174
active users, 26, 134, 274
ActiveX, 154–156
  ActiveX Automation, 154, 155, 156
  ActiveX Controls, 154–155, 156
    vs. Java applets, 177–179
  ActiveX Documents, 157, 175–176
  ActiveX Scripting, 154, 155, 156
  ActiveX Server Components, 166
    activating, 168–169
    deploying on transaction server, 173–174
    writing, 173
  component API standards, 45–46
  and Java Beans, 187
administrators, 133
ADO (Active Data Objects), 157, 167, 174
agents, 42–43, 141, 286–293
  and data mining, 98
  intelligent, 286, 292–293
  learning agents, 286
  simple agents, 286
  standard reporting, 289–290
  user notification, 290
airline reservation system, 56
aliasing, 277
analytic caches, 57–58, 102–105
APIs (application programming interfaces), 188–194
application objectware, 143–144
application partitioning, 98–99, 101–102
application programming interfaces. *See* APIs
applications
  architecture, 28–32, 98–102
  strategy, 18, 140, 142, 308
Arbor Software Corp., 105
ASP (Active Server Pages), 157, 160, 166, 179–180
authentication, 258, 262
authorizations, 257, 269–270
authors 133
automating information searches, 273–274
average income calculation, 97

B

B-tree indexes, 216
behavioral data warehouses, 8
BIS (business intelligence systems), 93
Bogakos, Maria, 125
Boolean operators, 283
Brattin, Rick, 150–151
Brio Query, 228
browser
  receive requests from, 167–168
  return results to, 169–172
browsing, collapsible, 121
bugs, 256

Building the Data Warehouse, 6
business applications manager, 147
business intelligence systems (BIS), 93
Business Objects, 228
business requirements planning, 128–134
  identify decision points, 131–133
  identify users, 133–134
  mission statement, 129–131
business services layer, 159–161, 166–174
  active data objects, 174
  automating server components, 168–169
  deploying components, 173–174
  maintaining state, 172–173
  receiving user requests, 167–168
  return results to browser, 169–172
  writing server components, 173

C

cache, 57–58, 102–105
calculations, 278
  an average, 11
  cross-dimension, 120
capacity, 32
Cartesian product, 215, 217
case studies. *See also* example
  A.C. Nielsen, 87–89
  Dayton Hudson's use of OLAP, 124–126
  Fidelity Investments Incorporated, 49–52
  Land 0 Lakes, 19–22
  Tyson Foods, 150–151
casual users, 26, 134, 274
categories within a data warehouse, 70–71
central warehouse, 137–139
CGI (Common Gateway Interface), 36, 101, 179, 195, 203,
    266
channel, 192
ciphertext, 262
client/server vs. intranet deployment, 24–34
client-side scripts, 163
closed-loop decision support, 43
clusters, 237–239, 241
Codd, E.F., 8–9, 92
collaboration, 141
collapsible browsing, 121
COM (Component Object Model), 155–156, 159, 160
  business services layer, 166–169, 173
Common Gateway Interface. *See* CGI
Common Object Request Broker Architecture). *See* CORBA
competitive advantage, 3–4, 14
competitive intelligence 7
complexity, 32
component API, 45–46
Component Object Model. *See* COM
components, 46–49, 187–188
  development tool, 183–187
Computer Security institute, 254
concurrency, 32
confidentiality, 262